# 100
# Natural Wonders
# of the World

Writers: Nishat Fatima, Pradipta Sarkar, Sankar Sridrar

Maps and text © Automobile Association Developments Limited 2007
Relief maps created from an original supplied by Getty Images/The Studio Dog

Published by AA Publishing (a trading name of Automobile Association
Developments Limited, whose registered office is Fanum House, Basing View,
Basingstoke, Hampshire, RG21 4EA; registered number 1878835).

Design layouts for AA Publishing by IL&FS Education & Technology Services
Origination by Keene Group, Andover
Printed and bound by C&C Offset Printing Co., Limited

The contents of this book are believed correct at the time of printing.
Nevertheless, the publisher cannot be held responsible for any errors,
omissions or for changes in the details given in this book or for the
consequences of any reliance on the information provided by the same.
This does not affect your statutory rights.

ISBN-13: 978-0-7495-5378-4
ISBN-10: 0-7495-5378-2

A03315

# 100
# Natural Wonders
# of the World

# Contents

Europe

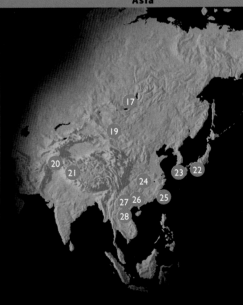

Asia

## Central & South America

## Australia & Oceania

# Introduction

## NATURAL WONDERS

How does one decide which natural feature or phenomenon is a "wonder" and which is "more (or less) awe-inspiring" than the other? For those who have seen Niagara Falls but not the Iguaçu Falls, Niagara would win hands down for its sheer beauty, even though it is dwarfed in both size and magnificence by its South American counterpart. Similarly, the Andes stretching for 4,500 miles (7,243km) may be the longest range in the world, but does that make it any more spectacular than the Rocky Mountains, the Alps, the Caucasus Mountains, or the Himalayas? And should one really be guided by the long and the short of it, or by any other relative measure?

Most of the the planet's natural features are undergoing constant changes, some natural and some caused by man's intrusion into the environment, or by irreversible occurrences such as climate change. The wonderful Great Barrier Reef—which boasts some of the most enchanting and colorful corals and equally mesmerizing marine life—is slowly dying due to global warming, with many of its corals turning into dead debris. North America's celebrated Arizona desert may soon turn into an oasis of green if the rainfall patterns do not change—as has happened to the Gir National Park in India, where the Indian lion struggles to adapt to a new environment in which savannah grasslands are turning into lush jungle.

It's a difficult choice to make as to which wonders to include, more so since we are not dealing with one to ten, but one to thousands of natural wonders that exist on our planet, each more magnificent and significant than the other. The selection of natural wonders in this book is, therefore, a slightly subjective one; one on which the editors have worked to balance the old with the new, so that you as the reader can get a broad picture of all those places that have kept us and continue to keep us linked to this wonderful planet, Earth..

## MAN AND NATURE

Man's affinity with nature is intrinsic to human evolution. From the pre-historic age to the present, we have always revered nature and celebrated its wonders. If animal life on land, sea, and air has made us conscious of our evolutionary link to the rest of the animal kingdom, the mighty expanse of oceans, mountain ranges, deserts and polar caps has made us aware of our own possibilities and limitations.

Most of what we know today is the result of human exploration that has sought to map the world we live in. While our adventurers and explorers have brought many amazing things to our notice, our scientists and naturalists have helped us to understand and explain their origin, evolution, and importance. The discovery and study of the Galapagos Islands, for example, has helped us to value this natural phenomenon more than we would a few crocodiles in a zoo. Reptiles may not be man's most-loved creatures, yet the probable extinction of "Lonely George"—the last survivor of the Galapagos Islands species of giant tortoise—is no less a loss. Caught gaping at the Blue Mountains in Australia, we have been made wiser by the information that the wonderful blue haze that envelops this craggy outcrop is caused by the oil exhaled into the atmosphere by the area's eucalyptus trees.

Many of our natural wonders have also survived because of the sacredness with which our ancestral tribes have regarded them. American Indians have warned tourists and administration against indiscriminate "recreational climbing" of Devils Tower, which has already caused considerable damage to this monument; in Australia, the Aboriginal tribes have come forward with a similar demand to protect Uluru (Ayers Rock), and in India and Nepal, hill people have traditionally regarded the Himalayas as the sacred abode of the gods and were aghast when man first decided to climb its highest peak, Mount Everest. Edmund Hillary's successful ascent of Mount Everest helped us to

appreciate human grit and Himalayan topography but nowadays it has also made us aware of the growing pile of non-bio-degradable garbage left behind by every climbing expedition that has sought to repeat the feat.

Fortunately, in most cases, our natural wonders have been protected by turning the surrounding areas into natural reserves, or simply by their relative inaccessibility, being situated in deep jungles, high mountain ranges, deserts, or icy landscapes. But today, we face a different enemy, a malaise born out of industrialization and our own thoughtless exploitation of natural resources and the environment—the phenomenon of climate change.

## CLIMATE CHANGE

Climate change is nothing new. Since the birth of the planet, the world has witnessed many cataclysmic climate changes that have altered the shape of continents and the flora and fauna that existed. However, while this change in the past was a result of natural causes, the current scenario has been largely caused by human behavior.

One of the most important causes of climate change in recent years has been the uncontrolled emission of greenhouse gases into the earth's atmosphere. The greenhouse effect relates to the gases that keep our planet warm; if they were to escape through the ozone, the temperature of our planet would drop to below freezing point. By trapping warm air, the greenhouse effect keeps the earth's surface temperature warm. Today, however, the additional greenhouse gases produced by humans—carbon dioxide, methane, and nitrous oxide—is overheating the stratosphere, causing temperatures to rise. This has led to a series of chain reactions that affect every living organism on earth.

Human beings are resilient. But, the animal world, and in particular plant life, cannot adapt as rapidly to the changes. Consequently, they face a bleak future. Less snow in winter, warmer temperatures in summer, and more winter rain have all had impact on our environment.

The effects of global warming in the Arctic and Antarctic regions—where ice is melting faster than Senator Al Gore's campaign to convince the world of the impending cataclysm—has already endangered the life of walruses, sea lions, penguins, and many sea birds. According to the 2007 report of the Intergovernmental Panel on Climate Change, the largest ice mass of the northern hemisphere is losing 12cu miles (5cu km) of ice per year, whereas in the Antarctic 1,160sq miles (3,000sq km) of the Larsen B ice shelf has already disintegrated. Lest we think these places and and their inhabitants are too remote to worry about, an exploration of our own backyards will reveal alarming facts. The traditionally warmer region of southern England is getting colder and already there are reasons to believe that its famous beech woodlands may not survive the change.

In Costa Rica, according to WWF, global warming has claimed its first victim, the Golden Toad, which is now believed to be extinct. In China, one of its mightiest rivers—the Yangtze—is facing shortages as glaciers that feed it are retreating. A similar fate awaits the Indian rivers that rise in the Himalayas. An increase in summer temperatures is causing frequent forest fires that could spell the end of the Valdivian rainforests of Chile and Argentina, not to speak of the rest of the Amazon—the lungs of the Earth—which, according to some estimates, may be half its size by 2050. Time, clearly, is running out—for us and many of the world's natural wonders.

# Europe

The epic story of Europe's natural wonders began three billion years ago. From then until now, humans have come face to face with many incredible features that have left us both excited and perplexed. Covering an area of 3,930,520sq miles (10,180,000sq km) of the westernmost Eurasian peninsula, who would have thought that thousands of years ago dinosaurs walked Oxford, or that the area occupied by some of France's most famous vineyards was a tropical sea? Some of the region's most stunning wonders are situated in the harsh icy landscapes of the Nordic countries, while others lie nestled in the great leafy Alps or the Caucasian Mountains and forests of Central and Western Europe. Still more survive along the coastal regions that touch upon the Atlantic Ocean, the Arctic Ocean, the Baltic, Mediterranean, and Black seas, and the innumerable lakes and mountain ranges that dot the continent.

In this section of the book you will have the opportunity to take a closer look at some of these wonders. Like the Giant's Causeway—a natural volcanic pathway on the Antrim Plateau in Northern Ireland; the icy region of Iceland's Lake Myvatn—the ecosystem of a stunning series of lakes and islets; the largest glacier mass in Europe, the Vatnajökull Glacier, which covers seven active volcanoes with a blanket of ice; or the underground giant ice cave tunnels of the Austrian Alps where you can come across an ice cathedral. And if that's not enough, the Cliffs of Moher will bring you close to some of the most amazing birdlife off the west-coast of Ireland; the Slovenian Skocjan caves and tunnels will explain the origin of a beautiful black stone that has so captivated women; and the coniferous plateau of Ardennes, full of valleys, swamps, and marshes will enchant you to return time and again to those pages or even plan a visit there.

- The blue-green algae (*Cyanophyta*) found in the lake lend a greenish-brown tinge to the waters of Myvatn during the summer months.
- Myvatn (midge) lake is named after the swarms of midges that thrive in its waters, forming an integral part of the food chain as they are consumed by fish as well birds.

**Lake Myvatn,** Iceland

# Lake Myvatn

The beautiful and serene Lake Myvatn lies in northern Iceland, 30 miles (48km) east of the town of Akureyri and is drained by the Laxa river which flows northward into the Greenland Sea. The fourth largest lake in Iceland, Myvatn is one of the most popular tourist attractions of the country.

Lake Myvatn is approximately 6 miles (9.5km) long with a width of about 4 miles (6.5km); the total surface area of the lake is roughly 14sq miles (37sq km). Despite this, Myvatn is a very shallow lake with an average depth of 8ft (2.5m)—the maximum depth of the lake is only about 13ft (4m).

The surface of Lake Myvatn is dotted with around 50 volcanic islands and islets, and numerous small bays and inlets indent its shores. Surrounded by countless hot springs and craters, the Myvatn area is famous for its volcanic topography. A variety of lava formations are found in the area. These extraordinary features and the geological peculiarities can be attributed to the heavy volcanic activity that the region has experienced over thousands of years. The

*Namaskard thermal area, Hverarond, near Lake Myvatn*

## MYVATN'S BIRDS

The Myvatn and Laxa area is reputed to house one of the largest concentrations of ducks in the world. All species of water birds in Iceland, including the Tufted duck, Harlequin duck, Red-breasted merganser, Red-Necked phalarope, Whooper swan, and Greylag geese, nest here. The most characteristic bird of the area is the Barrow's Goldeneye; a non-migratory bird, it nests in holes and crevices in the lava fields, and spends winter in holes in the ice. The Slavonian grebe is also found in the area, and nests in vegetation at the banks of the lake.

## CONSERVATION EFFORTS

The area of Lake Myvatn and the River Laxa has been demarcated a protected region according to laws of the Environment and Food Agency of Iceland since June 2004. The aim of the law is to ensure the protection of the biodiversity and geological formations and landscape, as well as active conservation of the area because of its sociological, scientific, and esthetic importance. Lake Myvatn and River Laxa are also listed as internationally important wetlands according to the Ramsar Convention.

*River Laxa flowing from Lake Myvatn*

area is situated on the boundary of two tectonic plates—the North American and the Eurasian. These plates drift apart by about 0.8in (2cm) every year; lava then forces its way up through the earth's crust and fills the widening rift. It is this phenomenon that is responsible for the intense geothermal activity of the region.

On the eastern edge of the lake is the Dimmu Borgir (meaning "dark castle") badlands, marked by magnificent dark lava pillars, some as tall as 213ft (65m). To the north of the lake is the vast Hverfjall crater—a smooth volcanic cone that is about 0.62 miles (1km) in diameter and 459ft (140m) deep. This stadium-shaped crater was formed by eruptions 2,500 years ago. The boiling mud pits of Hverarond form another one of the Myvatn area's strange but fascinating spectacles. The explosion crater of Viti showcases natural hot springs—people can bathe in the waters which are comfortably warm at 72°F (22°C). The most staggering of Myvatn's sights, however, is perhaps the absolutely barren lava field of Eldhraun (fire lava), where the Apollo 11 crew was trained in the 1960s for their impending moonwalk.

Created when a lava field blocked the course of a river, Myvatn is fed primarily by spring waters. Rainfall is quickly absorbed by the bedrock and surfaces as springs on the banks of the lake. This water is rich in minerals and is primarily responsible for the lake's flourishing ecosystem despite its altitude of 912ft (278m) above sea level. Salmon, trout, and the Arctic char abound in the waters of Myvatn and the Laxa river, and bird life is varied and abundant.

**Vatnajökull Glacier,** Iceland

# Vatnajökull Glacier

Aptly referred to as the "Land of Fire and Ice," Iceland is a land like no other. It continues to be built by nature—constantly being pulled apart because it happens to lie across the vast undersea split known as the mid-Atlantic ridge. The land is constantly being stretched and is subject to sudden upheavals. Such eruptions, due to the mid-Atlantic ridge, have included Eldgja (1896) and Laki (1783).

Vatnajökull, located in the southeast of Iceland, is the largest ice cap in Europe, covering several geothermal sources. The glacier covers an area of roughly 3,200sq miles (8,400sq km), about 8 percent of Iceland's total area. The sub-glacial landscape consists of an undulating plateau dissected by valleys and gorges, and lies up to 5,000ft (1,524m) above sea level. This frost-bound area is home to hundreds of rivers, some of the largest being the Skjálfandafljót, Jökulsá á Fjöllum, Thjórsá, and Lagarfljót. Of the numerous geothermal areas and active volcanoes that are scattered throughout the ice field, the noteworthy ones are Kverkfjöll, towering at 6,298ft (1,920m), which—along with its two calderas—is a potent, partly glaciated geothermal area that dominates the northern

## EXPLORING VATNAJÖKULL

The first man to cross the Vatnajökull was the Englishman W.L. Watts in 1875. Later, Bárðarbunga, the highest dome on the ice cap, was scaled by an Austrian-Italian expedition in 1935. Researchers, mountaineers, and travelers today crisscross the expanse of this slow moving ocean of ice. With the use of radio-echo depth soundings efforts are being made to formulate a complete picture of the land underlying Vatnajökull. Other scientific research being conducted in the region includes studies on mass balance, and movement and chemical research.

## THE 1996 JÖKULHLAUP

An eruption beneath the center of Vatnajökull on September 30, 1996, generated prodigious amounts of heat and rapidly melted the ice. Even though the eruption had effectively ceased by October 14, the melt water accumulating beneath the ice had raised the level of Grimsvötn's sub-glacial lake by 308ft (94m). In November,1996, this trapped water finally broke out onto the surface, devastating the Skeidarasandur region before ultimately draining into the Atlantic Ocean.

*Four-wheel vehicles atop the largest glacier in Europe*

margin of Vatnajökull; the Bárðarbunga Volcano, on the other hand, lies under the central portion of the ice cap, at an elevation of 6,560ft (2,000m), and has an ice-filled caldera.

The Grimsvötn, at a height of 5,638ft (1,719m), is the largest volcano under the Vatnajökull Glacier. This volcano contains a unique lake within the ice cap, of which the surface is usually frozen solid. Located in an expanse of high geothermal activity, Grimsvötn's periodic eruptions cause the surrounding ice to melt and the level of the lake rises until it breaks through the ice walls and partly empties itself in the form of a glacier flood called jökulhlaup, or "glacier run."

Nunataks, or the exposed summits of ridges, such as Grendill and Goðahnúkar in the east and Pálsfjall in the west, are the only structures that break up the immense white expanse of Vatnajökull. Esjufjöll and Mávabyggðir are two large massifs that rise high above the rest of the ice field, like islands emerging from a frozen sea. About 23 outlet glaciers which flow out from the accumulation area of Vatnajökull have been identified. Most of the outlet glaciers in the north and the west are either of the surging kind or flat, broad ice slopes.

*A section of the Vatnajökull Glacier*

**Jökulsárlón**, Iceland

# Jökulsárlón

Placed at the foot of Vatnajökull, the largest glacier in Europe, the Jökulsárlón lake forms one of the most spectacular sights in Iceland. Huge chunks of ice of innumerable shapes and assorted shades of blue dot the surface of this magnificent body of water. Jökulsárlón, the largest and most famous pro-glacial lake in Iceland, is situated at the southern margin of Vatnajökull, between Höfn and the Skaftafell National Park.

The retreat of the Vatnajökull ice cap from the southern coast of Iceland is responsible for the creation and growth of Jökulsárlón. Since the formation of the lake in 1934, it has been continuously growing in size. Occupying an area of 3sq miles (8sq km) in 1975, it is now more than twice its original size. The lake's dramatic growth can be attributed to the large volume of melt water from the Breidamerkurjökull, the outlet glacier of Vatnajökull that drains into Jökulsárlón.

Prior to 1950, the glacial river Jökulsá flowed directly into the sea from underneath. However, since then the tongue of the glacier has been retreating, leaving in its wake a vast and still-growing lagoon, further deepened by the scouring effect of Jökulsá on the basin. It is due to this that the size of the Jökulsárlón—which translates as "glacier lagoon"—has been constantly increasing. Clustered with ice floes, Jökulsárlón nestles today between the Breidamerkurjökull glacier and a ridge of glacial till, with only the narrow river Jökulsa as a channel of outflow.

Most of the pro-glacial lakes at the edges of Vatnajökull are freshwater lakes. However, increasing penetration of sea water into Jökulsárlón is responsible for the distinctive

*Sight-seeing boat sailing among icebergs, alongside a glacier*

## THREAT POSED BY THE SEA

The bridge over the Jökulsá river in Breidamerkursandur, which was built in 1967 and forms a part of the Iceland Ring Road, is close to being torn down by the constant erosion of the sea. The sea, it is believed, will continue to shorten Jökulsá and encroach inward, and convert the Jökulsárlón lagoon into a deep bay; and as the snout of the glacier retreats further, into an inlet of the sea. The road authorities launched a project in 2003 to prevent further erosion—attempts are being made to raise the level of the lagoon and construct sturdy boulder dykes to stall the erosion.

*Icebergs and coastline*

## THE GREAT SKUA

The sand and gravel dunes around Jökulsárlón form the primary breeding ground of a large seabird called the great skua. The birds usually nest around the lake and are often spotted during the summer months; they migrate to warmer climes during winter. These birds are predators, and often prey on smaller birds like puffins; fish and carrion are aslo part of their diet.

lagoon-like character of the lake. Ongoing erosion by the sea has caused the shoreline of the Breidamerkursandur area to recede, reducing the length of the river Jökulsá. Jökulsá was about 0.93 miles (1,500m) long in 1950; in 1998 a distance of only about 1,640ft (500m) separated Jökulsárlón from the sea.

Approaching 656ft (200m) in depth, Jokulsarlon is probably the second deepest lake in Iceland today. The lake is visually stunning, as the edge of the snout of the glacier floats on the surface of the water and large chunks of ice—over 1,000 years old with shades of blue and gray rather than white—break off and land in the water with a spectacular crash—and then slowly the icebergs float toward the sea. Boat rides allow visitors to experience this breathtaking waterscape from close quarters.

Over the years the steady infilitration of sea water, particularly after the end of the summer melting season when the volume of water discharged by Jökulsá decreases, has led to several species of fish such as herring, salmon, and capelin entering the lake, followed by harbor seals. A variety of birdlife, including the eider duck, Arctic tern, and great skua, can also be found around the lake.

- Encrusted with colorful minerals, the vent of the Great Geysir in Iceland is about 60ft (12m) wide.
- The Great Geysir has been known to spurt streams as high as 200ft (61m) at the peak of its activity.

**The Great Geysir,** Iceland

# The Great Geysir

One of Iceland's greatest natural attractions, the Great Geysir is a spouting hot spring situated in the Haukadalur Valley in southwest Iceland. The word "geyser"—the general term for erupting hot water fountains—has been in use since 1647 and is derived from the Icelandic word *geysir*, which means "to gush." Majestic columns of hot water shooting out from the mouth of the Great Geysir make it a spectacular geothermal phenomena.

The Great Geysir is the world's oldest known geyser. Though the exact date of its formation is not known, the first written record of the Geysir's activity dates from 1294, when the thermal areas of southwestern Iceland were modified to a great extent by earthquakes. As strong periodic tremors increased activity in the Geysir area, it gained fame and popularity since erupting geysers were unheard of in the rest of Europe.

For centuries, the outbursts of the Geysir were considered to be supernatural, with no concrete explanation for their occurrence. It was the German chemist Robert Bunsen who first came up with a scientific explanation for the Geysir's eruptions after visiting Iceland in 1846. He summarized the cause to be overheating of water below the surface in high temperature geothermal areas—areas of volcanic and seismic activity—where the subsurface temperature is greater than 392°F (200°C) at a depth less than 0.62 miles (1km).

Geysers are formed where subsurface hot water ascends to the surface through narrow channels in the

## THE GREAT GEYSIR AREA

Occupying roughly 1.2sq miles (3sq km) at the surface, the Great Geysir area is a thermal park atop a vast bubbling cauldron of geothermal activity. Hot and cold springs, hissing fumaroles, and sulphurous mud pots of unusual colors dot the surface. Beautiful and delicate silica sinters decorate the area around the hot springs. Other remarkable geysers in the area include the less majestic but very active Strokkur (Churn) and Litli Geysir (Little Geysir). Primitive plants are also found in the area. The small Laugarfjall mountain situated a short distance away offers a panoramic view of the Geysir area.

*Geothermal hot springs*

*A geyser erupting, Strokkur*

earth's crust. When water at considerable depth in the geyser pipe boils, it gets converted to steam, and expands to occupy greater volume within the pipe, forcing the water above to spurt out of the mouth of the geyser. The consequent decrease in pressure within the pipe allows more water to boil and form steam, and a chain reaction is set up.

The Geysir's activity has been interspersed with periods of dormancy. It lay silent for almost 40 years before being jolted out of its slumber by an earthquake in 1630. A long period of inactivity also preceded its reawakening in 1896 following a series of earthquakes. A period of extensive activity followed, leading to eruptions at a frenetic pace; the Great Geysir would erupt once every 30 minutes in 1910. However, it became almost dormant yet again in 1916. Artificial channels dug in order to lower the water table and clear out Geysir's silica-clogged channel failed to have much effect in reviving activity. Tourists tried to stimulate eruptions by throwing rocks into the vent, a practice which is strictly prohibited now. The earthquake of 2000, however, led to another awakening, and today the Geysir erupts every day, though not with the same force as before.

The Geysir has been drawing travelers, explorers, and naturalists from around the world for centuries. Despite its declining activity, no visitor to Iceland gives this majestic and powerful geyser a miss even to this day. Commemorative coins and stamps issued by the government have immortalized the Great Geysir.

## OWNING THE GREAT GEYSIR

Until 1894, the Great Geysir was part of the local farm, Laug. The owners sold the area to James Craig, who later became the prime minister of Northern Ireland. Craig fenced the land and collected entry fees from visitors for a year, and then gifted it to a friend who dropped the entry fee. The site was eventually purchased by the filmmaker Sigurdur Jonasson, who presented it as a gift to the people of Iceland.

- Included in the UNESCO World Heritage List, the Geirangerfjord and Naeroyfjord, enjoy as much prestige as is accorded to the Great Wall of China, the Great Pyramids of Egypt and the Grand Canyon in the United States.
- The passage through Naeroyfjord, one of the branches of Sognefjord, is so narrow that it looks like a tunnel into which ships disappear.

**The Great Fjords,** Norway

# the Great Fjords

Fjords, one of the most exquisite natural formations to be found in the world, are long, narrow inlets of sea that cut into land. Formed during the process of glaciation, they usually have high-walled sides with steep slopes. *Fjord* is a Norwegian word meaning "arm of the sea." Norway, the country to which the Vikings sailed and then settled in, is as rich in fjords as it is in myths and tales of Nordic gods. Its many fjords have earned for Norway the epithet, 'Land of Fjords.'

The Scandinavian fjords, formed as a result of heavy glacial erosion during the Ice Age, span most of Norway's 17,452-mile (28,148-km) coastline. Though geologists believe that glacial action was not entirely responsible for the creation of the fjords—some of the deepest fjords are too far below sea level to have been affected by the dredging masses of ice—they agree that these rivers of ice carved out most of the bays and inlets, and did the majority of the work in carving the U-shaped valleys as they gouged out mountains on their way to the sea. Patterned scars on the sheer cliffs that hem in the channels of water bear testimony to the ravages of the glaciers. Today, however, not much remains of these massive glaciers and ice caps apart from a few places places such as Jostedalsbreen, an isolated patch of ice to the north of Sognefjorden.

Thanks to the many fjords that cut into it, the actual Norwegian coastline, if stretched out straight, is more than half circumference of the earth. These so-called arms of the sea extend all the way from Stavanger in the south

## FJORD ROYAL

The well-known fjord Sognefjorden is known by two names—King of the Fjords and the Fjord of Kings. The first refers its size; it is Norway's longest and deepest fjord, stretching 112 miles (180km) and is more than 4,000ft (1,220m) deep. The second name is a reference to the fjord's royal connection; it is Norway's King Harald's favorite place for fishing.

*Elevated view, Aurlandsfjord*

## HOW GREEN IS THE VALLEY

Previous inhabitants of the fjords would seek out grassy patches near the floor of the valley and set up a pulley system at the top the mountain, similar to the ones used to draw water from wells. Instead of water, however, they would use the buckets to lower goats to the valley floor to graze, and adolescent children who would shepherd them. This system was followed in areas that could not be reached by shimmying down the almost-vertical rock faces. The risk involved and the meager pasture, however, forced an end to this practice.

*Red church on Lofoten islands, Nordland*

to the Russian border. The vast number of fjords make communicating by land in Norway a difficult task. For instance, villages sequestered in the curves of fjords which are only a few hours apart by boat would take far longer to reach if you were to travel by land.

The fjords also offer toursits a host of trekking trails. Four counties—Møre and Romsdal, Sogn and Fjordane, Hordaland, and Rogaland—make up the Fjord Norway area. Bergen is considered the gateway to this land of scoured rocks and sheer cliffs. About 150,000 off-shore isles dot the fjords, many of them inhabited by small pockets of population.

The very deep Geirangerfjord is considered by Norwegians to be the country's most beautiful fjord. With its many waterfalls—among them, the famous Seven Sisters—it is the second busiest destination in Norway for cruise ships, with more than 100 ships visiting in the summer. The *Hurtigruten* is one of the vessels that makes regular trips from Bergen to Kirkenes, a return voyage that takes 12 days. This vessel is also the only form of communication and source of supplies for some of the remotest islands.

The Seven Sisters is a single waterfall with seven separate streams—the tallest among them has a free fall of over 820ft (250m). According to folklore, the sisters dance naked as they gleefully splash down the mountain, while the Courtier—another waterfall on the mountain opposite the Seven Sisters—flirts playfully from across the fjord.

- Columns similar to the Giant's Causeway—though not as grand in scale, and formed in different ways—can be found in Armenia, California, Mexico, New Zealand, Russia, and Sicily.

- Though most of the columns in the Giant's Causeway are hexagonal, there are several which have five, seven, or even eight sides. The tallest columns measure about 39ft (12m).

# The Giant's Causeway

*Basalt rock formations, The Giant's Causeway*

Approximately 40,000 columns of basalt emerging from the base of the Antrim plateau makes up the magnificent Giant's Causeway in Northern Ireland. The colonnade stretches for about 300 yards (273m) across the coast from the cliffside and extends more than 448ft (146m) into the sea. It was declared a UNESCO World Heritage Site in 1986, and designated a National Nature Reserve by the Department of Environment of Northern Ireland the year after. The area is home to a host of birds, including the fulmar, petrel, cormorant, shag, guillemot, and razorbill. Exotic and endangered plant species such as sea spleenwort, hare's foot trefoil, vernal squill, sea fescue, and frog orchid grow here as well.

This natural pathway was born of a volcanic eruption some 50–60 million years ago, when the boiling basalt erupted through fissures in the chalk beds, and solidified to form a plateau. As the lava cooled, it contracted. Though the vertical contractions reduced the thickness without causing fractures, the horizontal contractions created hexagonal cracks throughout the lava layers. It was these cracks that were responsible for producing the incredible columns that we see today.

Sir Richard Bulkeley, a scholar at Trinity College, Dublin, announced the discovery of the Giant's Causeway in a paper presented to the Royal Society in 1693. It had, however, already been discovered by the Bishop of Derry a year earlier. The site garnered international acclaim only when Susanna Drury, an artist from Dublin, exhibited a series of watercolors depicting the landform in 1739.

According to legend, the Giant's Causeway finds its origin in a feud between two giants—Finn MacCool of Ireland and Benandonner of Scotland. Myth has it that Finn MacCool built a path so that he could walk to Scotland

to fight his rival. Upon finishing his task, Finn MacCool fell asleep. Meanwhile Benandonner, who was much larger than Finn, walked over to challenge him. Fearing for his life, Finn's wife, Oonagh placed a blanket over Finn, pretending that he was her son. The trick succeeded in fooling Benandonner, who assumed that the father of such a big baby would be an unbeatable adversary. He ran back to Scotland in terror, tearing up the rocks on his way so that Finn would not be able to cross the sea. The myth about the giants, it is believed, was propagated in the 18th century with the specific intention of attracting visitors to the area. Today, the Giant's Causeway is the most popular tourist attraction in Northern Ireland, drawing more than 750,000 visitors annually.

## OLDEST DISTILLERY

Before the construction of the famous coast road, visitors had to travel a long way on horseback to see the Giant's Causeway. The town of Bushmills, home to the world's oldest (licenced) distillery, was the last stop before the end of the journey. It had been a tradition for travelers to revive themselves with magnums of the King's whiskey. The Bushmills Distillery is still in business today.

## FINGAL'S CAVE

Columnar basalts are not confined to Northern Ireland alone. Another of the best known examples of this phenomenon is to be found off Scotland's west coast, in the Inner Hebrides. These columns are well developed over a large part of the island of Staffa, and a huge cave, where the sea has eroded the columns, is known as Fingal's Cave, after a mythical giant. The Cave has featured in many novels and poems over the centuries, and a rather rough boat trip to the island by the composer Felix Mendelssohn in 1829 inspired his famous orchestral overture *The Hebrides*.

- The Cliffs of Moher were featured as the "Cliffs of Insanity" in the 1987 film *The Princess Bride*.
- Blue and gold—the colors of County Clare—are what Brian Boru is said to have carried at the Battle of Clontarf in 1014.

**The Cliffs of Moher,** Ireland

# The Cliffs of Moher

**S**heer cliffs ascending majestically out of the Atlantic Ocean form the dramatic landscape of the Cliffs of Moher. Located on the west coast of Ireland, at the southwestern edge of the Burren area near Doolin, they extend for about 5 miles (8km)—from Luogh Point in the north to Cancregga in the south.

The rocks of Moher are a result of sediments deposited roughly 320 million years ago on an ancient sea bed. The sea shore then lay further north, and the rivers that flowed into it formed a series of deltas, depositing the silt that they carried onto the bed. With the passage of time and the intervention of geological processes, these sediments were converted into layers of Namurian shale, sandstone, and siltstone that lay on top of each other. As the level of the sea dropped, these rocks emerged out of the ocean as towering vertical walls.

The different rock strata are clearly defined in the face of the cliffs. The tier of rocks are partially inclined toward the southwest, and layers that are at the bottom of the cliff toward the south appear at the top edges a few kilometers to the north. Since sandstone is more resistant than the other rocks, they jut further out of the cliff-face than the intervening layers of shale and siltstone. The edges of the cliffs are naturally eroding areas, and many sections along the expanse of the Cliffs of Moher are severely undercut; chunks of the stone ledges thus often break off and drop into the ocean.

In 1835, local landlord Sir Cornelius O'Brien, a descendant of Ireland's High King Brian Boru, built an observation tower roughly at the mid-point of the Cliffs of Moher. It served as a viewing point for visitors who flocked to the cliffs to marvel at their grandeur. To this day, the tower stands proudly and the view from it extends beyond

## CREATURES OF MOHER

The Cliffs of Moher are famous for their abundant avifauna. Thirty thousand birds belonging to 29 varied species have been identified in the area. Nine species of nesting seabirds, including the guillemot, razorbill, puffin, kittiwake, and fulmar are present here. Most remarkable of these are the razorbill and the famous Atlantic Puffin, whose numbers are increasing in Moher in direct contrast to the decline in their population throughout the rest of Europe. The Atlantic Puffin nests in large colonies on the cliffs and the nearby islet called Goat Island. The edges of the cliffs are grassy and green, and rare lichens are found here.

Galway Bay to the Twelve Pins (or Twelve Bens) and Maum Turk Mountains in Connemara in the north, Loop Head at the southern tip of Clare, as well as the Kerry Mountains further south. The three Aran Islands to the west can also be seen unless visibility is exceptionally poor owing to bad weather.

Just below O'Brien's Tower is An Bhreannán Mór, a spectacular rock pillar or stack rising to a height of 230ft (70m), which provides a close view of the numerous birds that nest in the area. The cliffs at Hag's Head rise to a height of 394ft (120m) above the sea; a square stone ruin called Moher Tower, believed to be the remnant of a Napoleonic watch tower, is located here. The cliffs reach their maximum height of 702ft (214m) near O'Brien's Tower. A walking trail, mostly unenclosed, running along the top edge of the entire length of the cliffs—often perilously close to the sheer drop off the edge—provides a magnificent and impressive view of the whole area.

*A view of Doonagore Castle and O'Brien's Tower*

## CONSERVATION OF THE CLIFFS

Home to one of the major colonies of nesting seabirds in Ireland, the Cliffs of Moher were designated as a Refuge for Fauna in 1988 and declared a Special Protection Area for Birds (SPA) under the EU Birds Directive in 1989. The demarcated area covers 0.77sq miles (2sq km) and includes the cliffs, the fragile habitat formed by the cliff-top maritime grassland and heath, and a 656ft (200m) zone of open water in front of the cliffs in order to safeguard the feeding area of the birds. In 2006, the Clare County Council and the Burren and Cliffs of Moher Geopark Committee submitted an application to UNESCO to recognize the Burren and Cliffs of Moher Geopark as part of the European Geoparks Network. An interpretive visitor center called Atlantic Edge has also been established.

- The healing properties of mineral springs led to the opening of the world-famous health resort, Espa, which contributed the word "spa" to the English language.

- The Ardennes département of France has a nuclear power station in Chooz, and a plant that generates hydroelectric power from the Meuse river at Revin.

**Ardennes,** France/Belgium/Luxembourg

# Ardennes

The ancient wooded plateau of Ardennes comprises the western extension of the Middle Rhine Highlands and is spread across part of the Grand Duchy of Luxembourg, the Belgian provinces of Luxembourg, Namur, and Liège, and the Département of Ardennes in France. The product of a complex geological history, the plateau occupies an area of more than 3,860sq miles (10,000sq km), and encompasses the Forest of Ardennes consisting of an impressive 585sq miles (1,500sq km) of oak, beech, and ash.

A patchwork of diverse environments including barren lands, sparse heaths, dense woods, and rich meadows, the Ardennes has some of the most diverse and astonishingly beautiful landscapes in the world. Argonne in the east is a land of exquisite forests in which one can wander for calm and solitude. Bubbling streams run through pastures, and orchards neatly tucked away behind hills and farms bounded by copse hedges mark out the areas of human habitation. The Ardennes Hills are stumps of mountains, overgrown with forests of oak, ash, and birch, and with a thriving undergrowth of mosses and ferns; foxglove decorates the clearings. Orchids, the sundew, and the cotton grass are also found in abundance. Wildlife includes species such as roe deer, foxes, beavers, and the nightjar. The picturesque cliffs of Ardennes provide spectacular views of the surrounding lands.

Today, the name Ardennes is usually used to indicate the southern part of the area, where elevations vary between 1,150ft and 1,640ft (350m and 500m); the plateau reaches its greatest height of 2,277ft (694m) at Botrange, south of Liège. Made up of sandstone, quartzite, slate, and limestone, the rounded summits of the Ardennes are interspersed with shallow depressions

## CASTLES, FORTS, AND CHURCHES

Fortified castles, fortresses, and bastions have been built in the Ardennes since the early Middle Ages because of its location on a traditional invasion route. A majority were destroyed during the Hundred Years War, though some ruins still survive. Though most were built in semi-medieval styles, some excellent examples of brick and stone architecture from the Louis XIII period can still be seen. Residential chateaux started appearing in the 18th century. A fortified castle at Sedan, built in the 15th century, remains the largest in Europe. Churches—Romanesque, baroque or fortified like the castles—are found in every village. Remarkable among these are the Church of Asfeld, the abbey church of Mouzon, and Saint-Juvin en Argonne.

*Church of Asfeld, France*

containing peat bogs and narrow winding valleys carved out by the rivers that rise from them. The desolate uplands are characterized by heavy rainfall, low clouds, fog, and frost. Though forests cover half of the area, the thin acidic soil is mostly waterlogged, and can sustain only heath. The relatively lower northern portion of the Ardennes—measuring between 655ft and 985ft (200m–300m)—is, in contrast, covered by green pastures and cultivated farmlands. The high Ardennes forms a watershed between rivers which flow toward the Meuse and the Moselle rivers.

The Ardennes was formed as a result of intense tectonic activity involving folding, faulting, uplifts, and denudations, with older strata of rocks being thrust over newer layers. Part of the Hercynian orogenic belt that extends from western Ireland to Germany, the Ardennes region was formed approximately 300 to 400 million years ago, during the second half of the Paleozoic era. The plateau is cut extensively by the Meuse river and its tributaries, and has poor drainage in the higher areas, which are more conducive to the growth of swamps, bogs, and mossy patches than crops and trees. A large depression, which is known east of the Meuse as the Famenne and west of it as the Fagne, marks out the geological and topographical separation of Ardennes from the northern foothills.

*The lush green Ardennes forests*

## BATTLES AT ARDENNES

The Ardennes region—despite its difficult terrain—has been the scene of many battles since the French Revolution. Remarkable encounters include the campaign of 1794 and the Franco-German War, when Napoleon III surrendered at Sedan in 1870. Ardennes was also affected by the World Wars—the Battle of the Ardennes took place during World War I, and a bitter US-German encounter broke out in Argonne in 1918. The German breakthrough occurred near Sedan in 1940, marking the Battle of France. Ardennes was also the site for the final offensive action by the Germans in France during World War II, in December 1944— the famous encounter known as The Battle of the Bulge.

- The Eisriesenwelt Caves are not lit by electric lights. Visitors have to wear carbide lamps, and the most spectacular sights are illuminated with magnesium ribbon strips.
- The Eisriesenwelt Caves represent the largest accessible ice caves in the world today

**The Eisriesenwelt Caves,** Austria

*Tourists entering the Eisriesenwelt ice cave*

## SKIING AT TENNENGEBIRGE

The Tennengebirge range can be scaled at any time vof the year but the best months are September and October. Summer months are known for thunderstorms and in June many of the higher peaks are covered with snow. During this time the snow bridges over vertical caves get so thin that it is dangerous to ski. Skiers come here between February and April, although world climatic changes are forcing many to follow weather reports rather than traditional winter timings. It needs to be kept in mind that to enable skiing or snowboarding, karstic areas require far more snow than other mountains.

# The Eisriesenwelt Caves

The "Giant Ice Caves"–the Eisriesenwelt Höhle–were first discovered in 1879 when a natural scientist from Salzburg, Anton Posselt, stumbled into a giant cave on the Tennengebirge plateau and came face to face with the incredible wonderland of ice chambers and natural ice sculptures. It was not until the 1920s, when the speleologist Alexander von Mörk pursued the matter, that the uniqueness of the Eisriesenwelt ice caves was recognized and the first scientific expeditions and climbing routes established. Situated 25 miles (40km) south of Mozart's birthplace (Salzburg), the Tennengebirge range dominates the Salzach Valley to the west and offers one of the most stunning views of the Austrian Alps in the Hohe Tauern region.

The Eisriesenwelt Höhle, of which 26 miles (42 km) has been explored, and roughly only half a mile (0.8km) is open to visitors, are constantly being shaped and reshaped by the circulation of air and water precipitation caused by innumerable crevices, tunnels, and cave openings in the Tennengebirge range. The average temperature inside the freezing caverns is largely dependent on the outside temperature. In winter, the air inside the mountain is warmer whereas in spring, it is cooler. Located on the 7,976-ft (2,432-m) high triangular Tennengebirge plateau, the caves are part of the impressive set of cave ruins (partly collapsed and eroded caves) known as the Giant Caves Niveau. The plateau itself is devoid of any vegetation and is criss-crossed with tectonic faults and large ditches that are treacherous to cross during summer when the snow melts. In winter, however, it is possible to trek the area from east to west in a single day.

Geologically younger and found at higher elevations—4,920ft to 5,904ft (1,500m to 1,800m)— than the older Eiskogel Eishöhle, the Eisreisenwelt caves are part of the Austrian Alps formed during the Pleistocene Epoch. Its unique cave system is the work of the Central Alp rivers, which tore through the limestone and karst deposits to carve out one of the most astounding labyrinth's of natural wonders in the world.

When Posselt first stepped into the Eisriesenwelt entrance cave, a huge ice wall blocked the entry beyond the first chamber; today visitors can explore an entire series of caves connected with gangplanks, stairs, and handrails. Mörk, who likened his expeditions to that of Thor's journey to the Ice Giants, named the caves' chambers after characters from Norse mythology. These include the magnificent Hall of Hymir, Frigga's Veil, the Odin Room, the Ice Palace, and the 120-ft (36-m) high Alexander von Mörk Cathedral. In acknowledgment of his work and wishes, an urn containing his remains was placed here after he died during World War I.

*Hikers on the Tennengebirge mountain range, Salzburg*

## EXPLORING THE LIMESTONE MOUNTAIN RANGE

An interesting fact about Tennengebirge is that it is not a single mountain but a huge limestone karst range. It has steep slopes and a vast plateau that covers approximately 18sq miles (45sq km). The total mountain range extends over 94sq mile (240sq km). The highest peaks in this range are located at the western and southern rim of the Tennengebirge plateau. To get here one can follow the marked paths that often lead to huts located on the margins of the mountain range. Though the range is only 7,872ft (2,400m) high, the vertical distance between the surrounding valleys and the peaks exceeds 5,904ft (1,800m). The Tennengebirge is squeezed between the valleys of the River Salzach in the west, River Lammer in the north, and River Fritzbach in the south. Although it is one of the wettest places in Austria, its plateau resembles a desert during summer. This is due to karstification during which all water immediately disappears into the open joints, shafts, and caves of the limestone massif.

- The 49ft (15m) tall Orjak stalagmite, in the Velika Dvorana Hall, is the largest of its kind found in the Skocjan Caves.
- The Martel Chamber—479ft (146m) high, 394ft (120m) wide, and 1,010ft (308m) long—is the largest underground chamber in Europe.

**Skocjan Caves**, Slovenia

# Skocjan Caves

The Skocjan Caves is an extraordinary system of vast limestone caverns that lie in a region called Kras, or Karst, in southwestern Slovenia. It is from this karst plateau that the geological phenomenon derives its name. Comprising one of the largest underground canyons in the world, caves that are more than 66ft (200m) deep, underground passages extending for 3 miles (5km), dramatic collapsed dolines or sinkholes, and numerous picturesque waterfalls, the Skocjan Caves are a world-renowned site for the study and research of karst limestone phenomena.

The Skocjan Caves Regional Park, or Regijski Park Skocjanske jame, is situated 8 miles (13km) east of Trieste. Occupying an area of 1.6sq miles (4.13sq km), the park stretches from the area in the east where the River Reka first makes its appearance in a shallow canyon to a highway to Italy in the west. It encompasses the lower portion of the River Susica, the Skocjan Caves, and the area above the caves. First protected as a 0.3sq mile (0.8sq km) natural monument in 1980, the area was inscribed as a UNESCO World Heritage Site in 1986. It was expanded to its present size in 1990 and established as a

*Woman standing on a bridge in cave Zelske Jame in Rakov Skocjan*

## FLORA AND FAUNA

Though the surface of the caves consists primarily of dry grasslands, a variety of natural habitats are found within the caves. The disintegrated galleries and shallow chasms of the river valley experience microclimatic conditions, and thus different vegetations such as Mediterranean, sub-Mediterranean, Dinaric, and Illyrian thrive next to each other. Endemic species include the giant dead nettle. The speleofauna consists of creatures such as the snow vole, and a number of species of bats. Rare and endemic invertebrates, crustaceans, and cave beetles also abound; the cave salamander is one of the more remarkable and endemic vertebrates found in the Skocjan Caves.

*Stalagmites and stalactites in the Skocjan caves*

## CULTURAL HERITAGE

Excavations in the area of the Skocjan Caves demonstrate that the region has been occupied for more than 10,000 years. About 30 archeological sites are situated within the Skocjan Caves Regional Park, and 18 more such sites exist in the neighboring areas. According to the findings from the sites, the area was continuously inhabited from the middle Stone Age to the Iron Age; a fort was erected where Skocjan stands today during this latter period. The same place also saw the construction of another fort during the period of Roman settlement, and a fortified rural settlement was established during the Middle Ages. The written records of the Skocjan Caves date back two millennia, when Pozidonius of Apamea (135-50BC) wrote of them.

regional park in 1996. The Ramsar Convention established it as a Wetland of International Importance in 1999.

The underground passages carved out by the River Reka are among the most fantastic examples of large-scale karst drainage and topography. Entering the Skocjan grotto through a 1,148-ft (350-m) long subterranean passage, the Reka reappears at the bottom of two chasms which are 492ft (150m) deep and 98ft (300m) long. The river then disappears into one of the largest underground canyons in the world

The network of underground passages of Skocjan extends right up to Timavo on the Gulf of Trieste in Italy. The collapse of the gallery surfaces on various levels has produced many magnificent deep chasms, including the Sokolak in the south, Globocak in the west, and Sapen dol and Lisicina. The cave system also includes the Mahorcic grotto with its many underground lakes and five extraordinary cascades. Other striking features within the subterranean network include a narrow canal and five side galleries, including a 1,64-0ft (500-m) long gallery that leads to the surface. Breathtaking stalactites and stalagmites adorn these underground grottos, which reach a maximum depth of around 754ft (230m).

This impressive karst network also contains 25 waterfalls; among them is a magnificent cascade that is 535ft (163m) high. The most exceptional dripstone formations have many limestone pools and natural bridges that span the river at various points. The karstic terminology for a flat-floored depression with steep sides—doline or dolina—owes its origin to the two famous sinkholes of Mala dolina and Velika dolina. A number of species considered endangered the world over are preserved within the safety of the ecosystems of the dolinas and grottos of the Skocjan Caves.

- Kraft Foods in Switzerland, the makers of Toblerone, say that the triangular shape of their chocolate bar has been inspired by the Matterhorn.

- The Matterhorn Museum has on display the original rope used by the first successful expedition to the summit of the Horn in 1865. Of the seven-member climbing team, four lost their lives when the rope tore during the descent.

e **Matterhorn,** Switzerland

# The Matterhorn

The Matterhorn is a classic rock pyramid, with steep narrow ridges that jut out of the surrounding glaciers. The distinctive shape of this dramatic peak makes it a favorite with photographers and tourists around the world. Straddling the border between Switzerland and Italy, the mountain towers over the Swiss village of Zermatt and the Italian village of Breuil-Cervinia. Soaring to a height of 14,692ft (4,478m), it is the most famous mountain of the European Alps. While it is known as Mont Cervin in France and Monte Cervino in Italy, the residents of Zermatt call it Horu. The name Matterhorn is believed to be a combination of the German words Matt, meaning 'valley' or 'meadow,' and Horn, meaning 'peak.'

The peak that we see today was formed as a result of the dual action of tectonic movements and glacial activity. The process of formation began about 180 million years ago with the collision of the African and European plates. It reached a climax about 40 million years ago when the African plate convulsed, as it slid under the European plate, and mountains emerged out of the earth's crust—among them, the framework for today's Matterhorn. Around 2 million years ago, glacial activity took over, chiseling

## ALPINE PEAKS

The Alps have fascinated generations of visitors for their beauty and for the challenge they present. The highest mountain is Mont Blanc in France, which is 15,771ft (4,807m) high. The Jungfrau is considered one of the most spectacular of the snow-capped mountains.

The Eiger has achieved a place of importance because of the difficulty of its climbs: the almost sheer north face, 1 mile (1.8km) high, was not mastered until 1938. In Austria, the towering Zugspitze is the tallest of the Bavarian Alps and is popular with skiers and climbers. In the valley below, Garmisch-Partenkirchen—site of the 1936 Winter Olympics—has tramways to the crest of the mountain.

*The Matterhorn as seen from Zermatt*

the mountain—made up of granite, mica schist, gneiss, sandstone, and other rocks—and shaping it to form four tapering faces, converging at the peak. The steepness of the gradient keeps snow and ice from clinging tightly to the mountain, and any excess is regularly shed in the form of avalanches.

Although it is not the highest peak in the Alps, the shape of the Matterhorn has been a deterrent for mountaineers. The first serious attempts to scale the mountain from the Italian side were made in as late as 1857. The weather and the extremely challenging climb forced all parties back. The peak was finally conquered on July 14, 1865 by a team of seven men led by the British explorer Edward Whymper. They attempted the ascent from the Swiss side and began their climb along the now famous Hornli Ridge. Though the team managed to reach the peak, four of its members lost their lives during the descent. Three days after Whymper's team reached the peak, on July 17, 1865, four men led by the Italian guide Giovanni Carrel reached the summit via a ridge on the Italian side. After more successful summit attempts over the next few years, Lucy Walker became the first woman to ascend the mountain in 1871, and a few weeks later, Meta Brevoort followed suit.

Today, all the ridges and faces of the Matterhorn have been scaled, and in all seasons. Yet, it would be unwise to underestimate the perils inherent in attempting to conquer this peak. The difficult conditions and bad weather often lead to many climbers losing their lives to the mountain every year.

## SCALING THE MATTERHORN

The Matterhorn is one of the world's most frequently climbed mountains. Every part of it has been tackled, and the most popular routes have fixed ropes, ladders and huts. However, this should not fool anyone into thinking of it as an easy climb: the Matterhorn also has one of the highest death rates.

Local guides now take most climbers along the easiest and first ascent, Hornli Ridge and Lion Ridge, which have sections of fixed climbing aids. More experienced climbers go to the Zmutt and Furggen ridges, and the North Face presents the greatest challenge of all. Inexperienced climbers are advised to leave this mountain to the experts.

*A climber tackles the Matterhorn*

- Formed by the union of the Leschaux and the Geant glaciers, the Mer de Glace is one of the longest glaciers in the Alps, and extends for 3.5 miles (5.6km) on the northern side of Mont Blanc.

- Conifers and grasslands cover the Mont Blanc Massif, which is also home to many animals including the Alpine ibex, chamois, mountain pheasant, royal eagle, and the white Alpine partridge.

**Mont Blanc,** France/Italy

# Mont Blanc

The highest peak in the French Alps, and also the highest point in Europe, Mont Blanc stands tall at 15,771ft (4,807m). Part of the Savoy Alps, and variously referred to as The Roof of Europe, Mecca of Alpinism, and The Royal Summit, Mont Blanc straddles the Aosta Valley in Italy and Haute-Savoie in France. Though it is called Monte Bianco in Italy, the mountain is better known to the rest of the world by its French name, Mont Blanc. Both names translate as "white mountain," and are derived from the 40sq miles (100sq km) of the massif that is covered by glaciers.

Chamonix, a French town located at the foot of Mont Blanc, shot to worldwide fame when it was chosen as the venue for the first Winter Olympic Games in 1924. The area, however, had been well-known in scientific circles since the early 18th century, when glaciers such as Mer de Glace (sea of ice) and the Argentiere Glacier—which is the second largest in France—on the Mont Blanc Massif became a subject of research undertaken to understand the process of mountain formation. Glaciers spread across more than 66sq miles (170sq km) around Mont Blanc form a natural museum of dazzling beauty. There is great diversity in the glacial structures as well, ranging from glaciers such as the

*Climbers descending Mont Blanc, Rhône-Alpes, Haute-Savoie*

## HEIGHT OF MONT BLANC

A thick blanket of ice and snow covering the Mont Blanc is the cause of the instability of the summit height of the mountain. The peak has been under constant observation since the 1980s, and though the official height has been kept at 15,771ft (4,807m), according to GPS and satellite measurements, the height actually fluctuates between 15,771ft (4,807m) and 15,781ft (4,811m). In 2001, the height was recorded as 15,748.6ft (4,810.4m); following heat waves in Europe, the height was recorded as 15,770ft (4,808m) in 2005. Not only does its height vary, the snowy peak is also known to shift position very slightly. The rock summit of the mountain, under the layer of ice and snow, measures 15,718ft (4,792m), and is situated about 131ft (40m) away from the snow summit.

## MONT BLANC TUNNEL

The Mont Blanc Tunnel passes through the mountain and links Haute-Savoie in France and the Aosta Valley in Italy. This tunnel is a lifeline for Italy, which depends on it for the transportation of around 33 percent of its freight to northern Europe. Built at a height of 4091ft (1,247m) on the French side and 4,530ft (1,381m) on the Italian side, the construction of this 7.3-mile (11.7-km) long tunnel began in 1957, and it was finally opened to traffic in 1965. Subsequent plans of expansion of the tunnel have, however, been shelved because of protests about the detrimental effect of heavy vehicular traffic. The tunnel was closed for three years after a disastrous fire broke out inside in March 1999, but was reopened in March 2002.

*A view of Rhône-Alpes, Haute-Savoie*

Le Tour, which terminates in a stunning hanging glacier, to the Les Bossons, which exhibits a magnificent vertical drop of 11,152ft (3,400m) from the top of Mont Blanc to the valley at its base.

The evolution of Mont Blanc is divided into three phases, with the first dating back almost 500 million years. This period of evolution spans the Jurassic and Tertiary Ages, and tracks of dinosaurs found in the region now known as Emosson, give credence to the theory. Scientists believe that a massive body of water—Tetide—appeared at the site of the Alps during the Second Phase, between 250 and 60 million years ago; the Alps lay buried under a sea bed several hundred meters thick, formed from marine sedimentation. During the Third Phase, the African and European plates collided with each other, causing the Alps to rise from the ocean bed approximately 30 million years ago; the Mont Blanc Massif emerged about 28 million years ago.

Mountaineers, too, were drawn to Mont Blanc from the early 18th century. However, climbing as a sport grew in stature only when Horace Bénédict de Saussure, a scientist from Geneva, took it upon himself in 1760 to declare a reward for anyone who could climb the peak. The money was finally claimed more than two decades later, on August 8, 1786, by Chamonix doctor Michel-Gabriel Paccard and his porter Jacques Balmat. In 1808, Marie Paradis became the first woman to reach the summit. Today, more than 20,000 people climb the mountain annually.

**Plitvice Lakes,** Croatia

• Though temperatures at the Lakes Prosce and Kozjak climb up to 75°F (24°C) in summer, the entire Plitvice is snow-covered from November to March, and the lakes freeze December–January, creating a pristine and magical landscape.

• The "Milka Trnina Waterfalls" have been named in recognition of the famous Croatian opera singer's contribution to the Society for Protection and Embellishment of the Plitvice Lakes in 1897.

# Plitvice Lakes

An unbroken chain of beautiful lakes, caves, and cascades make up the beautiful Plitvice Lakes (or Plitvicka Jezera in Serbo-Croatian) in western Croatia. Divided into the Upper Lakes (Gornja jezera) and Lower Lakes (Donja jezera), the lakes are mostly fed by the waters of the Black River and the White River which form a confluence near Plitvicki Ljeskovac, and then run together to the first of the lakes as the Matica River. The 16 lakes of Plitvice form a chain that is 5 miles (8km) long.

The Upper Lakes comprises 12 picturesque lakes, starting with Proscansko (Lake Prosce). Situated 2,096ft (639m) above sea level, this is the highest of them, and is linked to the other lakes by numerous waterfalls. Kozjak, the very last in the Upper Lakes section, is also the largest of the Plitvicka Jezera. Measuring nearly 150ft (46m), these are also the deepest water bodies in the area. The Upper and Lower Lakes have different geological origins. While the former occupies a wide, gently sloping dolomite basin in the Korana Valley, the smaller and shallower Lower Lakes

*Waterfall, Plitvice Lakes National Park*

## HERITAGE OF PLITVICE

Also called the Land of the Falling Lakes, the Plitvice Lakes area was the cradle of the prehistoric Illarian tribe of Yopuds, from around 1,000BC Roman settlements followed the Yopudic society, and the area has been continuously occupied by the Slavs since the 8th century. Tools dating back to the Bronze Age, as well as ceramics and remnants of fortifications, have been found in the area.

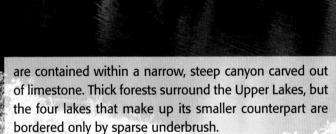

## PLITVICE NATIONAL PARK

Though the Plitvice Lakes were accorded the status of a national park as early as 1928, the region's boundaries were only finalized and properly designated and developed in 1949. The Croatian Parliament expanded the area of the park further by 39sq miles (100sq km) in 1997, leading to its present size of 114sq miles (295sq km). The Plitvice National Park was inscribed as a UNESCO Natural World Heritage Site in 1979. The Balkan War in the 1990s led to the park being placed on a list of World Heritage sites in danger in 1992, but it was removed in 1996.

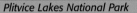

*Plitvice Lakes National Park*

are contained within a narrow, steep canyon carved out of limestone. Thick forests surround the Upper Lakes, but the four lakes that make up its smaller counterpart are bordered only by sparse underbrush.

Waterfalls at the Plitvice Lakes range from "splashers", which are only a few feet high, to huge "tumblers" that drop from heights of over 82ft (25m). The Novakovica Brod, separated from another lake by a travertine barrier only 6.5ft (2m) high and at an elevation of 1,650ft (503m), is the last and the lowest of the Plitvice Lakes. Waters from this lake form numerous waterfalls that tumble over the edge to a wide stone depression called Sastavci. The waters then continue to the Plitvice Brook, where a vertical fall—measuring 249ft (76m)—into a rocky scar marks the beginning of the flow of the Korana River.

The formation of this exquisite landscape is largely attributed to the deposition of phytogenetic travertine, (calcareous tufa), over the last 4,000 years. These deposits grew thickly in places, creating barriers behind which the water was barricaded, and thus the lakes were formed. A number of caves and vaults are scattered over the lake area. Fourteen limestone caves and six travertine caves have been discovered in the cliffs that surround the lakes and border the Korana River. The most remarkable among these is the Supljara Cave, situated just above Kaluderovac Lake in the Lower Lakes region. A dark tunnel that leads into the mountainside, this cavern was formed by the dissolution of porous limestone by the water that seeped in, and showcases ancient fossil clams that once lived in the shallow sea that covered this area millions of years ago.

This isolated corner of Croatia was once called Lika, or "Land of the Wolf", by its native inhabitants; even today gray wolves roam the forests of beech, fir, maple, elm, and spruce that surround the lakes. Brown bears, lynx, olms, the European pond turtle, the black stork, and Ural owls also inhabit the area.

- The Transylvanian Alps are known as *Carpatii Meridionali* in Romanian.
- First established in 1935, the Retezat National Park today covers 218sq miles (559sq km) of the mountainside and provides refuge to many creatures including the chamois.

# Transylvanian Alps

S cattered villages beneath a soaring mountain range make up the almost medieval landscape of the Transylvanian Alps. Arching across the country of Romania, the wild and rugged Carpathian Mountains are Eastern Europe's backbone. The southernmost section of this sprawling mountain system, from the Prahova River valley in the east to the valley of the Cerna and Timis rivers in the west, forms the picturesque Transylvanian Alps in south central Romania.

Formed during the Tertiary Age, the Carpathians are a part of the Alpine-Himalayan system and the eastern segment of the European Alpine fold chain. Composed primarily of dense crystalline and volcanic rocks, the Southern Carpathians have a rather looming character that distinguishes them from the other sections of the Carpathians. One of the final bastions of untamed nature in Europe, the Transylvanian Alps have a total length of about 155 miles (250km). The average elevation of the mountain range is between 4,920ft and 5,740ft (1,500m and 1,750m). Higher and more continuous than the other sections of the Carpathians, the Transylvanian Alps are also more impassable and bridged by only four passes. Brezoi, Hateg, and Petrosani form the notable lowland depressions in the area.

## TRANSYLVANIAN WEATHER

Winter in the mountains lasts from November or December through May or June, and temperatures often dip below freezing point. The Transylvanian Alps remain covered by snow and ice, and the area is the sole preserve of well-equipped veterans of Alpine mountaineering. Skiing in the mountains, however, is restricted to the eastern slopes of Bucegi. The summer months herald the return of hikers and walkers, even though the weather can often be unpredictable, and mist and rainfall is common.

*Winter view of a village and steepled church, Bukkloka-Fagetel, Transylvania*

The Fagaras, Bucegi, Parang, and Retezat-Godeanu massifs form the major subdivisions of the Transylvanian Alps. Ease of access makes Bucegi the favored destination of holidaymakers since the main road from Brasov to Bucharest passes through the Prahova Valley, which forms the eastern boundary of this massif. While three main routes through thick forests allow walkers and trekkers to explore the mountains, other tourists can use the two cable cars that serve the area. The mountain paths pass along rocky precipices carved out by the wind and through Alpine meadows, finally leading to Mount Omu, which at 8,216ft (2,505m) is the tallest peak in the mountain chain.

Squeezed between Bucegi in the east and Fagaras in the west is the ridge of the Piatra Craiului. One of the most beautiful sights in the Transylvanian Alps, this closely arranged sliver of white limestone peaks is only 11 miles (18km long). Walking trails begin from the north and then follow a precarious path along the tapering spine of the ridge, before descending southwards into an area of remarkable karst topography, with deep gorges, pitted slopes, and a series of caves carved into the mountainside.

Overlooking the Fagaras depression through which the Olt River gently flows south to the Carpathian foothills, the steep northern face of the Fagaras massif rises 8,000ft (2,450m) above sea level. This range—the highest in the Transylvanian Alps—runs for about 30 miles (48km), and is heavily glaciated, with scalloped peaks and moraine deposits. A relatively inaccessible and isolated section of the Transylvanian Alps, this massif also contains the two of the highest points in Romania: at 8,346ft (2,544m), Mount Moldoveanu is the tallest of the Southern Carpathian peaks, followed closely by Mount Negoiu, which measures 8,317ft (2,535m).

Covered with lush and abundant vegetation, the Transylvanian Alps also provide sanctuary to a rich and varied wildlife, including wolves and bears.

## COMMUNICATION AND POWER

Though the high passes of Bran, Novaci-Sugag, and Valcan allow communication at elevations reaching up to 7,400ft (2,256m), the main roads and railways that connect the Transylvanian Alps are located in the scenic river valleys of Olt, Jiu, and Danube. A joint Romanian-Yugoslav navigation and power project has harnessed the fast-flowing waters of the Danube at the Iron Gate (Portile de Fier) gorge. This power station has greatly improved navigation facilities in the area and is capable of generating a few million kilowatts of power. Deposits of iron, coal, and lignite have also been discovered in the southern Carpathians.

*Bran Castle (Vlad the Impaler's alleged castle), Bran, Transylvanian Alps*

- The wine produced on the slopes of Mount Vesuvius is known as "Lacrima Christi." In ancient Pompeii, wine containers would often be labeled with the name Vesuvinum.

- The sudden explosive bursts that have come to characterize Vesuvius's eruptions are called "Plinian" because of the description of the AD79 explosion by Pliny the Younger.

## FLIRTING WITH FIRE

The Osservatorio Vesuviano was founded in 1841 by Ferdinand II of Bourbon. It was housed in the side of an old building called Eremo, a resting spot for travelers who intended to climb the mountain. Situated on the southern border of the Somma caldera, it was sandwiched between two deep valleys. The aim was to observe the manner in which the mountain evolved and to understand it better. The observatory has weathered eruptions since the 1850s without any significant damage.

# Mount Vesuvius

Located in the Campania region of Italy, Mount Vesuvius looms large in the background of the beautiful landscape of the Bay of Naples. Part of the larger Campanian volcanic arc, it is the only volcano on the European mainland to have erupted in the last century.

Though it shows no signs of life today, Vesuvius is considered one of the world's most dangerous volcanoes for the threat it poses to the dense population of the surrounding area. More than 200,000 people crowd around this volcano, drawn by the fertile soils which are perfect for growing a variety of crops.

Mount Vesuvius rose as a result of the collision between the African and Eurasian tectonic plates, which caused the earth to buckle and fold, and finally rise as the African plate slid under the other. The friction in turn caused the crust to melt, forming magma that found its way to the earth's surface and resulted in the formation of the volcano we see today.

Vesuvius was considered sacred by the Greeks and the Romans because of its association with the god Hercules; the town of Herculaneum was constructed at its base. The volcano's most famous eruption in AD79 resulted in Herculaneum as well as Pompeii being buried under molten lava, ash, and dust several feet deep. An estimated 20,000 people were killed.

Over 50 eruptions have been recorded since the catastrophe of AD79, though none can match the severity of the devastation caused during that cataclysmic explosion. The height of the eruption column is estimated to have risen a staggering 20 miles (32km). The impact of the 1906 eruption blew away the top of the mountain itself, leading to the death of several hundred people. The 1944 eruption resulted in the height of the mountain being raised by approximately 492ft (150m), and the size of the crater increased threefold. Today, at its highest point, Vesuvius reaches 4,200ft (1280m).

The vineyards and orchards that cover the slopes of Vesuvius make way for groves of oak and chestnut further up along the gradient. The forests extend to the peak on the northern side, and higher up on the western side undulating plateaus are covered with broom. Inside the caldera the slopes are almost barren except for clusters of meadow plants. During the long period of dormancy before the violent eruption in 1631, the crater once held forests and lakes. Volcanic gases given off during periods of eruption, however, destroy all vegetation on the slopes.

*A view over Pompeii toward Mount Vesuvius*

## PRESERVING POMPEII

Parco Nationale Vesuvio, or the Vesuvius National Park, is the smallest park in Italy. Occupying only 34.7sq miles (84.8sq km), it encompasses the areas surrounding the mountain and the Somma caldera. It was set up in June 5, 1995 with the aim of preserving the flora and fauna of the area, and the many geological irregularities and paleontological formations that have been uncovered by archeologists over the years. Regulated tourism has also been promoted in the area to ensure that the local residents can earn a living and to increase awareness regarding the need for preservation of the ruins.

*Restored buildings in the Roman town buried in AD79 by ash flows from Mount Vesuvius*

- The name Cappadocia derives from the Persian word *Katpatuka*, which means "Land of Beautiful Horses."
- Today, many visitors choose to view Cappadocia from hot air balloons; floating gently over this incredible vista can be a unique experience.

**Cappadocia,** Turkey

*Church site cut into the rocks in the Göreme Valley; ropes are used to climb the ancient steps*

## CAPPADOCIA'S CHURCHES

The Apple Church and the Church of the Buckle (Tokali Kilise) are among the well-known churches in Cappadocia. The largest church in Göreme, Tokali Kilise, was restored to some of its early glory in the 1960s. The ninth-century frescos contained in the main nave make this church a remarkable one; also showcased are 11th-century frescos painted in the metropolitan style. These include depictions of the 12 apostles, the saints, and scenes from the life of Jesus.

# Cappadocia

Myriad shapes and contours carved out by the elements over millennia have earned Cappadocia in Anatolia (ancient Asia Minor) the name "Lunar Land." Situated in modern-day Turkey, there is something alien and lunar about the bizarre stone towers and cones, and the mysterious crags that dot the landscape of this ancient land.

The formation of Cappadocia began millions of years ago, as volcanic eruptions shook the earth. A long chain of lava-spewing eruptions during the Cenozoic era (between 30 and 60 million years ago to the present) are believed to have been responsible for the creation of Cappadocia. The lava from the upheavals were converted over eons to form a malleable stone called "tuff"—a mix of volcanic ash, lava, and mud. Elements eroded and molded this stony land, creating deep valleys bordered by steep undulating cliffs and giving rise to the structures that are seen today—formations that resemble palaces, steeples, towers, and sometimes even giant-headed mushrooms. Wind and water worked on these structures, smoothening and polishing them until they evolved into the present day visual wonders that they are. These magnificent stone façades are multi-hued, their colors ranging from bone white to blue to tan, orange, and pink.

The most unusual and famous of Cappadocia's natural formations, however, are the "fairy chimneys."

A photographer's delight, the fairy chimneys are scattered all over the Cappadocia landscape. These amazing structures are nothing but cones of tuff and volcanic ash covered with protective slabs of hard basalt at the top, which resemble cut columns with hats. Spectacular from all angles, these stone columns look particularly beautiful at dusk, burnished by the glow of the setting sun.

When man first arrived in the area, he dug, dredged, and carved the stone, leaving behind a sculpted record of life dating back to the Hittites of the late Bronze Age. Cappadocia hosts treasures below the ground too—subterranean cities more than 10 stories deep have been discovered here. Built as a defense against attacks, the cities boast mazes and labyrinthine tunnels—which often lead to inescapable pitfalls—constructed to bewilder and dispose of particularly persistent enemies. The cities of Kaymakli and Derinkuyu have today been opened up to visitors; however, because of the many treacherous passages they are strongly advised to follow directions and signs. The discovery of both Hittite artifacts and a Roman tomb at Derinkuyu suggest that these cities were expanded and occupied by Christians fleeing Arab persecution. They were used as recently as 1839, when the Turks, facing an Egyptian invasion, sought refuge in them.

Above ground, Cappadocia's rocks were converted into churches, monasteries, and sanctuaries adorned with Byzantine art. This ranged from the primitive icons of the seventh century to geometric designs derived from the cross during the Iconoclastic period (726–843) and 13th-century art (when a Mongol invasion and Islam severed Cappadocia's connection with Byzantium).

Thus, Cappadocia, with its magnificent lunar landscape and its hidden subterranean cities, remains one of the world's most fascinating natural as well as historical attractions.

## GÖREME

Situated in the "fairy chimneys" region of Cappadocia, Göreme has been inhabited constantly for at least 16 centuries. The presence of spectacular rock formations, evidence of Byzantine art, dwellings, troglodyte villages, and underground towns led to the Göreme Valley being declared a historical national park in 1986. Göreme National Park and the Rock Sites of Cappadocia were inscribed on the UNESCO World Heritage List in 1986

*View of Göreme with houses carved in conical rock formations (troglodyte dwellings)*

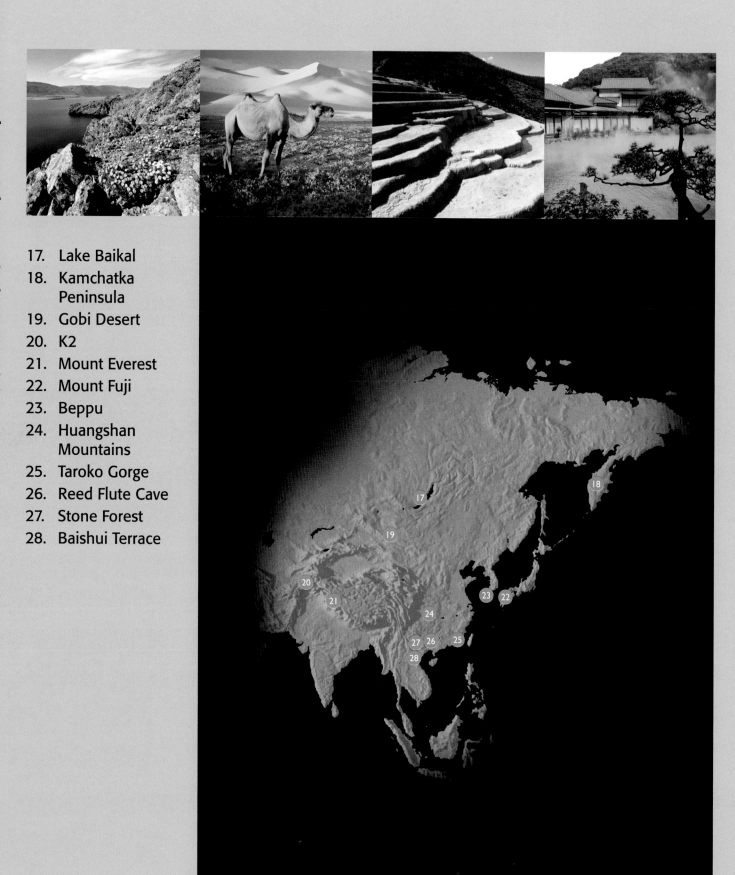

# Asia

Occupying four-fifths of the great Eurasian landmass, Asia is the world's largest and most diverse continent. Bound by the Arctic Ocean to the north, the Bering Strait and the Pacific Ocean to the east, the Indian Ocean to the south, and the Mediterranean and Red Sea in the southwest, it encompasses mighty civilizations and wildlife kingdoms in a vast area of 4.7 million sq ft (439,100 sq miles).

The highest point on earth, Mount Everest is to be found here, as is the most active volcanic site, the Kamchatka Peninsula in Siberia where 29 active volcanoes stage one of the most spectacular shows witnessed by humankind. In the continent's waters south and southeast of the mainland lies an entire realm of water-bound countries—archipelagos and islands—that extend to the Oceanic and Australian realms—Sri Lanka, Java, Sumatra, Borneo, Indonesia, the list is long.

The latest studies conducted by the American Museum for Natural History in 2006, and published in the acclaimed journal Nature, point to some startling discoveries in the region. Not only is this landmass home to some of the most ancient civilizations, it could also be the planet's original laboratory of mammals!

Like other parts of the globe, Asia is home to some magnificent splendors of nature. The "blue eye" of Siberia, Lake Baikal, one of world's deepest lakes, has as many as 330 rivers flowing into it; the chain of isles off the Indian east coast, the Andaman and Nicobar Islands, is home to one of the nomadic tribes that is close to extinction; the only three rivers to run parallel to each other—the Yangtze, the Mekong, and the Salween—cut through Yunnan Province in China and form one of the richest regions in the world in terms of biodiversity; and in Japan, the Beppu Hot Springs set the trend for "onsen culture" (thermal spring saunas in manicured Japanese gardens) that's as old as people can remember. Charlie Chaplin tried it, as did Mother Teresa, and the hordes of tourist that make their way to the springs every year.

- It would take approximately one year for all the major rivers—Volga, Don, Dnieper and Yenisei, Ural and Ob, Ganges and Orinoko, Amazon and Thames, Seine and Oder—to fill up the basin of Lake Baikal.

- Age and isolation are responsible for the unique freshwater fauna of Lake Baikal, which has earned it the name the "Galapagos of Russia." Eighty percent of the species that inhabit this lake are endemic.

**Lake Baikal,** Russia

# Lake Baikal

Flanked by mountains that rise higher than 6,600ft (2,000m) above the surface of the sea, Lake Baikal is situated in a depression in southeastern Siberia, within the Republic of Buryatia and the Irkutsk province of Russia. Created approximately 25 million years ago, Baikal is the oldest existing freshwater lake in the world. With a maximum depth of 5,315ft (1,620m), it is the deepest continental body of water.

The largest freshwater lake in the world in terms of volume—approximately 5,500cu miles (23,000cu km)—it holds about 20 percent of all the freshwater on the earth's surface. The lake measures 395 miles (636km) in length and has an average width of 30 miles (48km).

*Baikal Seal resting on a rock, Zabaikalsky National Park, Lake Baikal*

## NATURE RESERVES

The Barguzinsky Nature Reserve on the northeastern shore of the lake and the Baikalsky Nature Reserve on the southern shore were established in 1916 and 1969 respectively, in order to protect and conserve the lake and its environs. Between the two of them, the reserves protect over 1,000sq miles (2,564sq km) of territory, and help maintain the Baikal ecosystem in an undisturbed condition. Apart from protecting the area's vegetation and wildlife, these reserves also carry out research in the area of natural sciences. Since their creation, another nature reserve, two wildlife reserves, and two national parks have also been created in the area.

## BAIKAL'S HERITAGE

Around 1,200 archeological sites have been discovered around Lake Baikal, including rock drawings, stone walls, and remnants of ancient settlements; 1,000 of these monuments are legally protected. Mentioned in ancient Chinese, Muslim, and Russian writings, the Lake Baikal Basin has been inhabited in the past by tribes such as the Huns, ancient Turks, Uighurs, Kidanhs, and the Kaganates of Zhouzhanhs. The area also has a rich heritage of Mongolian culture, and the 13th-century Mongolian leader Genghis Khan is believed to have been born on Ol'khan Island. Today, the area is inhabited primarily by the Sayat and the Buryat people, many of whom lead very traditional lifestyles.

*About 50 species of edible fish live in Lake Baikal's icy waters, and are fished by locals*

The basin of Lake Baikal has been formed by a complex of grabens—that is, portions of the land dropping considerably lower than their surroundings along fault lines in the earth's crust. Faults are common in the area, and account for the presence of many hot mineral springs. The region is also prone to occasional but severe earthquakes, such as the one in 1862 that flooded a very large area in the northern Selenga delta, and created the new Proval Bay in Baikal.

The basin of this vast lake is asymmetrical—the steep western slopes provide a dramatic foil to the gently sloping eastern shore. The shoreline meanders for almost 1,300 miles (2,100km), and indents at the bays and inlets. The lake is fed by 336 rivers and streams, including the large Selenga, Barguzin, Upper Angara, Chikoy, and Uda rivers; however, only one river, the Angara, flows out of it again. About 45 islands and islets dot the surface of the almost crystal-clear water of the lake; Olkhon, occupying 270sq miles (700sq km), is the largest among them. Though Baikal's climate is milder than that of its surrounding territory, the surface of the lake freezes in January, and thaws only in May or June. In the deeper areas of the lake, waves can rise as high as 15ft (4.6m).

The great depths of Lake Baikal are a treasure house of an incredible variety of flora and fauna. While hundreds of plant species, most of which are endemic to Baikal, survive on or near the surface, between 1,500 and 1,800 animal species roam its depths. As many as 50 species of fish—with 25 species of gobies forming the majority—swim the lake. The golomyanka, a species of fish that is extraordinary for giving birth to live young, is endemic to Lake Baikal; so is the Baikal seal, or nerpa, the only mammal to live in the lake. More than 320 bird species have been discovered around the lake.

Covering an area of 33,980sq miles (88,000sq km), the lake and its surroundings, were declared a UNESCO World Heritage Site in 1996.

• The first official expedition to the Kamchatka Peninsula was commissioned by Tsar Peter I of Russia in 1725.

• The rivers of Kamchatka are said to contain the world's greatest diversity of salmonid fish, 11 species of which are known to co-exist peacefully in a single river.

**Kamchatka Peninsula,** Russia

## FLYING HIGH

In 1994 the eruption of the Klyuchevskoy Volcano in north Kamchatka, blasted a 49,000-ft (14,935-m) ash column into the sky. Winds of 150mph (240km/h) blew the ash cloud more than 620 miles (1,000km) southeast over the Pacific Ocean at altitudes of 31,000ft to 38,000ft (9,500m to 11,500m), sweeping across vital air routes in both Russian and US air space.

# Kamchatka Peninsula

The sight of bears dashing across the steaming thermal terrain is unforgettable, as are the fuming volcanoes, geysers, and hot springs of Russia's Kamchatka Peninsula. The geological uniqueness of Kamchatka is that it lies at the junction of major tectonic plates in an area of active volcanic activity where contemporary processes and the history of our planet cannot be separated from each other.

Jutting into the North Pacific Ocean and located in the northeast corner of Siberia, with Alaska to its northwest, Kamchatka—a 4,920-mile (1,500-km) long peninsula, roughly the size of Germany, Austria, and Switzerland put together—currently has 29 active volcanoes, plus 300 hibernating giants, looming over a wilderness of more than 150 thermal and mineral springs, geysers, and

grizzlies. The region is also home to some unique species of animals, amphibians, birds and fish, such as salmon fish, sea otters, brown bears (the Kamchatka subspecies is one of the largest bears in the world), white-tailed eagles, gyr falcons, and Stellar's sea eagle. Out of the 1,168 plant species, 10 percent are not found anywhere else.

The remoteness and ruggedness of Kamchatka has prevented many from exploiting the land and defiling this beautiful landscape. Though it was first discovered by the Cossacks, it escaped attention until a Soviet strategic military base was set up here during the Cold War. It was only after the collapse of the Soviet Union that the area was opened to the public. The region today includes three federal reserves—the Kronotsky, Koryaksky, and Komandorsky, and four natural parks, Bystrinsky,

A brown bear mother and her cubs in a river at the foot of a volcanic mountain, Kamchatka Peninsula

Yuzhno-Kamchatsky, Klyuchevskoy, and Nalychevo—and has been included in the UNESCO World Heritage site list since 1996. The nature reserve's greatest draws are the Uzon Caldera and the Valley of Geysers.

The Kamchatka is exceptionally beautiful—with large symmetrical volcanoes interspersed with lakes, wild rivers, and a spectacular coastline. It also boasts the unique phenomena of salmon-spawning areas and major concentrations of sea bird colonies along the coastal zone of the Bering Sea. The interior areas, such as Uzon Caldera, formed 40,000 years ago by a volcano that is now extinct, present a living on-site geological museum—containing hot springs, cold rivers, poisonous mud cauldrons, as well as pristine lakes full of fish, a berry tundra and birch forest, mountains, bogs, animals, and birds

Though untouched so far, the Kamchatka Peninsula is today facing increasing environmental degradation caused by gold mining, unregulated tourism, forest logging, and oil extraction.

## VALLEY OF GEYSERS TRAGEDY

On June 3, 2007 the Valley of Geysers was seriously damaged by a massive slide of boulders, gravel, snow, and ice. Fortunately, the main geyser field Vitrazh (Stained Glass) and the largest geyser Velikan (The Giant) escaped the devastation. At the same time, however, the famous entrance to the valley and some of the most beautiful geysers including Pervenets (The Firstborn), Sakharny (Sugar), Sosed (The Neighbor), and Troynoy (The Triplets), were lost forever. It was the largest landslide ever to have taken place on the peninsula.

The world-famous Geyser Valley in the Kronotsky Nature Reserve. The valley is one of the few places in the world where geysers jab holes through the earth's surface to spew boiling hot water into the air.

• It was during the expeditions to the Gobi Desert—which took place between 1922 and 1925—that the first fossil dinosaur eggs were discovered.

• The American explorer Roy Chapman Andrews and his adventures in the Gobi are believed to have been the inspiration for the fictional character, Indiana Jones, the intrepid archeologist and adventurer.

**Gobi Desert,** Mongolia

*A camel in the Gobi Desert National Park, Khongoryn Els Dunes*

# Gobi Desert

Not unlike the waves that rise and fall in a vast ocean, the sand dunes of the great Gobi ripple and sing smoothly, belying its reputation of being one of the harshest and coldest deserts in the world. It is from this land, spread across 500,000sq miles (1,295,000sq km), dotted with flat hills, dry lakebeds, and arid grasslands that Genghis Khan and his fierce armies rode out to conquer new worlds.

In the 13th century Marco Polo crossed the Gobi Desert on his legendary travels to Asia and China; the renowned Venetian traveler went on to spend several years in the service of the Great Khan, Kublai Khan. Centuries later, between 1922 and 1930, explorer Roy Chapman Andrews staved off thirst and dehydration, thanks to leather pouches filled with water his party was carrying, and fought off brigands with his pistol as he scoured the dunes for the bones and nests of dinosaurs. Today, friendly Mongolian nomads, with their herds of sheep and camel, roam Gobi, the planet's northernmost desert.

Stretching more than 1,000 miles (1,613km) wide across northern Asia, the Gobi, meaning "waterless place," straddles the border of Mongolia and the area of northern China that makes up Inner Mongolia. Legend has it that this desert was created by a spell cast by a Mongolian chief accomplished in the art of necromancy. Forced to flee his village, with the Chinese army in hot pursuit, the Mongolian chieftain, unable to shake off his foes, employed black magic to shrink and shrivel the land behind him. Trapped in this harsh land devoid of water and vegetation, his Chinese adversaries died a slow and painful death.

The Gobi holds a special place in the hearts of prehistorians. It is one of the richest sites in the world for discovering dinosaur bones and eggs, with some of them being found mere inches below the surface. Gobi's hidden treasures include among others the well-preserved remains of the Oviraptor, a flying dinosaur, brooding over its eggs. It was the discovery of this skeleton that led paleontologists to consider for the first time that dinosaurs did actually protect their offspring, providing precious insight into the social behavior of the creatures.

Though it appears barren of any life forms to the ordinary eye, the Gobi does have its residents. Khulan (wild asses), Saiga antelopes, takhi horses, the endangered snow leopard, and the Gobi bear—the only kind of bear known to live in any desert—call Gobi their home. It also has a large population of ibex. The Gobi Desert is also home to poisonous reptiles—in his autobiography, *Under A Lucky Star*, Chapman describes killing 47 vipers in a single night! Hardy creatures that they are, these animals have to withstand temperatures that soar to more than 104°F (40°C) in summer and drop to well below freezing in winter.

## EKHIINGOL

An abandoned oasis encompassed within the southern end of the arid Gobi Desert, Ekhiingol was once a significant agricultural research station during the communist regime. Today, the township is inhabited by less than 20 families. Basic vegetables and fruits that are grown here are sold locally. Also, the absence of air transport facilities make trade with the outside world an impossible task; even the provincial capital is roughly 248 miles (400km) away, with no easily accessible routes.

## GOBI GURVANSAIKHAN NATIONAL PARK

Established in 1993, the Gobi Gurvansaikhan is the largest national park in Mongolia. Covering an area of around 10,530sq miles (27,000sq km), it is situated at the northern edge of the Gobi Desert. The name Gurvansaikhan meaning "Three Beauties," refers to the three sub-ranges of the desert—the east, middle, and west. A host of rare plants and animals are found in this park, including wild herds of gazelles and Bactrian camels. The world's most endangered big cat, the snow leopard, and the Siberian ibex are found in this park as well. The Gobi Gurvansaikhan National Park also encompasses the Yolyn Am, a deep and narrow gorge containing an ice field. The famous Khongoryn Els, or the "Singing Sands," is an area of sand dunes surrounded by stunningly beautiful colored sandstone formations.

*Gurvansaikhan National Park, Gobi Desert*

- The base of the snow and glacier-clad K2 is at an elevation of 15,000ft (4,573m) on the Godwin Austen Glacier.
- The mighty Karakoram Range posed the biggest challenge to the early traders who had to use the Silk Road, which cut through the mountain chain to travel between Europe or the Middle East and China.

**K2,** China/Pakistan

# K2

Rising up from the heart of the Karakoram Range, the magnificent K2 stands tall at a height of 28,251ft (8,611m). The second largest peak in the world after Mount Everest, K2 stands at the head of the Godwin Austen Glacier, a branch of the famous Baltoro Glacier.

Situated partly in China and partly in Pakistan, this gigantic pyramid-like mountain is currently under the jurisdiction of Pakistan. K2 was discovered and measured by Colonel T. G. Montgomerie of the Survey of India in 1856. While surveying the mountains of Kashmir, Montgomerie first noticed a high and prominent mountain in the direction of the Karakorams, and assigned it the symbol K1 (K standing for Karakoram); consequently, this mountain turned out to be the Masherbrum in the Hushe Valley. Behind it, Montgomerie noticed another impressive summit, and christened it K2. Known as Chogori by the locals, K2 is also called Mount Godwin Austen, after the 19th century geographer Colonel H. H. Godwin Austen, the first surveyor of the peak.

A majority of the mountain ranges of Asia—the Hindu Kush, the Pamir, the Karakoram, and the Himalayas—are a result of the collision of the Indian and Asian tectonic plates. Karakoram and its surrounding ranges were created in the Eocene Epoch, approximately 40 million years ago, by the upliftment of the earth's crust. The series of Ice Ages that occurred during the Pleistocene Epoch (over the past one million years) and the erosion processes of the Holocene Epoch (in the last 12,000 years) covered the peaks with snow and gave the mountain range its current shape and topography.

The K2 area comprises some of the most astounding peaks in the world. Trekking on the Baltoro Glacier is distinctly rewarding, as it provides amazing views of the Masherbrum at 25,420ft (7,750m), the Uli Biaho Tower at 20,042ft (6,109m), and Grand Cathedral at 17,148ft (5,228m). From Concordia—the point where Baltoro is met by its tributary glacier Godwin Austen Glacier—a spectacular view of K2 is possible, as well as of Broad Peak, Gasherbrum Group, Golden Throne, and Chogolisa.

## K2's Walls

The towering north face of K2 is one of the biggest rock walls in the world; the right side of this wall is occupied by the enormous north pillar. The incredible east wall rises high over the Godwin Austen Glacier and houses the gigantic terrace of ice called "K2's Arm." The west wall of the mountain is divided into two parts by the west pillar—one section rises over the Negrotto Glacier, while the main part rises over the Savoia Glacier. A huge rocky section called the "Barrel" can be found here. The south face of the mountain comprises two spurs; while the right one extends to the Abruzzi Spur, the left spur combines with the southwest pillar over the hanging glacier de Filippi.

*Broad Peak above Godwin Austen Glacier, Karakoram mountains, Pakistan*

## KARAKORAM'S IMPORTANCE

The Karakoram Range is of immense significance to geologists and scientists for many reasons. Located at the boundary of two colliding continental landmasses, it is one of the most geologically active areas in the world, thus forming a valuable source of information and observation in the understanding of tectonic plate movements. It is also of importance to studies that concentrate on uplift and thrust processes of a smaller scale. Continuing research of the mountain range are predicated on some very compelling assumptions, including one that holds such young and swiftly eroding mountains responsible for alterations in the global climate since their formation. Precious gemstones and fossils have also been discovered in some areas of the Karakoram Range.

*A section of the formidable Karakoram Range*

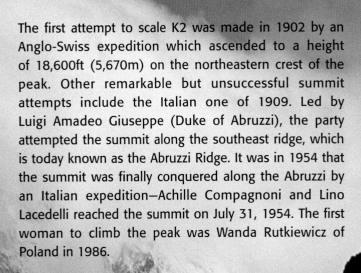

The first attempt to scale K2 was made in 1902 by an Anglo-Swiss expedition which ascended to a height of 18,600ft (5,670m) on the northeastern crest of the peak. Other remarkable but unsuccessful summit attempts include the Italian one of 1909. Led by Luigi Amadeo Giuseppe (Duke of Abruzzi), the party attempted the summit along the southeast ridge, which is today known as the Abruzzi Ridge. It was in 1954 that the summit was finally conquered along the Abruzzi by an Italian expedition—Achille Compagnoni and Lino Lacedelli reached the summit on July 31, 1954. The first woman to climb the peak was Wanda Rutkiewicz of Poland in 1986.

**Mount Everest,** Nepal/China (Tibet)

• The air at the top of Mount Everest is so thin that the human heart beats more than 170 times every minute to supply enough oxygen to keep the body functioning. At sea level the heart normally beats at around 70 times per minute.

• In 1852, Radhanath Sikdar, an Indian mathematician and surveyor, became the first person to classify Everest as the world's highest peak. Everest was then known by the name Peak XV.

# Mount Everest

Towering over the border of Nepal and Tibet, Mount Everest is the highest peak in the world at 29,035ft (8,850m). The peak is called Chomolungma, meaning "Mother Goddess of the Universe" in Tibetan, and Sagarmatha, meaning "Ocean Mother" in Sanskrit. The Everest massif is also the site for the fourth, fifth, and sixth highest mountains in the world—Lhotse at 27,939ft (8,516m), Makalu at 27,765ft (8,462m), and Cho Oyu at 26,906ft (8,201m). This cluster of peaks, joined by ridges that branch out from Everest, lies within the 56-mile (90-km) long subrange called Mahalangur Himal.

Everest was named in 1865 by the British Surveyor-General Andrew Scott Waugh after his predecessor George Everest. He said of his decision: "I was taught… by George Everest to assign to every geographical object its true or native appellation. But here is a mountain, most probably the highest in the world, without any local name… In the meantime the privilege… devolves on me to assign… a name whereby it may be known among civilized nations."

## THE WORST YEAR

In 1996, 12 people died because of unexpected bad weather while trying to reach the summit. The disaster gained wide publicity when John Krakauer, a journalist, wrote the bestselling book *Into Thin Air*. Later, it was made into a movie of the same name.

*Hiker on Mount Everest*

Ever since the peak gained popularity, conquering it has become a global obsession. Numerous summit expeditions were mounted, with the British spearheading with two unsuccessful attempts in the 1920s. George Leigh Mallory, a member of both the 1921 and 1922 British expeditions, along with Andrew Irvine, made an ill-fated summit attempt on June 8, 1924—the duo disappeared on the North Col route, never to return. His passion for peaks is perhaps best summed up in his famous retort to a journalist who asked him why he returned time and again to Everest: "Because it is there," he said.

In 1953, a successful assault on the summit was led by John Hunt, the leader of the ninth British expedition. Hunt selected two climbing pairs. The first pair, consisting of Tom Bourdillon and Charles Evans, turned back after coming close to the summit because of sheer exhaustion. On the following day, the expedition made its final attempt with its second climbing pair, Edmund Hillary and Tenzing Norgay, who approahed it via the South Col Route. They successfully scaled the peak on May 29.

By 1996, more than 15 routes had been charted to the peak, and by the year 2000, more than 1,600 people had achieved the precious feat of setting foot on top of the world's highest peak. The peak, however, has paid a heavy price for its popularity. Due to the increase in refuse, the area surrounding the base camp, as well as the peak itself, has earned the dubious credit of being referred to as the world's highest garbage dump.

## SAGARMATHA NATIONAL PARK

An area of 443 sq miles (1,148sq km) around the base of Everest on the Nepalese side was first declared a protected area in 1976, and given the name Sagarmatha National Park. It was designated a UNESCO Heritage Site in 1979 to protect it from increasing tourist incursions. The park is home to the Himalayan tahr, the Himalayan black bear, and the rare endangered snow leopard. The park also contains a variety of fauna, including the juniper and rhododendron, and more than 26 species of butterfly have been identified here. With its lowest point at 9,343ft (2,848m), the reserve is one of the highest in the world.

*View of a small village with Mount Everest in the background*

• Mount Fuji has been the inspiration for many artists and writers. One of the most celebrated artworks representing the mountain is the print series by artist Hokusai, depicting 36 views of the volcano.

• Owing to its religious associations, Mount Fuji is a popular site for pilgrimages. The devout not fit enough to undertake the climb up the mountain take lava soil from the base and fashion miniatures of it to worship in their houses.

**Mount Fuji,** Japan

# Mount Fuji

Situated within the Circum-Pacific volcanic chain, or the Ring of Fire, Japan has had a fairly dramatic history of volcanic activity. Long-dead lava fields, hot springs, and volcanoes—many of them still active—stand witness to this. Many of the country's volcanoes exhibit the classical cone shape, the most famous among them being Mount Fuji.

Fuji-san, better known as Mount Fuji, rises to an intimidating height of 12,388ft (3,776m). Situated on the island of Honshu, on the border of the Yamanashi and Shizuoka prefectures, Fuji is Japan's highest mountain, and also considered its holiest. The explosion crater Hoei-zan, halfway up the southern flank of the mountain, was formed during its last eruption in 1707. The eruption lasted 16 days, producing a 6-mile (10-km) wide cloud of smoke and ash that blocked the sunlight for days. The mountain's summit is actually its central crater, measuring around 1,600ft (500m) in diameter and 820ft (250m) in depth.

On the northern slope of the mountain lie the Fuji Five Lakes formed by the effects of lava flows—Lake Yamanaka, Lake Kawaguchi, Lake Sai, Lake Shoji, and Lake Motosu.

Mount Fuji's composition has been divided by scientists into four distinct phases of volcanic activity. The first, known as Sen-komitake, is composed of andesite—an igneous volcanic rock—that lies deep within the mountain. The second, a basalt layer, is called Komitake Fuji. Old Fuji, the next layer, was probably formed almost 100,000 years ago, over Komitake Fuji. What we see today is called New Fuji, believed to have been formed only about 10,000 years ago.

The geological history of the peak—the formation of a composite volcano by the deposition of successive layers of lava and ash—appears to almost mirror the peak's sacred past, shaped and affected by successive sects, religions, and beliefs. Shintoism, established around the sixth century, spawned the belief that natural features such as trees,

## WAITING TO EXHALE

In 2002, Japan issued a report hinting at a possible eruption of Mount Fuji, with projected damages of around $21 billion. Following the report, seismologists and volcano experts have been conducting tests and carrying out research, hoping to predict the route that the flowing lava might take and thus preparing evacuation plans on the basis accordingly.

*Mount Fuji from a distance*

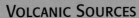
*Lake in front of mountain*

lakes, and mountains were the dwelling places of the Kami, spirits which could be invoked through prayer and ritual. The Buddhists considered Fuji a symbol of meditation, and named its summit *zenjo*—a term that describes the perfect meditative state. The Shugendo religious sect, which gained prominence in the ninth century, cemented the beliefs of those who wanted to commune with deities on mountain summits and gain supernatural powers. Historically, the Shugendo were also the first people to establish a climbing route all the way to the mountain's summit in the 14th century.

Mount Fuji's perfectly conical summit and the peak's startling beauty have inspired many works of art and literature, and attract millions of pilgrims every year. Apart from its religious heritage, Mount Fuji also has a rich warrior tradition. In ancient times, the Samurai would use the base of the mountain as a training area. The Japan Self-Defence Forces and the US armed forces have operated bases nearby since 2006.

## VOLCANIC SOURCES

The younger rocks of Japan are largely volcanic in origin. However, the country is not unique in this respect—all the lands and islands of the Circum-Pacific region experience some form of volcanic activity. The Pacific Rim is called the "Ring of Fire" by geologists. The expansion of the ocean floor is the reason for the creation of such a ring. When the ocean floor expands in one area, it needs to be accommodated elsewhere; this usually happens around the margins of the ocean, as the oceanic crust slides under the adjacent continental crust. But with the descent of the oceanic crust into the earth's mantle, it becomes heated due to friction between the two plates, causing melting and expansion. The resulting increase in pressure is reduced by volcanic activity, and the accompanying tension in the rocks is relieved by earthquakes.

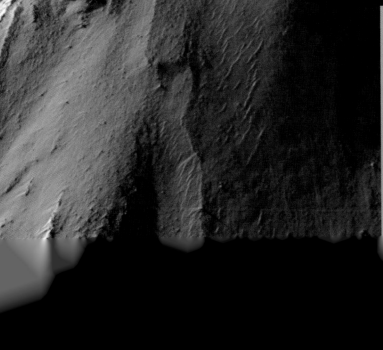

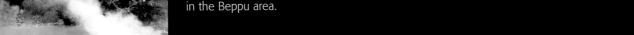

- The hot springs and geysers of Beppu emit over 2 million cu ft (56,000cu m) of water every day.
- There are about 3,500 fumaroles (vents which allow gases to escape), hot springs and geysers in the Beppu area.

*A thermal spa pool in Beppu*

## HOT HOUSE

Agricultural research facilities such as the Oita Research Station for Agricultural Utilization of Hot Springs also make use of geothermal water. The mineral-rich water is used to irrigate and heat the greenhouses all year round, and experimental crops of fruits and vegetables such as tomatoes, cucumbers, mangos, and bananas are harvested regularly. The breeding of species such as azaleas, rhododendrons, carnations, and so on is also being researched extensively at the facility.

# Beppu

Situated at the base of a steep slope of volcanic detritus flung out by one of the several volcanoes in its immediate neighborhood, the city of Beppu has been one of Japan's most famous tourist destinations since the end of the 19th century. Huge quantities of water are emitted every day by its hot springs and geysers. Visitors flock in from all over the world, eager to immerse their bodies in the hot sand baths and the healing, mineral-laden waters that Beppu offers.

Part of the Beppu-Shimabara graben, in Kyushu, Beppu is situated at its eastern end. One of the largest thermal areas in the world, Beppu, exhibits the typical volcanic features that are associated with the formation of a graben—an elongated and lowered portion of the earth's crust that lies between two fault lines.

The Beppu district has eight distinct areas of hot water springs: Beppu Onsen, Kannawa Onsen, Shibaseki Onsen, Myoban Onsen, Kamegawa Onsen, Kankaiji Onsen, Hotta Onsen, and Hamawaki Onsen. Apart from its spas, Beppu is also famous worldwide for its distinctive boiling ponds, or *jigokus*. Expelling mud high into the air, these steaming geysers are the most extraordinary of Beppu's natural attractions. The word *jigoku* means "burning hell", and the name is derived from ancient Buddhist scriptures.

Beppu's nine jigokus exhibit a fantastic range of colors and sizes. Boiling gray viscous mud that bubbles

## VOLCANOES AND THERMAL SPRINGS

Japan has been described as sitting on "Mother Earth's Cradle," and with more than 500 volcanoes on the main island, the description is apt. Many volcanoes are extinct but some remain active, including Fuji, Asama, and Aso. In addition to volcanoes there are hundreds of areas of thermal activity, the best known being Noboribetsu, Beppu, and Kusatsu.

Noboribetsu, on Hokkaido, Japan's largest island, is home to the Jigokudani Hot Springs. Geysers, boiling springs, and bubbling mud, as well as vents that give off a rather unpleasant sulphurous gas, occupy a volcanic crater 1.25 miles (2km) across.

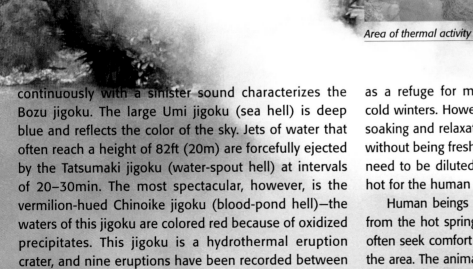

*Area of thermal activity*

continuously with a sinister sound characterizes the Bozu jigoku. The large Umi jigoku (sea hell) is deep blue and reflects the color of the sky. Jets of water that often reach a height of 82ft (20m) are forcefully ejected by the Tatsumaki jigoku (water-spout hell) at intervals of 20–30min. The most spectacular, however, is the vermilion-hued Chinoike jigoku (blood-pond hell)—the waters of this jigoku are colored red because of oxidized precipitates. This jigoku is a hydrothermal eruption crater, and nine eruptions have been recorded between 1875 and 1927.

Beppu's onsens cater to a diverse clientele, ranging from sophisticated vacationers to local workers. Since central heating is limited in Japan, Beppu's baths serve as a refuge for many people during the bitterly long cold winters. However, the baths are primarily meant for soaking and relaxation; nobody enters a bath unclean or without being freshly washed. Very often, Beppu's waters need to be diluted and cooled since they are often too hot for the human skin.

Human beings are not the only creatures that benefit from the hot springs of Beppu. In winter, small monkeys often seek comfort from the volcanically heated waters of the area. The animals head to Beppu's thermal pools, and sit submerged up to the neck in the warm water, while snow settles on their heads. Often, these clever creatures formulate a rota system—one or two delegates are sent to gather food while the others soak in the warm waters.

- The most famous Buddhist monasteries in the Huangshan Mountains—Xiangfu, Ciguang, Cuiwei, and Zhibo—are together referred to as the Four Big Monasteries.
- Mao Feng, meaning Fur Peak, named because of the downy tips of its leaves, is a world-renowned green tea from the Huangshan area.

# Huangshan Mountains

*Pagoda on Mount Huangshan*

The magnificent Huangshan Mountains, nestled in the southern reaches of the Anhui province in eastern China, were born of tectonic upheavals almost 100 million years ago. The movements of the earth's crust resulted in granite being thrust vertically upwards from the sea bed. Later, glacial erosion worked into the rock to carve out and shape the peaks and valleys that we see today. The scenic reserve spans an area of 60sq miles (154sq km) and encompasses numerous peaks, 77 of which are more than 3,280ft (1,000m) in height. The tallest peaks are Lian Hua Feng, or Lotus Flower Peak, at 6,114ft (1,864m); Guang Ming Ding, or Bright Summit Peak, at 6,035ft (1,840m); and Tian Du Feng, or Celestial Peak, at 6,000ft (1,829m).

## BUDDHA'S LIGHT

A frequent occurrence in Huangshan, Buddha's Light is better known as a "glory" or an anthelion. An optical phenomenon, it occurs when a combination of diffraction, reflection, and refraction scatters light back to its source. The Buddha's Light displays all the colors of the spectrum, and occurs only when mountains reach higher than the level of the lowest clouds. Seen in the direction opposite the sun, it sometimes forms a circle around the shadow, resembling a halo. According to legends, a person whose shadow is so encircled by Buddha's Light is led to the path of enlightenment. On average, Buddha's Light appears once or twice a month in the Huangshan.

## GUEST-GREETING PINE

The most photographed of the famous pine trees in the Huangshan Mountains is the Guest-Greeting Pine, which stands at the entrance of the Jade Screen Pavilion. The branches of the tree are like arms outstretched to embrace visitors in a gesture of welcome. This popular pine has become a symbol of hospitality and warmth of the Chinese people.

*The* Ying Ke Song *or Welcoming Guest Pine*

The unusual terrain of these mountains is responsible for a vertical change in its climate. Thus, the slopes of the mountains exhibit a distinctive vertical distribution of vegetation—the summit, the middle zones, and the foot of the mountains have plants that belong in the frigid, temperate, and subtropical climes respectively. Declared a World Heritage Site by UNESCO in 1990, this mountain chain nurtures more than 1,450 different plant species. The Huangshan also provides a natural habitat for a considerable variety of fauna. Monkeys, goats, deer, and many rare and exotic birds are among those who call these mountains their home.

These beautiful mountains have spawned countless legends over the centuries. The shapes given to the mountains by the actions of natural elements are often reflected in the exotic names of the peaks. Extraordinarily shaped natural formations such as the Immortal Showing the Way, Rooster Crowing at Dawn, Squirrel Jumping into Heavenly Capital, and Monkey Watching the Sea are shrouded in rich and colorful fables, and are also the reason why the Huangshan Mountains are considered a museum of natural sculptures.

This mountain range had been known as the Yishan since the reign of the Qin Dynasty (c. 221–207BC). The name Huangshan, which translates to Yellow Mountains, is credited to the famous Tang poet Li Bai, and it has been known as the Huangshan since AD747. The mountains have inspired artists and poets from time immemorial. The famous traveler and geographer of the Ming Dynasty (1368–1644), Xu Xiake, described Huangshan as the best of all mountains in China, unequaled by any other. Huangshan's stunning beauty and its fascinating and surreal atmosphere are estimated to have inspired more than 100 works of prose and almost 20,000 poems. The famous Four Wonders of the Huangshan—the peculiarly shaped pines, the rock figurines, the sea of clouds that swathes the peaks, and the clusters of hot springs—have been praised by many.

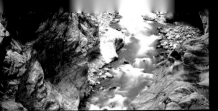

- More than half the area of the Taroko National Park is covered by mountains over 6,560ft (2,000m) tall; the most famous of these are Mount Nanhu, the Hehuan Snow Cap, and the Cilai Peaks.

- The name Taroko comes from the Aboriginal language *Truku*, which means "magnificent and splendid."

**Taroko Gorge,** Taiwan

# Taroko Gorge

Sheer marble cliffs and twisting tunnels make up the rugged landscape of the Taroko Gorge in Taiwan. Located in Hualien County on the eastern coast of the country, it is characterized by steep slopes and craggy ravines, through which the Liwu River flows.

The origin of this spectacular network of gorges can be traced back 230 million years to the formation of coral reefs in tropical shallows where Taiwan stands today. Over time, a process called lithification occurred and the coral reefs were transformed into limestone. Subsequently, the intense pressure and subterranean heat caused the limestone to metamorphose into marble. Approximately 70 million years ago, collisions between tectonic plates forced the sea bed to fracture and the Taiwan Mountain Range rose out of the ocean, along with the stratum of marble. The action of streams and rainwater over millions of years has since then eroded this layer of marble to carve out the breathtaking Taroko Gorge.

Much of Taroko's beauty is attributed to the Liwu river that rushes enthusiastically through the middle of the gorge. The erosive action of the river, coupled with the phenomenon of uplifting, has sculpted the layers of marble and forged through the 12-mile (19-km) long ravine resulting in incredible formations of sheer cliffs, dark tunnels, steep chasms, deep valleys, columns of marble, cascading waterfalls, and churning white water rapids. Together, these features combine to form the most spectacular natural landscape found in Taiwan.

## ETERNAL SPRING SHRINE

The Changchun or "Eternal Spring Shrine" is a Zen monastery that straddles a waterfall near the entrance to Taroko Gorge. This shrine was constructed in memory of the workers who lost their lives during the construction of the Cross-Island Highway that runs along the bottom of the gorge, commanding magnificent views of the Pacific Ocean and the mountains on either side. Behind the monastery are stone steps called the "Heavenly Stairs," which lead to the Guanyin Cave.

*The location of the Eternal Spring Shrine affords visitors a breathtaking panorama of mountains*

## ANCIENT HERITAGE

Seven prehistoric sites, which testify to human habitation of the area for 3,000 years, have been discovered within Taroko National Park. The most famous of these is the Taroko Site, which comprises 85 neatly-arranged monoliths. The artifacts found in this region indicate a blend of several ancient cultures such as the Pei-Nan, Chi-Lin, and Shih San Hang. Other relics found in the park include fragments of pottery, stone axes, stone spinning wheels, and coffins.

The Taroko National Park was set up in 1937 as the Tsugitaka Taroko National Park while Taiwan was still a colony of the Empire of Japan, and abolished after Japan's defeat in World War II. It was subsequently re-established on November 28, 1986. Running 22 miles (36km) from north to south and 26 miles (42km) from east to west, the park exhibits a great range of altitude—while the mouth of the Liwu River is close to sea level, the highest point is the peak of the majestic Mount Nanhu which rises to a height of 12,273ft (3,742m).

Numerous trails that traverse the park provide visitors with the opportunity to experience its astounding ecosystem and topography. Most famous of these is the Tunnel of Nine Turns Trail, which takes visitors through an area of cliff, canyon, tunnel, and waterfall, and provides a small but comprehensive taste of the park's scenic beauty. The Pai Yang, Yin Tai, Chang Chun, and Lu Shui are the most dramatic and exquisite of the park's waterfalls.

The natural habitats in the Taroko National Park remain generally undisturbed, and thus it is home to a great variety of wildlife. The different climactic zones of the park mean that its vegetation is very diverse, the variety of plants ranging from the alpine juniper to the dwarf bamboo. More than 1,200 native species of plants, 132 of which are endangered, have been discovered within the park boundaries. The park is also home to 144 species of birds and scores of other animals. On top of this, researchers have identified 251 types of butterfly.

- The Reed Flute Cave gets its name *Ludi Yan* in Chinese from the lush and verdant growth of *Ludi cao* (a reed grass—used for making flutes) that is found at its entrance.

- Large enough to accommodate a thousand people at a time, the Reed Flute Cave was used as an air-raid shelter during World War II.

**Reed Flute Cave,** China

# Reed Flute Cave

A dazzling array of stalactites and stalagmites in countless hues make up the extraordinarily mesmerizing Reed Flute Cave in Guilin. Located in the Guangxi Zhuang Autonomous Region of China, on the shores of the beautiful Lijiang River, Guilin is an ancient city surrounded by majestic mountains, sparkling waters, and exquisite limestone topography that adds to the natural beauty of the city. The Reed Flute Cave is situated on the southern shoulder of the Guangming Hill, to the northwest of the city, a short distance away from it.

The formation of the Reed Flute Cave (Ludi Yan) can be traced back millions of years. The area that is now Guilin was once occupied by a vast sea until about 190 million years ago, when movements of the tectonic plates thrust the sea bed up. The uplifted bedrock made of limestone has since then been weathered and eroded by water to form the fantastic karst features, underground streams, and caves that are characteristic of Guilin's topography.

## THE STRUCTURES OF LUDI YAN

Often called "A Palace of Natural Art," the formations within the cave resemble gemstones such as jade, agate, and amber in the colored light. Some of the more remarkable decoration (speleothems) of this cave include a huge stalagmite and a rather small conical stalactite—the peculiar combined shape of the two earns it the epithet "Fish Tail Peak." One of the grottos within the cave—an area that looks somewhat like a miniature Guilin—is called the Crystal Palace of the Dragon King. The cave also contains several drapery formations and exquisite reflecting pools.

*Stalactites and stalagmites, Reed Flute Cave, Guilin'*

The largest of the caves in the Guilin area, the Reed Flute Cave was carved out by an underground stream which left carbonate deposits that are responsible for creating the enthralling assortment of stalactites, stone pillars, and intriguingly shaped rocks that inhabit the cave. This dripstone cave is approximately 790ft (240m) long. Zigzagging paths have been laid down through the serried columns of stone so that visitors are able to get a closer look at every remarkable formation in the cave. The U-shaped sightseeing route enables tourists to enter the cave from one side and, after taking in the sights and sounds of the extraordinary structures and significnant areas, to exit from another cavern very close to the point of entry. A tour through the cave usually takes up to an hour.

The names given to the various features within the cave bear witness to the Chinese penchant for storytelling. Bearing picturesque and evocative names such as Virgin Forest, Flower and Fruit Mountain, Dragon Pagoda, Crystal Palace, and so on, several features within the caves are not unsurprisingly swathed in myth and fable. Imagination is required to associate the structures with plants, animals, and other creatures, and the stories associated with these features abound, further adding to the magic and romance of the stone formations.

The formations within the cave are artificially illuminated to create a mystical aura and enhance their attributes; many kinds of lights are employed in the different sections of the cave. Photography within the cave is usually not permitted because the light is not sufficient; however, certain spots such as the Crystal Palace and Flower and Fruit Mountain have arrangements for special illumination, and visitors are allowed to take photographs for a fee.

The Reed Flute Cave has been a popular destination for tourists for the last 13 centuries. Seventy inscriptions, believed to be travelogues and poems, dating back to the rule of the Tang Dynasty (AD618–907) have been discovered on its walls.

## GUILIN

Guilin has been the socio-political and cultural center of the Guangxi area for more than two millennia. Located in the northeastern part of the province, Guilin's claim to fame since long ago has been its astounding scenic beauty. While the city is a wonderful place to visit at any time of the year because of its mild subtropical climate, it is particularly attractive in autumn, when the fragrance of the sweet osmanthus in bloom pervades the air throughout the city; the name Guilin, in fact, translates as "forest of sweet osmanthus." Apart from the mountains, the Banyan and Fire Tree lakes, the Reed Flute, and the Seven Star Caves are the most outstanding and sought after tourist destinations around the city.

• The Sani is the largest tribe of the Yi ethnic group that has inhabited Yunnan for centuries. Other tribes of the group include the Axi, Heiyi, Baiyi, Yiqing, and Ayizi.

• The Lunan Stone Forest Scenic Zone has been on the tentative list at UNESCO, to be considered as a World Heritage Site, since 1996.

**Stone Forest,** China

# Stone Forest

Fantastic peaks, pillars, stalagmites, depressions, underground rivers, caves, and spectacular stone pinnacles make up Shilin, or the Lunan Stone Forest, in the Yunnan Province of China. Located in the Lunan Yi Nationality Autonomous County, 78 miles (126km) southeast of Kunming city, the area derives its name from the magnificent natural formations crowding together like a dense jungle of stone.

A popular tourist destination, this region of magnificent karst topography attracted attention as early as the 12th century. Its popularity can be traced back to the days of the Ming Dynasty (which flourished between 1368 and 1644). It was during this period that the Stone Forest was termed the "First Wonder of the World," a moniker that is often used even today. Steeped in myth and legend, this stony wilderness occupies about 156sq miles (400sq km), and is roughly divided into three sections—the Greater Stone Forest, Lesser Stone Forest, and Outer Stone Forest.

The area of densest karst formations is known as the Greater Stone Forest. Resembling a strange fairyland carved out of stone, this area is covered with bizarre formations that look like castles, trees, ancient fortresses, birds, and animals. Adjoining the Greater Stone Forest, an area of odd shapes interspersed with lush lawns and clusters of trees and bamboos, make up the Lesser Stone Forest. Surrounding these sections is the Outer Stone Forest, an area across which various stone peaks of myriad shapes— such as the Lion Hill, which resembles a lion squatting— are scattered. Many of the stone structures found in the area bear fantastic names, such as "Cluster of Pinnacles Propping Up the Sky" and "Stone Singing Praises of Plum," and have marvelous legends attached to their formation.

*Limestone pinnacles, Shilin*

## SHILIN'S CAVES

The Zhiyun and Strange Wind caves are two of the most remarkable karst caves in the Stone Forest Area. Zhiyun encompasses several caverns and grottos, many of which have astounding acoustic effects. It also showcases the wonders of underground lava topography at its best, with columns and pillars of strange and unique shapes. The Strange Wind Cave is remarkable for the short gusts of air that blow intermittently out of the cave during the months of August through to November every year. A peculiar conjunction and positioning at different levels of an underground river and a siphon spring are responsible for this odd phenomenon.

Geologist have attributed the formation of the Stone Forest to uplift and erosion. About 270 million years ago, during the carboniferous period of the Paleozoic era, the Shilin area was a shallow sea overlying a bed of sandstone and limestone. The sea retreated due to tectonic upheavals and triggered movements of the lithosphere, which in turn caused it to crumple and rise. Over eons, these clusters of hunkering rock were subjected to erosion by the elements, resulting in the formation of the incredible structures that we see today.

The Lunan Stone Forest region also houses several ponds, reservoirs, waterfalls, and five underground rivers. The most striking of these include the Long Lake, Moon Lake, Feilong Waterfall, Da Dieshui Falls, and the Dadie Waterfall.

The picturesque Stone Forest area has been inhabited by the Sani people of the Yi ethnic group for thousands of years. The lifestyle of these warm and kind people is closely interlinked with the environment, and they live in perfect harmony with nature. With their many festivals of song and dance, the Sani people themselves have become a major attraction for tourists visiting the area.

*The Stone Forest, Yunnan Province*

## THE LEGEND OF ASHIMA

According to a popular legend that surrounds the Stone Forest, Ashima, a young Sani girl defied the will of a tyrannical landlord who wanted to marry her. While trying to flee her tormentor, Ashima was turned into a stone peak at Shilin. The subject of a folk poem, the story of Ashima has gained such popularity that it has to date been translated into more than 20 languages, including English, Russian, and Japanese, and has even been adapted as a movie. The word *Ashima* translates into "girl as beautiful as gold," and is today considered a symbol of the virtues that the people of the area try imitate

- The pristine white terraces of Baishui are marred in places by streaks of cream and yellowish brown. These patches are caused by the deposition of dissolved minerals other than calcium.

- The Baishui Terrace is referred to as the White Water Terrace—*bai* meaning "white" and *shui* meaning "water."

**Baishui Terrace,** China

## BAISHUI AND THE DONGBA CULTURE

The Baishui Terrace is of immense religious significance to the Naxi people of the Dongba culture, and is considered a sacred site by the locals. Three traditional pieces of Dongba literature were discovered in the Baishui Terrace area—*Chongbangtong* (an account of the world's creation), *Dong'aishu'ai* (an epic about Naxi heroes), and *Lubanlurao* (a description of the ancient Naxis' quest for their current home).

# Baishui Terrace

A magnificent karst terrain composed of calcite minerals, the Baishui Terrace is ranked among the most beautiful scenic spots in China. Located near the Baidi Village at Sanba, 63 miles (101km) south of the county seat of Zhongdian, the Baishui Terrace is one of the most spectacular examples of its kind.

Geologists believe that the formation of the Baishui Terrace dates back 200,000 to 300,000 years. This dazzling sinter was formed by the deposition of calcium bicarbonate by flowing spring water rich in minerals over hundreds of thousands of years. The subsequent piling up of calcite sediments after the decomposition of the calcium bicarbonate led to the creation of this impressive landform.

The sparkling white Baishui Terrace is situated on a slope at the foot of the Haba Snow Mountain at a height of 7,806ft (2,380m) above sea level. Occupying a total area of 1.2sq miles (3sq km), it is actually made up of a series of short terraces. These individual levels taken together make Baishui one of the largest terraces in China and the world. Stretching for about 525ft (160m) at its widest point, the Baishui Terrace runs 459ft (140m) down the slope of the mountain.

Spring water flows down from the top of the mountain into a semi-circular pool at the top of the terrace, and then trickles slowly over the rim of one row of the terrace to another, right to the bottom, leaving behind patterned tracks of exquisite beauty. The terrace, with its gleaming wet, marble-white walls, and the sparkling water that fills the shallow basins behind the terrace walls, looks like a silver waterfall arrested and frozen in time and place.

Baishui Terrace is believed to be the place where the founding father of the Dongba culture settled on his way back from Tibet and first started preaching his beliefs. Every year, on the eighth day of the second month of the lunar calendar, the Naxi people gather together at

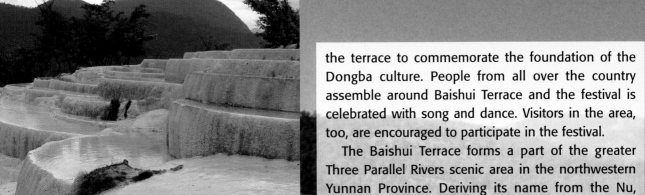

*Series of limestone terraces, Baishui Terrace, China*

the terrace to commemorate the foundation of the Dongba culture. People from all over the country assemble around Baishui Terrace and the festival is celebrated with song and dance. Visitors in the area, too, are encouraged to participate in the festival.

The Baishui Terrace forms a part of the greater Three Parallel Rivers scenic area in the northwestern Yunnan Province. Deriving its name from the Nu, Jinsha, and Lancang rivers, the Three Parallel Rivers area is spread over 13,260sq miles (34,000sq km) and encompasses a wide range of geological features and biological environments, including the mesmeric and mystical Shangri-la. With its high mountain glacier lakes, karst topography, waterfalls, grassy marshlands, and other such stunning natural formations, the area was inscribed as a World Heritage Site by UNESCO in 2003.

## PAMUKKALE

The pristine white Pamukkale in Turkey is the only other outstanding example of a limestone terrace in the world. Formed in much the same way as Baishui, the Pamukkale is also characterized by mineral springs, to which tourists were granted free access until recently. Ill-managed tourist activity in the area has led to the discoloration of the white stone basins and choked the natural drainage. Visitors are now allowed to walk only along carefully demarcated pathways.

*Pools in eroded limestone terraces, Pamukkale, Turkey*

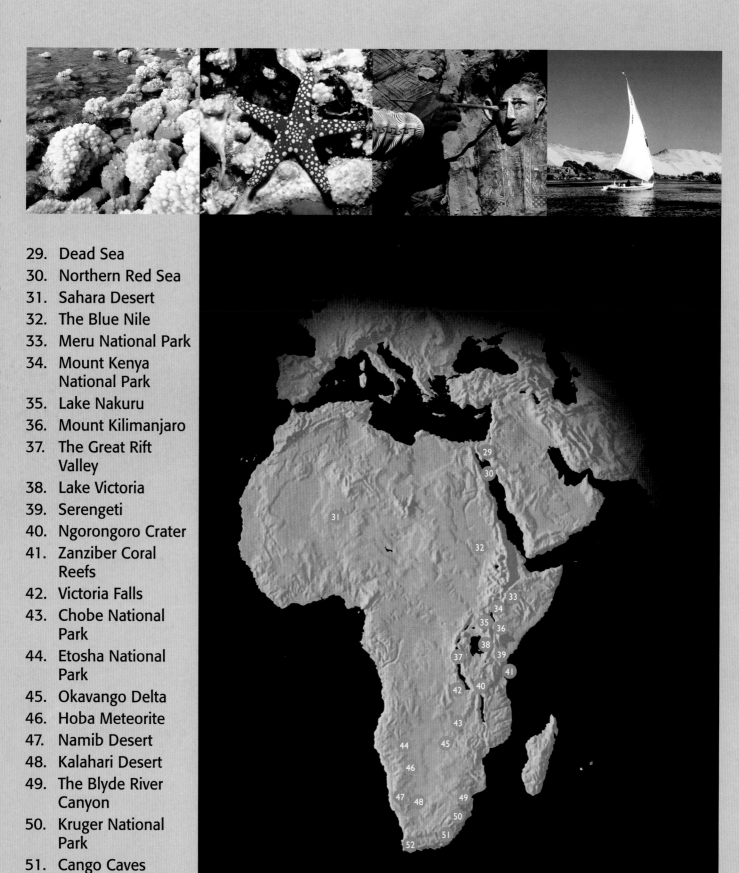

# Africa & Middle East

The Dead Sea, North Sea, Mediterranean Sea, the indomitable Kalahari and Namib deserts, the mighty rivers Nile, Tigris, Euphrates, Lakes Victoria, and Nakuru, Mount Kenya and Mount Kilimanjaro are just a few of this region's wonders. There are many, many more natural monuments and national parks located in what is often described as the "cradle of civilization"—Africa, and the area known as the Middle East. Africa boasts the largest combinations of natural diversity and wildlife density in a single continent. With the help of exciting safaris in the region one can explore its hot deserts, sweeping savannahs and wet rainforests, and meet its illustrious, but often endangered, residents, such as the elephant, giraffe, zebra, lion, black rhino, cheetah and gazelle.

And this vast region is still on the move—the Great Rift Valley in east Africa is growing wider by the year, tearing a chunk of land from the African continent in a tectonic process that has been going on for 20 million years. It is predicted that one day, not in our lifetimes, the country of Somalia will be set adrift from the rest of the African mainland. Meanwhile, archeologists continue to find the remains of our earliest ancestors, revealed by this constant upheaval.

From the southern and eastern shores of the Mediterranean Sea extending from Morocco to the Arabian Peninsula and Iran, fed by the Nile and the Euphrates rivers, the Middle East is not short of spectacular attractions. In its Elburz Mountains, in central Iran, lies one of the most intriguing deserts—the Great Salt Desert, made entirely of salt. Meanwhile, in Oman's Wadi Dawkah, UNESCO has come forward to protect the only known group of frankincense trees that supplied exotic smells to the world in ancient and medieval times. And who can ignore the wonders of the Dead Sea—the only place where the crust of Earth actually sinks 1,364ft (416m) below sea level!

- Seven million tons of water evaporate daily from the Dead Sea; figures for the sea's salinity vary from 26 to 35 percent.

- Since the 1960s, the flow from the Jordan River has reduced by 90 percent, reducing the surface level of the Dead Sea by 82ft (25m).

# Dead Sea

The lowest body of water on the earth's surface, as well as the most saline and buoyant, the Dead Sea is a salt lake of which the minerals have served as a natural spa for thousands of years. Forming part of the Israel–Jordan border, it is 50 miles (80km) in length and 11 miles (18km) wide, and at 1,371ft (418m) below sea level, the lowest point on the planet. A dramatically beautiful landscape formed of the blue sea and otherworldly salt deposits on the shore and rocks, the Dead Sea is flanked by majestic desert mountains and rolling hills rising to the east and west, which are believed to have been home to the Biblical cities of Sodom and Gomorrah. Subtropical oases outline the sea, and mineral-rich springs, primarily sulphur, rise from deep down into little ponds along the Dead Sea shores.

The name Dead Sea aptly describes this body of water; no plant or animal life can survive in its waters, though a negligible measure of bacteria and microbial fungi manage to withstand the hypersalinity. Humans can float effortlessly on the surface of the sea; in fact, it is so buoyant that most swimmers can't put their feet down. It is, however, dangerous to swallow the water. The shores of the Dead Sea are an ideal place to sunbathe because the more harmful ultraviolet rays get filtered out, and the surrounding atmosphere is high in oxygen due to the high barometric pressure.

## HARVESTING THE DEAD SEA

The salts and minerals of the Dead Sea caught the eye of chemists in the early part of the 20th century and it became an economically important source of potash, bromine, gypsum, salt, and other chemical products, which could be extracted inexpensively. Today, potash is the most valuable of the minerals extracted, used in the manufacture of fertilizers. The Dead Sea Works Ltd. harvests the valuable minerals in Israel, while the Arab Potash Works does the same in Jordan.

*Eastern shore of the Dead Sea, with a salt concentration of more than 30 percent*

A landlocked body of water, fed primarily by the river Jordan, it owes its existence to the 22,960ft (7,000m) fault line that links Asia and Africa's Great Rift Valley. As the water has no outlet and can only evaporate, what is left behind is saturated with salts and minerals. As a result, salt precipitates and piles up at the bottom of the sea. So the mysterious depths of the sea serve up a cocktail of chloride salts—magnesium, sodium, potassium, and others.

Its surface being least saline, the sea turns saltier as its depth increases. At 130ft (40m) below the surface, each liter of water contains about 12oz (300g) of salt, making it ten times more saline than a regular ocean. Below 300ft (91m), however, the salt content for similiar quantities of water increases to 13.2oz (332g) of salt per liter. The Dead Sea does not restrict itself to supplying salts, and regularly spits out black pebbles of asphalt. Little wonder then that the ancient Greeks referred to it as "Lake Asphaltites."

Though the lake itself is devoid of life, its surrounding mountain areas are home to a number of animals, including the Nubian ibex, the caracal, jackals, foxes, and the Arabian leopard, as well as hundreds of bird species. Both Jordan and Israel have established nature reserves around the Dead Sea—the Mujib Nature Reserve located in the Wadi Mujib gorge in Jordan and the Ein Gedi Nature Reserve in Israel.

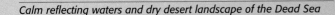

*Calm reflecting waters and dry desert landscape of the Dead Sea*

## DEAD SEA SCROLLS

On the northern shores of the Dead Sea, in the Judaean Desert (now the Qumran National Park), lie the ancient caves and settlement where, in 1947, a young Bedouin shepherd went searching for a stray goat. He instead stumbled upon a long-forgotten cave, and in it, jars filled with ancient scrolls, the oldest Biblical documents ever found. The search by the Bedouins yielded seven scrolls, but a decade of intensive search later thousands of scroll fragments were discovered from 11 caves. These scrolls outdate any other surviving Biblical manuscript by almost one thousand years. Named the *Dead Sea Scrolls*, they were well preserved because of the low atmospheric humidity. Many of the original *Dead Sea Scrolls* are displayed in the Shrine of the Book at the Israel Museum, Jerusalem.

• The Red Sea was formed because of continental rift that took place millions of years ago. However, in 2006, after another unusually large rift in Ethiopia, scientists have reason to believe that the Red Sea is widening and in future will extend further southward.

• It is not just the waters at Ras Mohammed that are rich in coral; the peninsula is also made up of a fossil coral reef, which is thought to have emerged from the waters some 75,000 years ago.

**rn Red Sea,** Egypt/Israel/Jordan

# Northern Red Sea

The Northern Red Sea follows the coastline of Egypt and extends its arms into the Gulf of Suez and the Gulf of Aqaba, where it touches Israel and Jordan. Its vast surrounding expanses of sand make it difficult to imagine that some of the planet's richest and most magnificent coral reefs rise from the floor of its northern reaches, especially at the confluence of the two gulfs. Here lies an underwater paradise, with dramatically lit caves and caverns, populated by an amazing diversity and richness of species, not just of coral but also of fish, from the deadly stone fish and butterfly fish to triggerfish and parrotfish, as well as dolphins, sea turtles, and sharks. Add shipwrecks, clear visibility, insignificant wave action, and warm temperatures all year long, and it is not surprisingly considered to make for some of the world's finest diving.

The many marine splendors of the Northern Red Sea are showcased in Egypt's Ras Mohammed National Park, home to some of the world's finest coral reefs. Such is their scale, and abundance, that they almost constitute a coral plateau. The intense sunlight of the region pierces the sea, causing an explosion of color on the reefs' swaying soft corals, which shine in a sunburst of shades from yellow to orange, purple to green. It is not just the corals that add color to the blue depths; sea anemones glow a bright orange and schools of shimmering tropical fish swim by in all hues, shapes, and sizes.

*Hawksbill turtle, Red Sea, Egypt*

## CORAL EXAMINATION

The Northern Red Sea boasts a thriving coral reef ecosystem. Reasons for this wealth of corals include the lack of sedimentation, which would have otherwise hindered coral growth; benevolent undersea currents that disperse larva and the coral fragments necessary for reproduction; intense sunlight that provides abundant solar energy for the photo-synthesizing zooxanthellae that live within the corals, and the fact that the area is relatively sheltered from powerful storms. Interestingly, coral growth is restricted by salinity, yet it thrives in the Red Sea, which is an extremely saline body of water.

A starfish feeding on coral in the Northern Red Sea

## LIFE AQUATIC

Thirty million years ago, the northern end of the Red Sea flowed into the Mediterranean Sea, but was closed at its southern end. Thus, hundreds of species of marine life from the Atlantic entered the sea to breed. Ten million years later, shifts in the earth's tectonic plates barricaded the Red Sea's northern end and opened its southern end to the Indian Ocean, letting in Indo-Pacific species of fish, which are now found in these waters. This explains the abundant marine life and the richness of species in its depths.

The reefs at Ras Mohammed are made up of hundreds of varieties of coral, from the tiny soft ones to the harder reef-building kind that form the backbone of these undersea wonders. More than 200 species of hard and 100 species of soft coral have been recorded in these waters. The corals that are exposed are dominated by the Acropora species, the sheltered ones by the Porites, and the semi-sheltered corals by the Millepora species. Even more astonishing is the amount of coral cover found around the islands near Ras Mohammed, which averages 70 percent.

It is not only the scale of the reefs that makes the Northern Red Sea so unique, it is also the way they have transformed the waterscape, forming everything from plunging columns that reach the ocean floor thousands of feet below and spreading gardens and lagoons, to oases of caves and plateaus. These reefs are made up of both fossil and live corals, whose age is mind-boggling—some of them are around two million years old!

- The Sahara is the largest desert in the world, which covers an area of 3,579,000sq miles (9,269,594sq km).

- Dunes in parts of the Sahara roll forward at the rate of 36ft (11m) per year.

# Sahara Desert

Occupying approximately 10 percent of the African continent, the Sahara stretches from Egypt and the Sudan to the west coasts of Mauritania and Spanish Sahara, to the Red Sea, and down to the highlands of Ethiopia.

The mere mention of its name summons images of vast, baking-hot sand dunes, interrupted all too infrequently by jewel-like oases of green. The immense area of the Sahara contains just about every kind of desert terrain, including sand seas and dunes (known as ergs); stony plateaus, gravel plains (serirs or regs), and dry valleys (wadis); salt flats and deeply dissected mountain massifs; and parched scrub land and underground aquifers that occasionally rise to the surface as oases. On a single swathe of land you will find Mount Koussi, towering over the desert at 11,204ft (3,415m) as well as the Qattara Depression in Egypt, which is 436ft (133m) below sea level. Over 25 percent of the Sahara's surface is monotonously covered with sand sheets and dunes.

The bulk of the desert is far inland, and the prevailing winds absorb any moisture from the air before it can reach the interior. Mountain ranges between the desert and the sea cause clouds to drop their rain long before they reach the interior. With scanty clouds in the sky, daytime in the desert is ferociously hot. Cloudless skies also allow the heat to escape into the atmosphere once the sun has set, and temperatures can drop to below freezing. One of the hottest places on the planet, at its worst temperatures during the day can soar above 122°F (50°C). Dust-laden gales and whirlwinds also disperse and destroy the precious fauna and flora of the desert.

Archeologists have discovered proof that just a few thousand years ago the Sahara actually possessed abundant resources of water, and was densely populated. Fossils, rock art, stone artifacts, bone harpoons, and shells as well as the remains of animals and even aquatic

## DESERT ART

The barren wastes of the Sahara are home to the earliest known African rock art. This treasure trove in the desert consists of more than 30,000 engravings and paintings on rocks. Carved around 7,000 years ago, many of these artworks represent the region's flora and fauna; at that time the Sahara was open savannah, which sustained animals no longer found in the desert but which were instead captured for posterity in art.

*An archeologist brushes away dirt from the figure of a child*

creatures have been found in areas which today are considered too hot and dry to inhabit.

Present day Sahara, however, is so harsh that it has one of the lowest population densities in the world. Most of this inhospitable land's inhabitants are nomads, largely the Tuareg, Tibbu, and Moors who survive by nomadic pastoralism, hunting, and trading. It is not just the human population that is scarce in the area, plant and animal life is negligible too, though the latter far outstrips the former. Some of its notable residents include the desert owls with wingspans of four feet, the well-camouflaged Houbara bustards, the iridescent scarab beetles, dama gazelles, and the scimitar-horned oryxes. Antelopes known as addaxes—with large, flat hooves that allow them to walk over the sand without sinking, high levels of tolerance for dehydration and high temperatures, and the ability to find shelter in depressions that they dig in the sand—are another species that have adapted extremely well to harsh desert life.

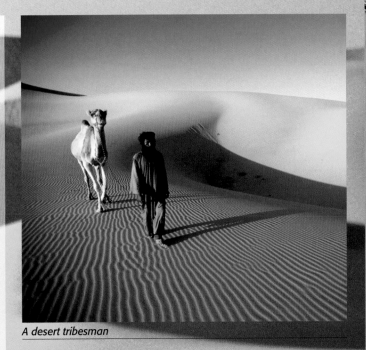
*A desert tribesman*

## DISCOVERY OF LAKE CHAD

Before the 19th century Europeans had very little knowledge of the interior of the Sahara. Their first accurate information came from attempts to solve the mysteries surrounding the source of the River Niger. The first significant exploration involved three British explorers—Dixon Denham, Hugh Clapperton, and Walter Oudney.

The small party left Tripoli in 1822, spent 68 days journeying through the uncharted desert and on February 4, 1823, they became the first Europeans to see Lake Chad. Denham went on to explore the area to the south, while Clapperton and Oudney turned west toward the Niger. Not long afterwards Oudney died but Clapperton reached the great towns of Kano and Sokoto, both of which are in Nigeria.

- Egyptians honored the Nile god Hapi during floods, for bringing fertility to the land.
- The Blue Nile derives its name from the color of its water, which is a clear blue in all seasons except the monsoons, when the river turns a muddy brown because of the sediment it carries.

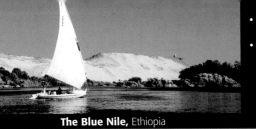

**The Blue Nile,** Ethiopia

# The Blue Nile

**M**eandering through thousands of miles of desert, plains, and swamps—sometimes gently, sometimes as rapids and cataracts—the Blue Nile forms the headstream of the Nile river, and is the source of more than half its water. The river originates from Lake Tana in the Ethiopian highlands. Though many small streams feed the lake, the sacred source of the Blue Nile is believed to be the Abay Wenz (meaning "Great River"), which starts off as a small spring at an altitude of approximately 6,000ft (1,800m) at Gishe Abbai. The river flows out of Lake Tana, over the lava barrier near Bahir Dar in the southeast, and plunges down 138ft (42m) to form the breathtaking Blue Nile, or Tisisat (which translates as "Water That Smokes"), Falls.

The river then cuts a 400-mile (644-km) long arc through the Ethiopian plateau. As it runs through Ethiopia, the Blue Nile also carves out a gigantic gorge through

## THE NILE CROCODILE

The ancient Egyptions revered the Nile crocodile. The god Sebek had the head of a crocodile, and the crocodiles were kept in temples and given gold bracelets to wear. Even a city, Crocodilopolis, was named after the creature. Archeologists have discovered thousands of crocodile graves, where the animals were buried with great care and sometimes expensive jewels.

The Nile crocodile no longer abounds on the shores of the Egyptian Nile and is in fact quite rare in Africa today. There are some conservation programs and small populations are being monitored and protected in places such as Lake Turkana in northern Kenya.

the middle of the plateau, reaching a depth of 1 mile (1.6km) and a width of 15 miles (24km) in some places. The river then drops down to the hot plains of Sudan and joins the White Nile at Khartoum to converge and form the Nile; it eventually flows out into the vastness of the Mediterranean Sea.

The volume of the Blue Nile peaks during the rainy season between June and September, when it contributes to almost two-thirds of the flow of the Nile. Together with the Atbara River, which also flows out of the Ethiopian highlands, the Blue Nile was responsible for the annual Nile floods that led to the fertility of the Nile Valley and the consequent flourishing of the great Egyptian civilization. The Aswan High Dam, which was completed in 1970, regulates the flooding of the river today. The Blue Nile is also a vital source of power and irrigation in Sudan, thanks to the two dams of Sannar and Roseires, completed in 1925 and 1966. respectively

The first European to have sighted the Blue Nile appears to have been a Spanish Jesuit priest, Father Pedro Páez, in 1618. However, better known is the Scottish explorer James Bruce, the first person to navigate the Blue Nile from Lake Tana to the Nile delta, in 1770. Bruce's comment regarding the Tisisat Falls is truly evocative: "It was a most magnificent sight, that ages, added to the greatest length

of human life, would not deface or eradicate from my memory." The course of the river, however, remained a vague dotted line on maps until the late 1920s. This changed when the British Consul Major R. Cheesman surveyed the river by walking along its banks and charting its course through the highlands. In 1968, a team led by the British explorer Col. John Blashford-Snell traveled the length of the river in Ethiopia.

The waters of the Blue Nile, people believe, have the power to cure a thousand ailments, break evil spirits, and bless the land upon which it is sprinkled with a good harvest.

## SEARCH FOR THE SOURCE

While the source of the Blue Nile is undisputedly Lake Tana, the search for the source of the White Nile was not so straight forward. It had become the world's greatest geographical challenge by the middle of the 19th century. In 1858 John Hanning Speke, on a diversionary journey from an expedition led by Richard Francis Burton, was the first European to reach Lake Victoria, which he proclaimed as the White Nile's source. Burton, meanwhile, insisted that Lake Tanganyika was the source. A number of explorers, including Scottish missionary David Livingstone attempted to resolve the question.

In the 1870s, Henry Morton Stanley circumnavigated Lake Victoria, proving that it did not have a major river running into it and that it had only one major outlet, Ripon Falls, where the Nile actually starts. Speke had been right all along.

*The Blue Nile Falls*

- The Meru National Park is part of a group of protected areas along the Tana River, the others being the Bisanadi and Mwingi National Reserves, Kora National Park, and Rahole National Reserve.
- The phrase "Big Five" was coined by game hunters to refer to the five large animals that were most sought after in Africa—the lion, the African elephant, the African buffalo, the leopard, and the black rhino. All of the Big Five can be found in the Meru National Park.

**Meru National Park,** Kenya

# Meru National Park

**L**ush grasslands and thick wild forests, crisscrossed by permanent streams and a diverse range of habitat and wildlife, make the Meru National Park a naturalist's paradise. Straddling the Equator, Meru lies in the northeastern lowlands below the Nyambene Hills in Kenya, 216 miles (348km) from Nairobi. Designated a national park in 1966, it occupies an area of 339sq miles (870sq km).

In addition to the countless streams that water the reserve, Meru National Park is bound by three massive rivers—the Tana to the south, the Ura to the southwest, and the Rojeweru to the east. The hilly northwestern section of the park is wetter with rich volcanic soils. Alluvial soils are found towards the flatter east side. River irrigation and adequate rainfall are responsible for the untamed wilderness that makes Meru so attractive.

Thirty years ago, the park boasted a diverse range of wildlife, housing more than 3,000 elephants, the black and white species of rhino, reticulated giraffes, Grevy's zebras, antelopes, elands, lesser kudus, gerenuks, leopards, cheetahs, and lions. Over 300 varieties of birds—rare species such as Peter's Finfoot and Pel's Fishing Owl—could be found here. Up until the early 1970s, the park managed to attract in excess of 40,000 tourists every year.

The fortunes of the park, however, took a tumble with a sharp rise in poaching activity. Meru supplied happy hunting grounds to poachers for whom the dense swamps and the riverine forests populated by fig trees, tamarinds, and doum plants provided an ideal cover.

Inadequate security resulted in rampant poaching that lasted more than a decade and decimated the park's

## ELEPHANT RELOCATION

The translocation of elephants from private ranches in Laikipia to Meru has been touted as the biggest relocation of its kind in all of eastern and central Africa. To help them adjust to the new surroundings and so that their social bonds were not the disturbed, the animals were moved in family groups. Sixty-six animals have been relocated to the Meru National Park. The successful translocation of the elephants was followed by the relocation of four rhinos. The efforts to replenish Meru's stock continue, with 20 rare Grevy's zebras having been brought in, and several species of antelope to follow.

## BLACK OR WHITE

The name "white" rhinos is misleading because its color is very similar to that of the black rhino. The name is said to have originated from the Afrikaans word "wyd," which in turn is derived from the Dutch word "wijd," meaning wide. The reference to the square lip of the animal—specially adapted for chomping on grass—was misinterpreted by English settlers who called the rhino "white" instead of "wyd." A more appropriate name for the animal, would be the square-lipped rhino.

animal population, depleting stocks of the larger beasts in particular. In the incident that was to eventually spur the government into action, poachers wiped out the five white rhinos in the park for their horns, and killed seven park rangers during their escape.

Today, the park has succeeded in reclaiming much of its former glory largely because of the efforts of African wildlife conversationists George and Joy Adamson. Through the touching story of Elsa, the orphaned lioness they hand-raised after her mother was shot dead in 1956 and later released into the park, the couple managed to make the park famous. Their book—and later, movie—*Born Free* has won them millions of admirers across the world. The couple later separated and in 1980 Joy Adamson was found murdered in the Shaba Game Reserve. Her husband paid the price for his unyielding stance against poaching when nine years later he was killed at the isolated Kora National Reserve.

With security arrangements now in place to protect its animals, Meru has launched an aggressive campaign to attract tourists. In order to replenish the stock in Meru, elephants and rhinos from nearby reserves have been translocated and brought in.

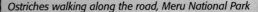
*Ostriches walking along the road, Meru National Park*

- Mount Kenya's summit was first scaled in 1899 by British geographer Halford John Mackinder, along with Swiss guides César Ollier and Joseph Brocherel.

- The Kikuyu people of Africa consider the mountain as the home of their god *Ngai*. They call it *Kirinyaga*, which translates as "mountain of whiteness."

**Mount Kenya National Park,** Kenya

# Mount Kenya National Park

Straddling the equator, a single mountain soars into the sky, its snow-covered summit thrown into sharp relief by the bare rock and glaciers below and the dense forests and high moorland on its lower reaches. This is Mount Kenya, an ancient extinct volcano, and the second highest mountain in Africa. The mountain was inscribed as a UNESCO World Heritage Site in 1997 and as an international Biosphere Reserve in 1978.

Mount Kenya National Park encompasses this mountain and its unique ecosystem, covering all ground above 10,500ft (3,200m) and sprawling across 279sq miles (715sq km). The park offers a uniquely dramatic landscape, one that has been crafted by its combination of hot and cold, volcanic and glaciated, and equatorial and alpine. Erosion too has played a major part in the formation of this awe-inspiring mountain scenery: from the enormous steep-sided valleys and fantastically rugged rock formations to the fields filled with huge rocks. There are waterfalls, streams, and tarns (small lakes); grasslands and bamboo forests; and flowing down its surface, the waters of the melting snow and glaciers form the country's most important river, the Tana. Last but not least is the giant Afro-Alpine vegetation.

The Afro-Alpine vegetation is a memorable, almost otherworldly sight that unfolds on moorlands where plants must adapt to the mountain's unique climate and conditions; they do so by breaking all known botanical rules. These plants—heather, senecios, and lobelias—tower over humans and can reach heights of up to 30ft (9m). There are 13 species of endemic plant found in the park,

## PEAK PERFORMANCE

Mount Kenya's summit is made up of a number of steeply jagged peaks, the most important—and the tallest—being Batian at 17,058ft (5,199m), Nelion at 17,022ft (5,188m), and Point Lenana at 16,355ft (4,985m). While it is possible for trekkers to reach Point Lenana without difficulty, Batian and Nelion can only be scaled by professional mountaineers. All the peaks were originally part of the "plug" that filled the volcano and are made of an igneous rock called nepheline-syenite. More evidence of the mountain's volcanic origins is found on the lower slopes, where lava has been largely responsible for fashioning the rock.

*Sunrise on Batian, the highest peak on Mount Kenya*

*Rock climbing 17,000ft (2,134m) up the top pitch of Mount Kenya*

## WHERE PARK MEETS PEOPLE

Mount Kenya National Park is spread over the districts of Meru, Nyeri, Kirnyaga, and Embu in the Eastern and Central Provinces. Electrified fences, to ensure that there is no damage to either farmlands or inhabitants from the wildlife, and also to protect the animals from poachers, surround a small portion of the Park.

which include the giant thistle and giant groundsels. The Afro-Alpine vegetation is unique to East Africa and is found only on the region's highest peaks—Mount Kilimanjaro, Mount Elgon, and the Aberdares.

Game to be spotted at the park range from hyraxes, rhinos, and the black and white colobus monkeys to waterbuck, genets, giant forest hogs, hyenas, and zebras. There are also a number of endangered species of fauna in the park. These include animals such as the albino zebra, sunni buck, bongos (a number of which are being reintroduced to the area from zoos in America), Mount Kenya mole shrew, skinks (lizard), as well as birds like the Abyssinian long-eared owl, the scarce swift, and the green ibis. The park is enclosed within the Mount Kenya National Reserve.

**Lake Nakuru,** Kenya

- Archeological evidence suggests that the earliest settlers on the banks of the lake appeared about 30,000 years ago—a small hunter-gatherer tribe called the Eburran. Later residents of the area were the Masai, who live in areas of the basin even now.

- Among the seasonal rivers that flow into Lake Nakuru, the most important ones are the Njoro, Makalia, Nderit, and Lamudhiak.

# Lake Nakuru

Situated in the Rift Valley in west-central Kenya, Lake Nakuru is the site of one of the most impressive ornithological spectacles in the world. This hypersaline lake is located at an altitude of 5,768ft (1,758m), within the national park of the same name which was established in 1961. It plays host to as many as 2 million flamingos—of the greater and lesser variety—which flock to the lake in order to feed on the abundant algae that thrives in its warm waters.

In the Masai language, Nakuru means "dusty place"—a name that can be explained by the nature of the lake itself. The lake, which does not have a major outflow, is fed only by rain and a handful of small seasonal rivers. The waters of the lake are used by the locals for various purposes, and levels of evaporation are also fairly high. Because of this, Lake Nakuru's water levels tend to fluctuate drastically.

Between 1951 and 1953, the lake dried up completely and it came close to drying up in 1990. The size of the lake can thus vary from a mere 2sq miles (5sq km) to 12sq miles (30sq km); the mean depth is 8ft (2.5m). The lake receives around 38.6in (98cm) of rain annually.

Lake Nakuru is bordered by the Menengai crater to the north, the Bahati hills to the northeast, the Lion Hill ranges to the east, Eburu crater to the south, and the Mau escarpment in the west. The lake and catchment area of the basin are composed primarily of volcanic rock dating from the tertiary age. The soil is composed of volcanic ash, making it very fertile, but highly porous. Thus it fractures easily during and after rains, causing immense erosion.

The salinity of the waters of Lake Nakuru is a result of the high levels of carbonates and bicarbonates present. This has ensured that only the most adaptable and

## LIFE CYCLES

Scientists believe that the flamingo population at Nakuru consumes about 550,000lbs (250,000kg) of algae per 2.5 acres (1 hectare) of surface area every year. The beta-carotenes in the plankton are responsible for the birds' brilliant plumage. The plankton, on the other hand, survives on the droppings of the flamingos.

*Lesser flamingos washing and eating in a freshwater stream*

resilient aquatic species can survive here. Six species of phytoplankton, five species of zooplankton, four species of water boatmen, two varieties of midge larvae, and a calanoid copepod have been identified here. The phytoplankton forms the lowest rung of the food chain—among them, the blue-green alga *Spirulina platensis* is so prolific that it turns the water dark green, thickening it like a broth.

However, the limited variety in water species is more than compensated for by the explosion of bright color that the flamingos of the lake showcase. These graceful birds, which the lake provides feeding and nesting grounds to, are siphon feeders, using their upturned bills to sieve plankton from the water. Apart from the lesser and greater flamingo, more than 400 species of birds have been identified in the lake area, including pelicans, smaller species such as little grebes, white-winged black terns, stilts, avocets, and many species of duck. And each winter, migratory birds seek refuge here too. The lake has been designated a Ramsar (Wetland of International Importance) site.

The Nakuru National Park is also home to several large animals including lions, leopards, hyenas, hippos, and otters. Only a single species of fish, introduced to control the mosquito population in the 1960s, live in the lake. The diminutive *Tilapia grahami*, with its high salinity tolerance, has thus thrived in the lake and is the only source of food for the pelicans.

## MORE THAN A LAKE

The park was declared a rhino sanctuary in 1983. Under the ensuing rhino stocking program, white rhinos from South Africa were introduced to the park. Currently, the sanctuary has approximately 45 of the black and 31 of the white variety—the highest combined population of rhinos in Africa. The park is also a sanctuary for the Rothschild's giraffe translocated from South Africa. The borders of the park are fenced in order to prevent the animals from wandering and falling prey to the bullets of poachers.

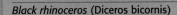

*Black rhinoceros* (Diceros bicornis)

85

**Mount Kilimanjaro,** Tanzania

- The Mount Kilimanjaro National Park was created in 1973 with the aim of protecting the mountain and its forest corridors. The park was designated a UNESCO World Heritage Site in 1987.
- Ernest Hemingway's classic 1936 short story, *The Snows of Kilimanjaro*, is set against the backdrop of Mount Kilimanjaro.

# Mount Kilimanjaro

The spectacular snow-capped peak of Mount Kilimanjaro, Africa's tallest mountain, towers over the semi-desert of northern Tanzania. Rising to 19,350ft (5,899m) above sea level at its highest point—the Uhuru Peak on the Kibo volcano—Kilimanjaro rises just east of the Rift Valley on the border of Tanzania and Kenya, and is one of the largest volcanic massifs in the world.

Relatively young in geological terms, the formation of Kilimanjaro began approximately 750,000 years ago due to tectonic activity. The mountain has three summits—each of them a volcano—joined together by a complex history of eruptions. Shira, the oldest of them, rises to a height of about 12,500ft (3,810m). Believed to have been taller in the past, geologists are of the opinion that the mountain collapsed as a result of an eruption, leaving behind a much shorter, flattened plateau. The second oldest volcano is Mawenzi at a height of 17,500ft (5,334m). Kibo, the youngest, was formed during a series of eruptions and is topped by a caldera about 1.2 mile (2km) wide. Subsequent eruptions created a second volcanic cone inside the caldera, within which another cinder cone was formed during further eruptions.

The caldera of Kibo is what forms the distinctive elongated and flattened summit of the mountain. Though the older peaks have undergone heavy erosion and retain only their jagged peaks, Kibo, in all its permanently snow-clad glory, continues to captivate visitors. However, only a small fraction of the mountain's glacial cover remains today, an event that can be attributed primarily to global warming. It is believed that at the current rate of glacial recession, the

*View of Mount Kilimanjaro*

## AGRICULTURE

The Kilimanjaro region happens to be one of the leading producers in Tanzania of mild coffee, barley, wheat, and sugar. Other crops produced in the area include sisal, maize, beans, bananas, cotton, pyrethrum, and potatoes. The Chaga, Pare, Kahe, and Mbugu peoples are the native inhabitants of the area. Located at the southern foot of Kilimanjaro, the town of Moshi is the chief trading center for the area, and also the base for ascent.

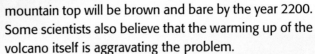

mountain top will be brown and bare by the year 2200. Some scientists also believe that the warming up of the volcano itself is aggravating the problem.

Kilimanjaro displays a whole range of vegetation zones—the semi-arid scrub of the surrounding plateau, the cultivated irrigated southern slopes, dense cloud forest, open moorland, alpine desert, and moss and lichen communities. The giant lobelia and the giant groundsel are two notable species of plants that grow in the moorlands. The forests of Kilimanjaro's southern slopes are also home to elephants, buffalo, eland, many species of monkey and duiker, among other creatures. A whole host of bird species, including the rare Abbot's starling, are also to be found here.

The first serious attempts to scale the Kilimanjaro were made in 1848 by the German missionaries Johannes Rebmann and Johann Ludwig Krapf. However, reports of the presence of a snow-capped mountain so close to the equator were scoffed at by Europeans until at least a decade later. Rumor of a quartz, limestone, and crystal laden peak ran rife for 40 years before the German geographer Hans Meyer and the Austrian mountaineer Ludwig Purtscheller scaled the Kibo summit for the first time in 1889. Since the Kibo summit can be ascended without the aid of any mountaineering equipment, every year, thousands of ambitious visitors attempt the climb.

## MICROCLIMATE

The sheer size of Kilimanjaro is responsible for it being able to influence and create its own weather pattern. The summit is mostly crowned with clouds brought by the moisture-laden winds from the Indian Ocean—they rise up against the flank of the mountain and sprinkle its crest with water or snow. Though the average rainfall is only about 8in (20cm) a year, it is sufficient to enrich the soil on the slopes and support Kilimanjaro's varied botanical systems.

*Kibo peak bathed in clouds*

- The Great Rift Valley is home to spectacular highs and lows: the Danakil Depression in Ethiopia is one of the lowest points on the planet while Mount Kilimanjaro is Africa's highest peak.

- Water bodies in the rift include Lake Tanganyika, the Sea of Galilee (Lake Tiberias), the Jordan River, the Red Sea, the Gulf of Aqaba, and the Gulf of Aden.

**The Great Rift Valley,** Africa/Middle East

# The Great Rift Valley

It has been called the "cradle of civilization," and the "backbone of Africa" but neither adequately describes the Great Rift Valley, one of the most amazing geological features on the planet. The Great Rift Valley is a vast split in the earth's crust, one that stretches almost 4,000 miles (6,400km) from its northern tip in Jordan down through eastern Africa before finally exiting at its southern end into the Zambezi River in Mozambique. The result of tectonic activity, the rift was created around 20 million years ago when Africa and the Arabian Peninsula tore apart. In fact, Africa is still undergoing the process, and it has been predicted that Somalia will someday be separated from the rest of the continent.

The Great Rift Valley was named by the British explorer John Walter Gregory, although it was the German meteorologist Alfred Wegener who developed the theory of continental drift. He noticed that the opposing shores of the Red Sea formed a perfect match, and that the sea could be closed by sliding Africa against Arabia—except that Yemen would then overlap the Afar Triangle. Geologists now recognize that the volcanic rocks in both these areas are younger than the Red Sea, and so could not have existed before the Red Sea opened; thus the match would have been perfect. Active rifts are characterized by earthquakes and volcanic activity, and in the African rift, the Afar Triangle is currently the most active part.

## THE CRADLE OF HUMAN CIVILIZATION

There is evidence to support the claim that the Great Rift Valley is the place where evolution began, some three million years ago. In the Olduvai Gorge in Tanzania, in 1959, archeologists discovered a 1.75 million-year-old hominid skeleton. Further archeological discoveries have been made throughout the valley, including those at Awash River in Ethiopia.

*Olduvai Gorge, Tanzania*

*Lake Natron and Ol Doinyo Lengai active volcano, The Great Rift Valley*

The Valley is actually divided into two forks, the eastern rift and the western rift. The eastern arm starts to the east of Lake Victoria and continues northward for about 1,600 miles (2,574km). It goes from Tanzania through Kenya and into Ethiopia and the Afar Triangle. Here the rift divides, with one part continuing north toward the Red Sea, while the other strikes eastward into the Gulf of Aden. The western arm of the rift extends for about 1,900 miles (3,057km) from Lake Malawi in the south, close to the Mozambique coast, then northward along the line of the great African lakes to the west of Lake Victoria. This arm is not only surrounded by some of the continent's deepest lakes, such as Lake Tanganyika, but also by some of its highest mountains, including Mount Kilimanjaro, the highest peak in Africa.

For most of its length, the Rift Valley has a width of about 35 miles (60km), and in many places—from Kenya, for example—it is possible to look down and across its spectacular expanse. One of the few ecosystems to remain unchanged for centuries, the valley abounds with wildlife and is home to numerous national parks, including those in Kenya, Tanzania and Congo (Ngorongoro Crater Conservation Area being the most famous)—the definitive safari destinations in the world, where you can spot not only the Big Five, but also watch the annual Serengeti migration. Also interesting are the shallow soda lakes littering the valley floor that owe their existence to poor drainage. These are home to clouds of pink flamingos as well as dozens of other migratory birds that like to feed off the sulphuric algae and crustaceans.

## FRACTURED EARTH

A rift valley is formed by the tension in the earth's crust where the opposite sides of the valley are slowly moving apart. As the valley widens, the floor of the valley drops between two roughly parallel escarpments.

The fault systems along the valley margin are complex but generally result in wedge-shaped slices that slip downward to jam the widening gap.

Over millions of years, the valley gradually widens and deepens, but continued erosion blurs the sharp lines of escarpments and sediments accumulate on the valley floor. When the crust grows too thin, a new crust is formed by magma erupting from the underlying mantle.

89

• The greatest length of Lake Victoria measured from north to south is 210 miles (337km); while the width from east to west is 150 miles (240km).

• Of the 200 or so species of fish found in Lake Victoria, the Tilapia is the most important economically.

# Lake Victoria

The largest lake in the continent, and the second largest freshwater lake in the world, exceeded in size only by the North American Lake Superior, Lake Victoria occupies an area of 26,828sq miles (69,484sq km). The heavily indented coastline of this enormous lake runs for more than 2,000 miles (3,220km) through central Africa. Its waters are shared between three countries—Tanzania, Uganda, and Kenya. Also called Victoria Nyanza, it forms the chief reservoir of the Victoria Nile, or the White Nile; it is this river that converges with the Blue Nile to form the longest river in the world.

Shaped like an irregular quadrilateral, Lake Victoria occupies a shallow depression in the middle of a great plateau that is bordered on its two sides by the Eastern and Western Rift Valleys. The surface of the lake is situated 3,720ft (1,134m) above sea level; however, it is considered shallow for its remarkable size and the maximum depth has been recorded as being around 270ft (82m). Numerous archipelagos dot the surface of the lake, and several reefs are visible just below. The most noteworthy river that enters the lake is the Kagera; the largest of the rivers that feed Lake Victoria, it enters from the western side of the lake, just north of latitude 1° south. Flowing out from the northern coast of the lake is its only outlet, the Victoria Nile.

The shores of Lake Victoria showcase many kinds of natural features. While the southwestern coast consists of 300-ft (90-m) high towering cliffs and precipices, the western coast is characterized by swamps of ambatch and papyrus that mark the Kagera River delta. The northern coast is deeply indented, but flat and bare, with only a narrow channel that leads into the Kavirondo Gulf. The Emin Pasha and Speke gulfs are situated at the southwestern and southeastern corners respectively. The densely populated Ukerewe, situated north of the Speke Gulf, is the largest of the lake islands; wooded hills on

## THE OWEN FALLS

The Owen Falls is located just below the Victoria Nile's outlet from the lake at Jinja in Uganda. This waterfall serves as the site for the Owen Falls Dam, which utilizes a hydroelectric station to harness the water, and provides hydroelectric power to western Kenya and the industries of Uganda. Using Lake Victoria as a reservoir, the dam was completed in 1954. The dramatic Ripon Falls was submerged by the dam. The water channelling of the lake through this waterfall accounts for only 20 percent of the total outflow of the lake; the rest of the water is lost by evaporation.

*Owen Falls Dam*

## DISCOVERING VICTORIA

Even though the early charts of Ptolemy delineated Lake Victoria as a vague patch of water, it was not until 1858 that it was first sighted by a European. The British explorer John Hanning Speke discovered the lake on his quest for the source of the Nile, and in 1862 located the exit point of the river and named it Ripon Falls. The vast lake was first circumnavigated by Sir Henry Morton Stanley in 1875, and later explored by him and others. Sir William Garstin, in 1901, conducted a detailed survey of the lake. Previously known as the Ukerewe, the lake was renamed by Speke in honor of Queen Victoria.

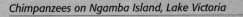

*Chimpanzees on Ngamba Island, Lake Victoria*

the island rise to a height of 650ft (200m) above the surface of the lake. The northwestern corner of the lake houses the 62 islands of the strikingly beautiful Sese archipelago. The northern coast of Lake Victoria is the site for the Ugandan cities of Kampala and Entebbe.

One of the most densely populated areas in Africa, the Lake Victoria region is inhabited by approximately 30 million people, most of whom depend on the lake for subsistence—shipping and the catching, preparation, and sale of the cichlids (fish) in the lake form the most important industries. Local steamer services around the lake serve as the mode of transportation and communication. Most of the native inhabitants are Bantu-speaking; many of them, particularly the Ganda and Tutsi tribes, have developed the decorative arts to levels of great distinction.

- The Serengeti region encompasses the Serengeti National Park, the Ngorongoro Conservation Area, Maswa Game Reserve, the Loliondo, Grumeti, and Ikorongo Controlled Areas, and the Masai Mara National Reserve in Kenya.
- Considered a jewel in the crown of Tanzania's protected areas, the Serengeti altogether accounts for approximately 14 percent of the country's land area, an unmatched conservation record.

## Salt of the Earth

A few million years ago, during the Pleistocene Epoch, rock and ash from the volcanoes of the Ngorongoro area covered the present day Serengeti plains. The volcanic ash contains salts, such as potassium, sodium, and calcium that are washed down into the soil during the seasonal rains where they precipitate. In the Serengeti plains, the salts are deposited less than a foot below the surface, and form a hard layer called a hardpan, which prevents tree roots from going further into the soil. However, the hardpan is perfect for grasses—because it traps rainwater close to the surface and makes it available for grasses that grow thick and dense—as well as for animals.

*A lioness and her cub drinking water*

# Serengeti

Serengeti—a word that conjures up images of every kind of wildlife, of vast plains, and the great migration—is one of the oldest ecosystems in the world. The Serengeti's essential features, climate, and vegetation have remained almost unchanged for a million years. The Serengeti is not one place but many, all interlinked to each other in the ecosystem. To the north lies Kenya's Masai Mara; to the west Lake Victoria; to the east the soda lakes of the Great Rift Valley; and to the south the extraordinary Ngorongoro Crater and the highlands of Tanzania. Perhaps that's why the Masai called it *Siringitu*,

"the place where the land moves on forever." Occupying an area of 11,600sq miles (30,000sq km), it encompasses two World Heritage sites and two biosphere reserves.

The Serengeti is home to one of the greatest and most diverse variety of wildlife on earth as well as one of the last great migratory systems known to mankind. It is home to over three million large mammals, including more than 35 different species of land animals, more than 500 species of birds, as well as the most fierce and intimidating predators: lions, leopards, cheetahs, crocodiles, hyenas, rhinos, and hippos. A savannah made up of grasslands

and woodlands, plains, kopjes, marshes, and riverine forests, the Serengeti is a kaleidoscope of colors, particularly at the end of February when the plains near Olduvai Gorge and Ngorongoro Crater are green with fresh grass and teaming with wildflowers.

The single most arresting sight in the Serengeti is the migration of more than a million wildebeest, about 200,000 zebras, and other grazing ungulates. The greatest spectacle in the animal kingdom is driven by rain, responsible for grass and grazing. The wildebeest spend the rainy season from December to May in the open volcanic plains below the Ngorongoro Crater. With the end of the monsoons in May or June, the plains dry out, prompting the wildebeest to move west toward Lake Victoria in search of food. Still following the rains, the migration moves north, into the Masai Mara, where the rift wall catches the last rains even in the middle of the dry season.

Once the Masai Mara's grass has been devoured and Tanzania has been bestowed with fresh rain, the vast herds travel back across hundreds of miles to their breeding grounds in the Serengeti and Ngorongoro plains. There, the young are born in time to grow sufficiently strong to undertake the long march north six months later. But migration is not devoid of danger, as predators, from lions and tigers to hyenas and crocodiles, are on the look out for easy game. Thousands of the migrating animals meet their end en route, many in the jaws of crocodiles while crossing the Grumeti and Mara rivers. This is survival of the fittest, yet so strong is the ancient instinct to move that no drought, gorge, or crocodile-infested river succeeds in holding them back.

## RIVERINE FORESTS

Riverine Forests are a unique habitat within the Serengeti. Large rivers, which remain dry for most of the year, flood during the wet season. Higher water levels give rise to a dense forest of evergreen trees, transforming the environment below it and making it a special habitat for a variety of plants, insects, birds, and animals. On the forest floor live an amazing variety of frogs, lizards, and snakes. Plant-eaters such as dikdik, duiker, and bushbuck are common, while the rivers are home to crocodiles and hippos.

*A rhino in a field of tall grass in the Serengeti*

- The total elevation of the rim of the Ngorongoro Crater is 7,500ft (2,286m) above sea level.
- Ol Doinyo Lengai (Mountain of God) is an active volcano situated within the Ngorongoro Conservation Area; it is said to have last erupted in 1983.

**Ngorongoro Crater,** Tanzania

# Ngorongoro Crater

The spectacular bowl of the Ngorongoro Crater forms the largest intact caldera in the world. Located 75 miles (120km) west of the town of Arusha in northern Tanzania, this extinct volcanic caldera lies in the Eastern Rift Valley. The rim of the crater is shrouded in dense forests, and rises to a height of 2,000ft (610m) above the floor of the caldera. Estimated to have been formed about 2.5 million years ago, the Ngorongoro Crater is the result of the major eruption of a large active volcano, whose cone is believed to have collapsed inward with the subsidence of the molten lava.

Measuring between 10 and 12 miles (16 and 19km) across, the Ngorongoro Crater has an area of approximately 102sq miles (264sq km). This vast unbroken caldera houses a great variety of ecological environments. The floor of the crater comprises primarily open grasslands; swamps and forests also proliferate. Lake Makat, the soda lake situated in the middle of the caldera, is fed by the waters of the Munge River. Owning to its exceptional geographical characteristics, the Ngorongoro Crater and its surroundings, encompassing about 3,200sq miles (8,300sq km) of area around the crater, were designated a national conservation area.

Situated to the southeast of the Serengeti National Park in the Arusha region, the Ngorongoro Conservation Area was originally included as a section of the national park in 1951. However, it was demarcated as a separate and independent conservation area in 1959. Today, this remarkable conservation area provides refuge to a diverse array of animals, and serves as a stalking ground for up to 20,000 to 30,000 wild beasts at a time.

*Giraffes the in Ngorongoro Conservation Area*

## OLDUVAI GORGE

Located in the eastern Serengeti, within the Ngotongoro Conservation, Olduvai Gorge is the mystical place where the Leakeys uncovered the hominoid remains of a 1.75-million-year-old skeleton of Australopithecus boisei, an important link in the human evolutionary chain. In a small canyon just north of the crater, the Leakeys along with international archeologists unearthed the remains of at least three recognized hominoid species, and also chanced upon a series of hominid footprints estimated to be over 3.7 million years old. Its claim of being one of the oldest sites of hominid habitation in the world is well substantiated by the excavated fossils that have been discovered here.

The marvelous landscape of this conservation area is sprinkled with exotic forests, savannah woodlands, swamps and marshes, grassy plains, mountains, volcanic craters, rivers, and lakes. The wildlife that has made this extraordinary assortment of habitats their home includes leopards, cheetahs, spotted hyenas, elephants, buffalo, zebras, black rhinos, warthogs, wildebeests, and Grant's and Thomson's gazelles. The Ngorongoro Conservation Area is home to the densest population of lions in the world. Four hundred species of birds abound in the area including the uncommon silvery-cheeked hornbill, the superb starling, and bronze and tacazze sunbirds.

Apart from the Ngorongoro Crater, the other chief volcanic attractions within the conservation area are the Olmoti and Empakaai volcanoes, which were formed between 2 and 20 million years ago. The oldest volcanoes in the area—including the ones mentioned earlier, along with the Lemagrut, Sadiman, Oldeani, Sirua, and Lolmalasin—developed along the Eyasi Rift, which today forms sweeping cliffs at Lake Eyasi. Other striking features in the area include a remarkably deep soda lake that covers nearly half of the floor of Empakaai's caldera. A shallow soda lake called Magadi, surrounded by many extinct volcanoes, is famous as a habitat for large flocks of pink flamingos.

The Ngorongoro Conservation Area was inscribed as a UNESCO World Heritage Site in 1979. Even though cultivation is prohibited within the limits of the conservation area, the local Masai people are allowed to graze their livestock in the grasslands within the Crater.

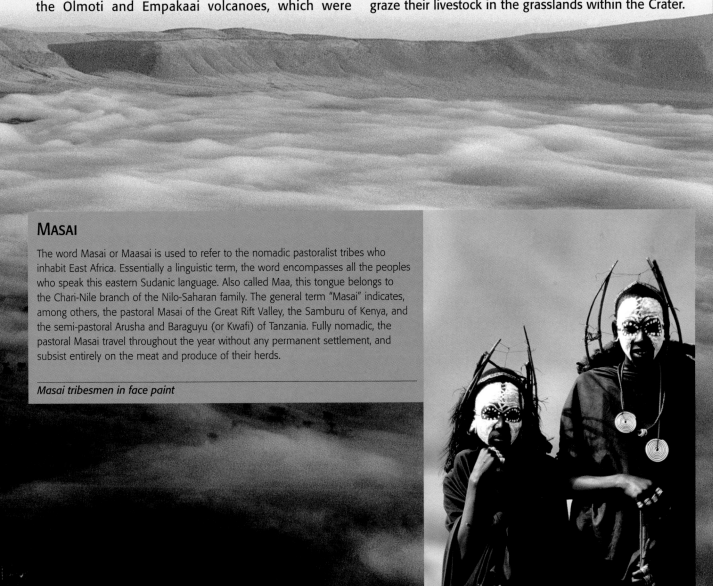

## MASAI

The word Masai or Maasai is used to refer to the nomadic pastoralist tribes who inhabit East Africa. Essentially a linguistic term, the word encompasses all the peoples who speak this eastern Sudanic language. Also called Maa, this tongue belongs to the Chari-Nile branch of the Nilo-Saharan family. The general term "Masai" indicates, among others, the pastoral Masai of the Great Rift Valley, the Samburu of Kenya, and the semi-pastoral Arusha and Baraguyu (or Kwafi) of Tanzania. Fully nomadic, the pastoral Masai travel throughout the year without any permanent settlement, and subsist entirely on the meat and produce of their herds.

*Masai tribesmen in face paint*

- Misali Island, just west of Pemba, has been singled out for having some of the highest recorded coral cover, and a high diversity of species, with 40 types of coral and 350 fish species.

- Fringing reefs, of the type found in Zanzibar, are relatively young and border land masses of islands and shorelines. They are found in shallow waters, not very far out to sea.

**Zanzibar Coral Reefs,** Indian Ocean

# Zanzibar Coral Reefs

**A**lso referred to as "Spice Island," Zanzibar is an alluring paradise with palm-fringed beaches and idyllic coves, fascinating dhows (sailing boats), and ancient Islamic ruins. An archipelago made up of three main islands—Unguja (also known as Zanzibar Island), and Pemba and Mafia islands—as well as many smaller islands and islets, Zanzibar boasts some of the world's finest coral reefs. With warm temperatures around the year and plenty of sunshine, the waters of the West Indian Ocean have the perfect conditions for coral formation, as seen by the extensive and luxurious fringing reefs off the islands.

In the clear blue and turquoise depths of the waters around Zanzibar is an ecosystem whose beauty defies description. Over millions of years, corals have formed gardens and caves, walls and gaps, mountains and overhangs, and even the backbone of many of the islands in the archipelago. Illuminated by sunlight, the corals paint the waters in vivid hues with reefs of green, gardens of rose, and caves of blue. Soft corals undulate in the waters while schools of fish swim around and through them. The reefs are made up of everything from columna and cabbage corals to honeycombs, gorgonian fans, and brain and plate corals. The waters guarantee sightings of barracuda, manta rays, moray eels, octopus, tuna, parrotfish, and pufferfish.

Two islands within the archipelago, Chumbe and Pemba, have already achieved world renown. Chumbe, an island created by fossilized corals (it even has a petrified coral forest), is home to the Chumbe Island Coral Park. Comprising 200 species of hard

*The beautifully filigreed gorgonian sea fans found among the Zanzibar Coral Reefs.*

reef-building corals, 400 species of fish, and visited by turtles, dolphins, and humpback whales, its reefs are considered to be the healthiest on the coast. Not surprisingly, it has been named the world's finest marine park by a host of authorities. In comparison, Pemba is unknown, yet the completely unspoilt coral reefs around it stretch far out to sea, where they can be found at a depth of 210ft (64m). The reefs around Pemba are considered unmatched in their beauty and variety. The numerous challenging dive spots they offer include such evocative names as Emerald Reef, Misali Coral Garden, and the Gauntlet.

Other islands in the Zanzibar archipelago whose coral reefs are worth a visit are Mafia Island and archipelago, home to the Mafia Island Marine Park, which protects the extensive coral reefs that surround it, as well the hundreds fish species that live in the waters. Mnemba Island, located off the northeastern tip of Zanzibar Island, is also rich in coral reef.

## HERITAGE CITY

In addition to its coral reefs, Zanzibar is famous for one of its towns, which is also a World Heritage Site. Stone Town is a coastal trading township whose architecture and culture is a testament to the many peoples that shaped Zanzibar—Arab, African, European, and Indian.

*Red starfish marooned after a spring tide on Zanzibar island*

## WRONG DIRECTIONS

The amount of coral cover found in the Zanzibar archipelago varies dramatically depending on the direction of the shore. Cover on eastern shores is much lower than on the western ones, and rarely reaches above 15 percent. This has been attributed to the vigorous and high-impact movement of the waves hitting the shore; coral thrives best in waters that are largely undisturbed.

Victoria Falls is known among the Kalolo-Lozi people as Mosi-oa-Tunya, meaning "the smoke that thunders."

The Scottish missionary and explorer David Livingstone, the first European to sight the towering falls in 1855, named it Victoria Falls after the British Queen, Victoria.

**Victoria Falls,** Zambia/Zimbabwe

# Victoria Falls

A thunderous roar and a veil of mist shrouds the waters of Zambezi as they tumble over the edge of a sheer cliff to form the magnificent Victoria Falls. Situated almost halfway down the river's course, on the border between Zambia in the north and Zimbabwe in the south, Victoria Falls plummets into a narrow chasm formed by the precipice and a barrier wall. Tiny islands, promontories, and depressions split the lip of the precipice into many sections, some of which remain dry during periods of low water flow of the river.

Victoria Falls is believed to have been created because of the diversion of the waters of the Zambezi caused by tectonic movements during an earlier geological period. This alteration led the waters over a massive bed of basalt and resulted in the formation of the waterfall; the heavy volume of water swiftly and easily eroded the soft rock with its many cracks and fissures.

Boasting a maximum drop of 350ft (107m) and spanning the complete breadth of the Zambezi at one of its widest points—more than 5,500ft (1,700m)—Victoria Falls forms the world's largest single curtain of falling water. Foggy columns of spray are visible from miles away as approximately 33,000cu ft (935cu m) of water plunges over the edge of this formidable waterfall every second. The spray from the falls has been known to rise upto a staggering height of 1,000ft (305m).

Today, Victoria Falls, with its awe-inspiring magnitude and its astonishing beauty, is one of Africa's greatest natural attractions, and a prime focus for conservation. The lands surrounding the waterfall have also been demarcated as protected areas. While the Victoria Falls National Park girds the waterfall on its Zimbabwean side, it is bounded on the Zambian side by the Mosi-oa-Tunya National Park, which was established in 1972. Together, the two national parks host an astounding variety of wild animals and vegetation.

*The mighty Victoria Falls*

## DEVIL'S CATARACT

Constant erosion of the soft material within the basalt in the Victoria Falls area has resulted in the creation of many fault lines along which the water is often diverted as it falls over the precipice. The Devil's Cataract, on the Zimbabwe side, is one instance of the sheer force of water cutting backwards along such a line of weakness. Approximately 69ft to121ft (21m to 37m) lower than the rest of the present waterfall, the cataract is probably a sign that another new line of flow for Victoria Falls will be established in the future because of the erosive action of water.

*A view of water rushing over Victoria Falls*

Dense forests with trees such as fig, ebony, teak, ivory palm, and acacia throng the region. There is also a considerable growth of ferns and mopane. More than 400 species of bird make up the area's rich avifauna; significant among them are the Taita and peregrine falcons, the black stork, the augur buzzard, and eagles. Elephants, lions, wildebeest, zebra, giraffes, and other creatures roam the grasslands and the rainforests. Antelopes and hippos are usually found close to the waterfall. Victoria Falls also marks a geological barrier between the distinct upper and middle river fish varieties of the Zambezi. Together with Victoria Falls, the two adjoining national parks were inscribed as a UNESCO World Heritage Site in 1989.

With its rich combination of a diverse animal population, a vast range of flora, and the breathtaking waterfall, the Victoria Falls region forms an amazing focal point of the African landscape. Thousands of tourists flock to the waterfall every year for a glimpse of one of nature's most spectacular creations.

## THE VICTORIA FALLS BRIDGE

The narrow gorge through which the waters of Victoria Falls cascades down is spanned by the Victoria Falls (Zambezi) Bridge. Commissioned by Cecil John Rhodes in 1900, the bridge is a part of Rhodes' dream of building a railway line from the Cape in South Africa to Cairo in Egypt. Though Rhodes died before the construction began, the bridge is today fully functional and people are transported between Zambia and Zimbabwe across it by rail, automobile, or on foot.

**Chobe National Park,** Botswana

- Chobe has the highest concentration of elephants in the world. However, the elephants here have smaller and more brittle tusks than those in other parts of Africa.

- As a national park, Chobe encompasses the most diverse landscape in Africa—from flood plains to savannah, from lush green stretches to arid desert.

# Chobe National Park

Home to more than 450 species of birds and a host of predators including lions, leopards, cheetahs, wild dogs, and crocodiles, Chobe National Park, the second largest game reserve in Botswana, boasts the greatest concentration of animals in the entire continent. This 4,121sq mile (10,566sq km) park in northwest Botswana provides sanctuary to possibly the largest continuous population of elephants in the world—the migratory herds are estimated to be around 120,000. This record has earned it the nickname Elephant Capital. The park is also considered the best place to spot four of Africa's Big Five—the lion, the leopard, the elephant, and the buffalo.

The first human inhabitants to arrive here were the hunter-gatherer Bushmen (Basarwa), also called San, which means "person." Though not much is known about their way of life, rock paintings discovered throughout the park give us glimpses of their lives. The San later shared space with other tribes such as the Basubiya, and later the Batawana, who moved to the area sometime in the early 20th century. The park can be divided into four distinct ecosystems: Serondela in the northeast, with its lush plains and dense forests through which the Chobe River flows, is a favorite watering hole for elephants and buffaloes during the dry season. Lion prides roam the marshlands of Savuti in the west. The Linyanti wetlands in the northwest have

## ELEPHANTS OF CHOBE NATIONAL PARK

Though listed as a threatened species, the elephants of the park are faring well enough to make park authorities fear that they might strip the park bare and irrevocably alter its landscape. The authorities had considered culling in order to control the population and reduce pressure on the parkland. Large-scale protests against the proposed plan of action, however, have kept them from executing it, and the elephants continue to thrive.

*African Elephant, Chobe National Park*

## THE CAPE BUFFALO

Often considered more dangerous than the lion by park rangers, the Cape buffalo is the biggest of the buffalos. It can weigh as much as 1,984lb (900kg), has horns that can reach 3.28ft (1m) in length, and stands 5ft (1.5m) at the shoulder. It is known to turn on its aggressor and hold its ground or charge at hunters even after being shot. Living in herds of sometimes more than several hundred, the Cape buffalo has no natural enemies and has been documented attacking—and on occasion, even killing—lions.

a similar landscape. In between Savuti and Linyanti lies a hot dry hinterland.

The idea of cordoning off the land as a protected reserve was first raised in 1931. A year later, 9,360sq miles (24,000sq km) around the Chobe district was set aside as a no-hunting zone. An additional 2,730sq miles (7,000sq km) was added to this in 1933 in order to make space for the growing number of animals. The initiative suffered a huge setback about a decade later, when a deadly tsetse fly attack resulted in the decimation of the animal population. The future of the park remained uncertain for the next 10 years after which the animal numbers soon began to stabilize. The project of creating a national park to protect animals and boost tourism was revived in earnest. However, the reserve was not formally designated a national park until 1967.

Since many industrial settlements dealing in timber dotted the landscape of the selected area, it cost the government a great deal of time and effort to enforce restrictions that a protected reserve park demanded. The last of human settlers were finally moved out of the park in 1975, and plans for spreading out continued. The last expansion took place in 1987. The remnants of the abandoned industrial sites can still be seen at Serondela.

**Etosha National Park,** Namibia

- The Etosha National Park harbours the largest and only protected-area population of the extremely rare and endangered black-faced impala.

- Etosha is one of the few reserves in Africa that has been able to provide sanctuary to the black rhino, which had been hunted to the point of extinction for its horns. Fortunately, thanks to the tough anti-poaching measures that the park authorities have adopted, the population of the animal in the park is now on the rise.

# Etosha National Park

The Etosha National Park in Namibia, home to myriad exotic creatures, covers an area of more than 8,500sq miles (22,000sq km). Designated a national park in 1907, this game reserve is inhabited by 114 species of mammals, 340 species of birds, 110 reptile species, and 16 of amphibians. Lions, elephants, leopards, cheetahs, and the endangered black rhino are among the larger animals that populate this reserve. The elephants at Etosha are believed to be the largest of all species of pachyderms found on earth, with some males measuring more than 13ft (4m) at the shoulder, which is 3ft (0.9m) more than the normal size.

Etosha translates literally as Great White Place; it is also known as the Place of Dry Water or the Great Void. The massive silvery white mineral pan that covers a quarter of the reserve—around 1,930sq miles (5,000sq km)—is probably responsible for the park being referred to by that name. Part of the Kalahari Basin, the pan is estimated to have been formed about 1,000 million years ago. The pan was once a perennial body of water, thanks to the Kunene River that flowed into it. But today, all that remains of the lake is a dusty, salt-crusted depression. The process of drying began thousands of years ago when tectonic movements forced the river

to change its course, which in turn cut off the source of water for the depression.

Folklore, however, offers a less mundane theory for the lake's creation. The formation of the pan is attributed to a tribal woman who lost her husband and children during a raid in which everyone, save the women of the village, were killed by the assailants. So grief-struck was she that she cried inconsolably for days on end. Her tears drenched the soil until the earth was saturated, and slowly the lake was formed. The tale does not tell of what happened to the woman afterwards; it only says that when the tears finally dried up, this pan of caked earth was all that was left.

The dryness of the saline pan, however, does not mean there is an absence of wildlife. During the monsoon months, the mineral-rich waters of this lake lure hundreds of species of wading birds, including the flamingo—one of the greatest tourist attractions. The area also attracts other magnificent animals such as elephants, lions, herds of wildebeest, and the black-faced impala—Etosha's most prized resident. In the summer months, the dry mineral deposits found on the lake's bed are scattered by the winds and serve to fertilize the lands surrounding the park.

Decades before this area was set aside as a protected reserve for animals, American trader G. McKeirnan visited it in 1876 and was captivated by the stunning range of wildlife to be found in this flatland. "All the menageries in the world turned loose would not compare to the sight I saw that day," wrote a fascinated McKeiran.

## THE HAUNTED FOREST

The peculiarly shaped Moringa trees that cluster around the saline pan are a great tourist draw. The trunks of these trees are thick and swollen, with branches that are bare except for a few leaves at the tips—they look as if they have been planted upside down, with the roots reaching for the sky. Owing to this eerie appearance, this part of the reserve is called The Haunted Forest.

## CUTTING DOWN

When the idea of protecting animals for conservation and tourism was first discussed and implemented, the Etosha game reserve was spread over an unbelievable 38,600sq miles (100,000sq km), making it the largest reserve on the planet. Political pressures in the 1960s, however, forced a reduction of the area, bringing it to down to less than a quarter of its original size.

*White rhinos at Ongava Camp, Etosha National Park*

• The Scottish missionary David Livingstone is believed to have been the first European to reach the swampy delta of the Okavango in 1849.

• The *mokoro*, a dugout canoe, forms the primary mode of transportation in the Okavango Delta.

**Okavango Delta,** Botswana

# Okavango Delta

The fourth longest river in southern Africa, the Okavango runs for about 1,000 miles (1,600km); rising as the Kubango in the highlands of central Angola, it flows southeastwards to the Kalahari in Botswana, and then disappears into the dry, arid sands of the desert before it has a chance to meet the sea. The slow-moving waters of the Okavango River pass through an intricate network of channels as it terminates in this enormous inland delta—the largest of its kind in the world.

Taking its name from the Kavango people of northern Namibia, the Okavango forms a triangular-shaped delta that covers a core area of around 6,000sq miles (15,540sq km), which during periods of floods can increase to 8,500sq miles (22,015sq km). More than 95 percent of the water of the Okavango Delta is lost by evaporation. The remaining waters travel either southward via the Boteti River to the Makgadikgadi Pans or to Lake Ngami in the southwest.

## CHANGE AND MANAGEMENT

The delta's grassy plains are inhabited by cattle-herding tribes. In the past their livestock was confined to the margins of the delta because of attacks by tsetse flies, carriers of sleeping sickness. Aerial spraying has all but eradicated the fly, allowing cattle and herdsmen to enter the swamps. The unfortunate side effect of this success has been to reduce the range available to the antelope, by disturbing its habitats and making it compete with cattle for grazing. The numbers of antelope are thus in decline and the fragile integrity of this wilderness is threatened. This risk has been recognized by the local people, and the Moremi Wildlife Reserve, covering 1,500sq miles (3,885sq km), is the first wildlife sanctuary in southern Africa to be created and managed by the local people.

*Lechwe sprinting at Okavango Delta*

*Zebra herd at a waterhole*

The unique character granted to the Okavango Delta by the curious juxtaposition of the prolific wetlands and arid wastelands makes it an extraordinary chunk of the African wilderness. The delta provides sanctuary and sustenance to a wide variety of flora and fauna. An extensive growth of dense reeds, predominantly papyrus, covers the upper reaches of the delta. Interspersed with the beds of reed are areas of permanent water. Large masses of water lilies sprout in these standing waters; they are a great favorite of the pygmy goose, who feeds almost exclusively on the lily fruit.

The wetland habitat offered by the Okavango Delta is ideally suited to the needs of hippos, crocodile, and several species of antelope. The sitatunga is the most remarkable of these species; related to the bushbuck and kudu and having specifically adapted to an aquatic lifestyle, this creature remains largely confined to the impenetrable reaches of the delta, and occupies other similar areas in Africa. The kobs, including the waterbuck and the lechwe, are species of antelope that have adapted to water and can be found only in southern Africa. The delta serves as the last refuge of the largest remaining number of the red lechwe antelope; at least 20,000 of these animals thrive in the grasslands.

A great number of birds, among them some of Africa's rarest species, also call the reed swamps and open waters of the Okavango Delta their home. The spectacular African fish eagle, with its distinctive piercing cry, hunts here. Many other species such as the little bee-eater, malacite kingfisher, varieties of heron and egret, and the African fishing owl feed and nest in the delta.

Reeds make way for scrublands of acacia thorn and grassy flood plains in the lower reaches of the delta. Many migrating herds of plains animals, including creatures such as the elephant, buffalo, and zebra, thus make their way to these areas, and predators such as the hyena, wild dog, leopard, and lion also follow them in pursuit.

## LAKE NGAMI

Situated at the southwestern corner of the Okavango Swamp, Ngami is a shallow lake fed by the Okavango River after it has lost most of its water due to evaporation in the marshes of the delta. Situated at an elevation of 3,057ft (932m) above sea level, the lake was first sighted by the explorer David Livingstone in 1849. The circumference of the lake was then estimated to be more than 170 miles (275km); however, by 1950, the lake had been transformed almost entirely into a sea of grass. During a particularly severe drought in1965–66, the lake dried up completely. The village of Maun, the traditional capital of the Tswana people of Botswana, and the centre of the safari industry, lies to the northeast of the lake.

**Hoba Meteorite,** Namibia

# Hoba Meteorite

Discovered only in the early 20th century, the famous Hoba Meteorite has been sitting unmoved at the Hoba Farm near Grootfontein in northern Namibia for thousands of years. Though there are rumors of the presence of a larger meteorite in Mauritiana, the Hoba Meteorite has the distinction of being the largest known meteorite in the world.

According to legend, J. Brits, the erstwhile owner of Farm Hoba West, chanced upon the meteorite in 1920 while he was ploughing his field. The ox-driven plough apparently ground to a halt with a grating metallic sound when it came across an obstruction; digging around the area the farmer uncovered a huge boulder of iron. Assuming a roughly quadratic shape, this slab of iron measures approximately 9.76ft (2.95m) in length, and 9.64ft (2.94m) in breadth; the average vertical thickness of the slab is 3.28ft (1m), with a maximum thickness of 4ft (1.22m) and a minimum of 2.5ft (0.75m). This giant block, which gleams with a metallic luster, is estimated to be roughly 66 tons—it is because of this immense weight that no one has seriously attempted to move the meteorite from its original site.

The composition of the meteorite is believed to be 82.4 percent iron, 16.4 percent nickel, and 0.76 percent cobalt, with faint traces of other metals; the surface of the slab is sometimes covered with iron hydroxides because of the formation of a thin oxidation layer. Despite its large size, the Hoba Meteorite belongs to a rare category of

## THE LARGEST METEORITES

Due to the greater stability of iron meteorites over stony or stony-iron meteorites, the largest meteorites in the world usually belong to the former category. The latter two types of meteorites fracture upon entering the earth's atmosphere, and are responsible for the creation of the spectacular meteor showers that we often see. However, they also suffer greater ablation and disintegrate almost entirely upon impact. The iron meteorites, on the other hand, are less susceptible to ablation, have greater resistance to the effects of terrestrial erosion, and can thus be preserved almost intact for thousands of years.

*A view of the single largest meteorite known to mankind sitting in its enclosure*

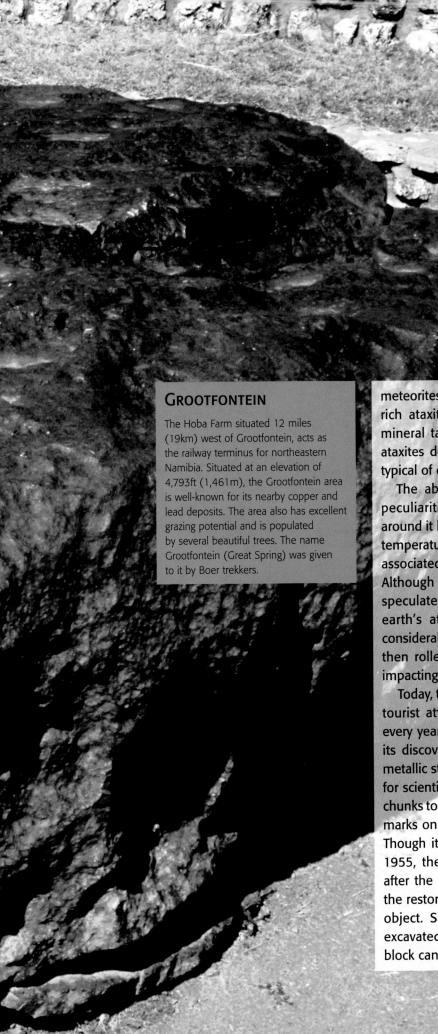

## GROOTFONTEIN

The Hoba Farm situated 12 miles (19km) west of Grootfontein, acts as the railway terminus for northeastern Namibia. Situated at an elevation of 4,793ft (1,461m), the Grootfontein area is well-known for its nearby copper and lead deposits. The area also has excellent grazing potential and is populated by several beautiful trees. The name Grootfontein (Great Spring) was given to it by Boer trekkers.

meteorites, and is scientifically classified as a nickel-rich ataxite. Composed of a dense packing of the mineral taenite (a combination of nickel and iron), ataxites do not exhibit the Widmannstätten patterns typical of other meteorites.

The absence of an impact crater is one of the peculiarities of the Hoba Meteorite. Excavations around it have shown a marked absence of the typical temperature and pressure induced features that are associated with the crashing impact of a meteorite. Although no definitive explanation exists, scientists speculate that the meteorite probably entered the earth's atmosphere at a very low trajectory, was considerably slowed down by atmospheric drag, and then rolled or bounced to its current location after impacting somewhere several miles away.

Today, the Hoba Meteorite is one of Namibia's major tourist attractions, and draws thousands of visitors every year. Unrestricted access to the meteorite since its discovery, however, resulted in vandalism of the metallic structure. Apart from samples that were taken for scientific research, the meteorite also lost bits and chunks to tourists eager to return with souveniers; saw-marks on the meteorite bear witness to this damage. Though it was protected as a national monument in 1955, the vandalism only came to an end in 1985 after the Rössing Uranium Ltd. Foundation took over the restoration and preservation of this extraterrestrial object. Since then, the entire meteorite has been excavated, and all the exposed surfaces of the iron block can be studied in detail.

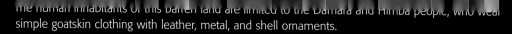

The human inhabitants of this barren land are limited to the Damara and Himba people, who wear simple goatskin clothing with leather, metal, and shell ornaments.

• Dune 45 and Big Daddy are the two most famous dunes in the Namib. Big Daddy is the largest, towering at 1,000ft. (305m). Below it lies the Dead Vlei, a dry lake bed.

## FAIRY RINGS

A curious feature of the Namib Desert are the circles found on the desert floor, known as "fairy rings," which are clearly visible from the air. They occur near the eastern border of the desert, and while their presence has generated much interest over the centuries, their origin was only recently attributed to termites.

*A view of fairy rings in the Namib Desert*

# Namib Desert

The oldest, driest, and perhaps the richest, the Namib, with its towering sand dunes is one of the most spectacular deserts on Earth. Arid for the past 55 million years, the Namib stretches for 1,200 miles (2,000km) along the southwestern coast of Namibia, averaging a width of only 70 miles (113km). It is bordered by the Atlantic Ocean whose cold Benguela current is instrumental for the desert receiving negligible amounts of rain, between 0.08in to 3in annually (0.2cm to 7.6cm). Coastal fog, however, sometimes rolls inland and is the only form of moisture that parts of the desert receive over the years. The Namib is so intensely dry that, though sloping downhill, no watercourse meets the ocean.

The word Namib comes from the Hottentot word, meaning desert or "place of no people." Due to its inaccessibility, the desert remains largely unpopulated. It occupies an area of around 31,000 miles (50,000km) and

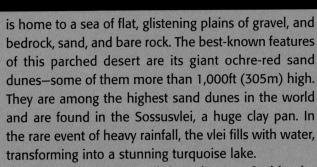

is home to a sea of flat, glistening plains of gravel, and bedrock, sand, and bare rock. The best-known features of this parched desert are its giant ochre-red sand dunes—some of them more than 1,000ft (305m) high. They are among the highest sand dunes in the world and are found in the Sossusvlei, a huge clay pan. In the rare event of heavy rainfall, the vlei fills with water, transforming into a stunning turquoise lake.

The dunes of the Namib have been crafted by the elements over millions of years. They are thought to have been formed of sand that was dumped into the Atlantic Ocean by the Orange river, which in turn was moved northward by the Benguela current and cast back on to the land by the surf. Wind blew the sand inland, and created the dunes. Even now, it continues to reshape them, forcing grains of sand to fly upward to the crest of the dune, where they drop, resulting in the characteristically steep leeward slope.

Stability of its climate over time has ensured that the Namib contains a number of species of ancient origins, as well as those that have accustomed themselves specifically to the arid conditions. One of the most remarkable is the *Welwitschia mirabilis*, a two leaf plant with the longest-lived leaves of any species in the plant kingdom; some plants are about 2,500 years old. Also found here are 70 reptile species, including the wedge-snouted sand lizard, the small-scaled sand lizard, and the barking and day geckos. There are also rodents like the gerbil and the eyeless Grant's golden mole, which can swim through the loose sand of the dunes. Hartmann's zebras, gemsbok, and oryx (Namibia's national animal), are among the biggest animals found in the desert, while cheetahs, brown and spotted hyenas, and the cape and bat-eared foxes are the main predators. Six birds are endemic to this desert: the dune lark, Benguela long-billed lark, Gray's lark, bank cormorant, tractrac chat, and Rüppell's korhaan.

## BEETLE MANIA

Several varieties of beetles are found in the Namib Desert, especially those belonging to the *Tenebrionidae* family. These beetles have acclimatized to the aridity of the desert by evolving methods to use the condensing fog as their source of moisture. An example is the head-standing beetle, which finds its way to the crest of a dune at the site of fog. Positioning itself to face the wind, it stretches its back legs so that its body tilts forward with its head down. As the fog precipitates all over its body, it flows into its mouth, and quenches the beetle's thirst.

*Fog-Basking Beetle, or Darkling Beetle, sucking moisture from a drop of water in the Namib Desert*

- The second largest desert in Africa after the Sahara, the Kalahari derives its name from the word *Kgalagadi*, which in Tswana means "the great thirst" or "a waterless place."

- After the independence of Botswana, large diamond deposits were discovered in the country. The inauguration of the diamond mine at Orapa in 1971 marked the beginning of mining activity throughout the Kalahari.

*Quivertrees in the Quivertrees forest near Keetmanshoop*

## KGALAGADI TRANSFRONTIER PARK

The Kgalagadi Transfrontier Park comprises two adjoining parks—the Kalahari Gemsbok National Park in South Africa and the Gemsbok National Park in Botswana. A historic bilateral agreement was signed by South Africa and Botswana in 1999 whereby both countries agreed to undertake the management of these two parks as a single ecological unit; they agreed to jointly promote and cooperate in tourism in the region, and share profits and duties equally. Thus the Kgalagadi Transfrontier Park was born, and formally launched as southern Africa's first peace park in 2000. Together, these parks provide a safe haven for diverse and valuable wildlife.

# Kalahari Desert

The Kalahari, with its open woodlands and an evergreen and deciduous forest in the northeast, doesn't resemble most people's idea of a desert. Though the southwestern section of the desert receives less than 10in (25cm) of rainfall and is sparsely dotted with a few drought-resistant shrubs, the relatively high precipitation and density of vegetation found in the rest of the plain makes it more of a savannah than a desert in the true sense of the word.

Sprawling across an area of roughly 360,000sq miles (930,000sq km) that covers almost all of Botswana, the eastern third of Namibia and the northernmost part of South Africa's Northern Cape province, the Kalahari has an average elevation of 3,000ft (900m) above sea level. It runs for approximately 1,000 miles (1,600km) from north to south, and measures 600 miles (970km) at its widest east–west stretch, and merges with the Namib desert in the southwest.

The Kalahari is a gently undulating sanded plain made up of sand sheets and longitudinal dunes. While the sand sheets—formed by wind and rare flood action during the Pleistocene Epoch 1.6 million to 10,000 years ago, and usually deeper than 200ft (61m)—occupy the eastern part of the Kalahari, the western part of the plain is dominated by dunes that are at least 1 mile long, several hundred feet wide and 20ft (6m) to 200ft (21m) high. In places, kopjes, or low vertical-walled hills, rise up conspicuously, exposing the underlying rock. The most remarkable of the Kalahari features, however, are the scattered vleis (pans) or "dry lakes" formed due to ephemeral streams draining their waters into the depressions. Because of its loose and frequently thick sand covering, the Kalahari surface has no standing water. The reddish soil, too, is dry, and often calcareous or saline to the point of toxicity in the pans.

The desert encompasses three of the world's most remote game reserves—the Central Kalahari Game Reserve, the Khutse Game Reserve, and the Kgalagadi Transfrontier Park. The wildlife includes the famous Kalahari black-maned lion, leopards, cheetahs, brown hyenas, elephants, ostriches, and a host of antelopes including the gemsbok. The desert also provides sanctuary to a host of other creatures such as wild hunting dogs, foxes, jackals, hyenas, warthogs, baboons, badgers, porcupines, and numerous small rodents. There are also several types of snakes and lizards, and a wealth of birdlife too. As with the plant life, the fauna that is supported by the northern Kalahari is more varied and abundant.

The Kalahari today is inhabited by the Khoisan-speaking San and the Bantu-speaking Africans, along with a few Europeans. Due to its sparse population, the network of roads connecting various parts of the Kalahari is poor. Most of the infrequently used roads and tracks are negotiable only by trucks and four-wheel drives. However, administrative centers, major habitations, and mining areas are connected by proper roads; eastern Botswana, the Okavango Swamp, and mining areas in the south too, are linked by a regular network of roads.

San bushmen hunting

## VLEIS

One of the Kalahari's most striking and fascinating features are its pans. Formed from streams that drained their water into the sands of the Kalahari itself, the pans are made up of fine silt particles deposited by the streams, and soluble calcium salts and minerals precipitated when the water evaporates. Hardened by the cementing action of the minerals, these pans gleam white when they are dry. From time to time, the pans may be covered by a shallow sheet of water. Only in areas where the salt content is low do the pans display a cover of grass just after the rains.

- The Taita Falcon, one of the rarest birds in the world, was discovered in the Blyde River Canyon as recently as the 1990s.

- Blyde River Canyon is the point where the supercontinent Gondwanaland broke apart some 200 million years ago, separating Madagascar and Antarctica from Africa.

**The Blyde River Canyon,** South Africa

# The
# Blyde River
# Canyon

Carved out of red sandstone and set against the greater Drakensberg escarpment, the Blyde River Canyon showcases some of the most spectacular and dramatic landscapes in Africa. Erosion by wind and water through millennia has contributed in making this sprawling canyon one of the most stunning natural formations in the world. The third deepest canyon in the world—after the Grand Canyon in the USA and Namibia's Fish Eagle Canyon—the magnificent panoramic views offered by craggy cliffs that rise up to 2,624ft (800m) from the river bed defy description.

The Blyde River Canyon slices through the Drakensberg Mountains in South Africa. One of the seven major mountain systems in the continent, it was formed as a result of volcanic eruptions. Previously known as uKhahlamba (Barrier of Spears) by the local Zulu people, this massive stretch of mountain and gorge was recently rechristened Motlatse.

The Blyde River Canyon is a treasure house of astounding structures fashioned by nature. The Three Rondavels—three huge dolomite rocks that rise out of the canyon walls and then taper off to resemble the roofs of traditional African huts (called *rondavels*)—are considered sacred by the indigenous of the area. At the convergence of the Blyde and the Treur rivers, erosion of water has given rise to phenomenal spirals of rock—the Bourke's Luck Potholes, named after a pioneering gold prospector, Tom Bourke. Thousands of years of work on the rocks by the whirling waters has carved out incredible cylindrical rock sculptures embellished with streaks of white and yellow lichen. Scientists contend that these shapes were carved out when the churning waters of the rivers, laden with sand, silt, and debris, crashed through the rocks. In between these rock formations nestle smooth, dark pools of water.

## PILGRIM'S REST

Pilgrim's Rest was a gold mining town established in the early 20th century when gold was found along certain stretches of the Blyde River Canyon. Though the mines were exhausted by the mid 1970s, Pilgrim's Rest did not fall into disrepair. The provincial authorities developed it into a tourist attraction, and it remains a hugely popular destination for visitors even today.

*Blyde River Canyon, Mpumalanga Province*

Other remarkable features of the canyon include the Pinnacle, a startling single column of quartzite that rises out of the woods. The occasional rainbow stretching across the top of the rock bestows it with a rather mesmeric quality. The God's Window Escarpment, another popular vantage point where cliffs plunge more than 2,296ft (700m) to the Lowveld, opens out onto a vista of extraordinary beauty—the Wonder View is yet another spectacular viewpoint. Masses of waterfalls are also found along the canyon.

The extreme climate, the range of altitudes, and the varying soil conditions of the canyon ensure a rich variety of flora. The Blyde Canyon Nature Reserve houses plants such as orchids, lilies, tree ferns, and cycads. The diverse plant life of the Blyde River Canyon also supports varied fauna. The gorge provides a safe haven for creatures such as hippos, crocodiles, impala, kudu, blue wildebeest, waterbuck, and zebra, along with several species of primate and many birds.

## BIO DIVERSITY

The Blyde River Canyon Nature Reserve is one of the few areas in Mpumalanga where montane grass still grows. More than 1,000 species of flora are found in this reserve. Many of these are endemic to the escarpment, and not found anywhere else in the world. The reserve provides shelter to nearly 20 rare or endangered species, many of them being cycads.

• A "gold rush" explosion in the area of the Kruger National Park in 1869 decimated the animal population due to a rise in hunting and trading of animal horns and skins.

• The Great Limpopo Transfrontier Park—Africa's largest game reserve—was opened to the public in early 2003.

# Kruger National Park

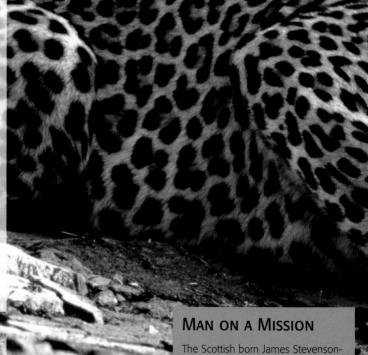

Low ranges of hills dot the otherwise flat terrain of the Kruger National Park in South Africa. Previousy South Africa's largest national park, Kruger is now part of the Great Limpopo Transfrontier Park. Comprising the Limpopo Park in Mozambique, Gonarezhou Park in Zimbabwe, and the Kruger National Park, this peace park was set up in 2002. About 200 miles (320km) long and between 25 and 50 miles (40 and 80 km) wide, Kruger individually occupies an area of about 7,523sq miles (19,485 square km)

Despite the fact that it is fed by six perennial rivers, drought is not unknown in the park. Vegetation in the park ranges from open veld to dense bush, including marula, acacia, mopane, and baobab trees. Wild beasts such as elephants, lions, leopards, cheetahs, buffalo, rhinoceros, zebra, wildebeest, and impala that roam the wilderness are among the 147 animal species, 114 species of reptile, and 507 varieties of birds that populate this untamed ecosystem. More than 1,986 types of plants can also be found in the park.

*Giraffes, Kruger National Park*

## MAN ON A MISSION

The Scottish born James Stevenson-Hamilton took charge as the first ranger of the reserve in 1902. His means of working—summary and often ruthless eviction of settlers to make more room for the animals in the reserve—earned him the nickname *Skukuza*, meaning "he who sweeps clean" or "he who turns everything upside down." The name of the main rest camp in the park was changed to Skukuza in his honor in 1936.

*Young hippos play in a river*

By the early 1800s, the region had turned into a fighting ground for the Difaqane tribal wars and inspite of the repeated introduction of hunting laws, the slaughter continued well into the late 1800s. It was Paul Kruger who started the uphill battle for conservation in 1884, demanding that the region be declared a protected area. Finally in 1898 he managed to convince the government to set aside a 1,794sq miles (4,600sq km) swathe between the Sabie and Crocodile Rivers as a game reserve. Prohibition on hunting did not succeed in deterring poachers who continued to skulk in the area. The final blow came in 1899—with the eruption of the three-year long Boer War, the animal population plummeted further because of indiscriminate killings. After the war, however, the park staged a comeback under the aegis of James Stevenson-Hamilton, who was appointed as game warden.

Stevenson-Hamilton and his team of rangers and scouts cleared the area of human habitation and brought an end to poaching. Because of their efforts, the Shingwedzi Game Reserve, between the Letaba and Luvuvhu rivers, was formed in 1903, and within two years the area of the park went up to 6,630sq miles (17,000sq km). It was on his insistence that the reserve came to be declared a national park in 1926 and was consequently named, in order to honor Paul Kruger's contribution to the cause of conservation. In the same year the park was further expanded and has thus reached its current size.

## SUCCESS OF TOURISM

Kruger's popularity skyrocketed soon after it was declared a national park in 1926. Compared to 1927, when three vehicles roamed the park, 900 vehicles loaded with tourists were scouring the park by 1930, and more than 310 miles (500m) of road had been laid. Today, millions of tourists visit the park each year, and nearly 5,000 miles (8,065km) of paved and gravel roads traverse the area.

- The Cango Caves were the first to be protected by environmental legislation and also the first natural wonder with a full-time tourist guide.

- Dripstone caverns, similar to the Cango Caves, are found in several places around the world; another example would be the Damlatas Dripstone Cavern in Alanya, Turkey, which was discovered in 1948.

**Cango Caves,** South Africa

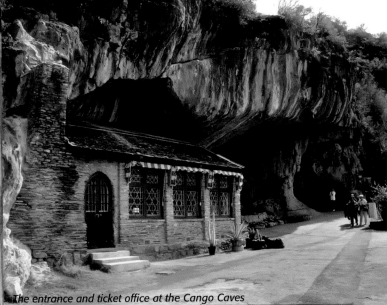

*The entrance and ticket office at the Cango Caves*

# Cango Caves

O ver time, water, limestone, and carbon dioxide have toiled to create one of the planet's most spectacular sights. The Cango Caves, situated near Oudtshoorn in South Africa's Western Cape, in a limestone ridge parallel to the Swartberg Mountains, are an underground marvel featuring some of the world's finest dripstone caverns. Ancient tools have been uncovered here which suggest that humans have inhabited these caves for at least 80,000 years. Not surprisingly, they are also South Africa's oldest tourist attraction.

Inside the Cango Caves are vast halls with towering formations of stalactites, stalagmites, helicites (columns sprouting in several directions), and stalagnates (various trajectories formed when stalactites and stalagmites join), that have been growing for the past one-and-a-half million years. The bizarrely shaped helicites are composed mainly

## CAVE PROTECTION

When the caves were opened to the public in the 19th century, vandalism was rife as people carried away parts of the delicate stalactites and stalagmites as souvenirs or defaced the cave walls. To put an end to this destruction, the governor of the Cape Colony, Lord Charles Somerset, published the first Caves Regulation in 1820, which became the first law in South Africa designed to protect an environmental resource.

of calcium carbonate that condenses as lime water drips from the stones and evaporates.

The caves were believed to have been first explored by a colonial farmer, Jacobus van Zyl, in the late 18th century, though no proof exits to substantiate this claim or the fact that somebody by that name even lived in the area in the 1770s. Nonetheless, the myth has lived on—the first chamber in the caves is called Van Zyl's Hall, a massive space measuring 321ft (98m) in length, 160ft (49m) in width, and 49ft (15m) in height. It is not clear just how much of the space he explored, but over the years a vast sequence of chambers—with imaginative names like Lumbago Alley, the Crystal Palace, Tunnel of Love, the Coffin, the Post Box, and the Devil's Chimney—were discovered and christened Cango One, and subsequently opened to the public. It ran 2,499ft (762m) from the entrance and then came to an abrupt halt, though draughts of fresh air convinced explorers that there were still more chambers to be discovered.

Cango Two, an 886-ft (270-m) extension of the existing cave sequence was discovered in 1972. In 1975, another extension of about 5,248ft (1600m) was revealed and named Cango Three. The natural colors, crystalline beauty, and formations inside the two caves combined are several times more magnificent than those of Cango One. However, in order to preserve the beauty of the limestone formations inside, neither Cango Two or Three are open to the public.

Some of the notable dripstone formations inside the caves are Cleopatra's Needle—a 29-ft (9-m) high and at least 150,000-year-old stalagmite—and Completed Column, which rises 410ft (125m) from the floor to the ceiling in the center of Cango One's second chamber. A remarkable feature of Van Zyl's Hall is its beautiful dark gray roof that has been smoothly sculpted into hollows and pendants—a dramatic contrast to the softer limestone walls that are a mellow yellow.

The Cango Caves are maintained at a constant temperature of 64.4°F (18°C) and are perfectly illuminated, making them the biggest showcave operation in Africa. Thousands of tourists are drawn to these natural wonders annually. In 1938, the caves were declared a national monument.

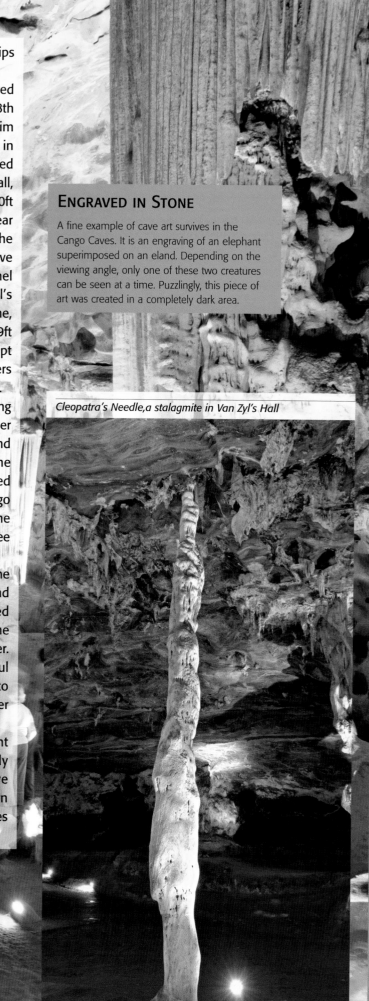

## ENGRAVED IN STONE

A fine example of cave art survives in the Cango Caves. It is an engraving of an elephant superimposed on an eland. Depending on the viewing angle, only one of these two creatures can be seen at a time. Puzzlingly, this piece of art was created in a completely dark area.

*Cleopatra's Needle, a stalagmite in Van Zyl's Hall*

- Maclear's Beacon—a stone cairn on the highest point on Table Mountain—was constructed by Sir Thomas Maclear in 1865 for the purpose of a trigonometrical survey.
- Table Mountain is one of the few places in the world with extensive sandstone caves, with the Wynberg Caves being the largest among them.

**Table Mountain,** South Africa

# Table Mountain

The imposing figure of the Table Mountain looms over the hustle and bustle of Cape Town in South Africa, often obscured from view by white clouds. Draped in mist, when viewed from the bay the mountain appears to be a monolith—with a perfectly flat summit and steep cliffs which rise abruptly—that shimmers gently in the heat. Table Mountain was referred to as *Hoerikwaggo*, meaning "sea mountain" or "mountain in the sea," by the original inhabitants of the Cape, the Khoekhoen and San tribes.

One of the oldest mountains in the world, Table Mountain rises to a height of 3,560ft (1,085m). Millennia of erosion of almost horizontal layers of sandstone by strong winds and water have given the mountain its unusual tabular shape. While the 2-mile (3.2-km) long northern face of the mountain is desolate and scarred, the summit plateau is crisscrossed with small streams and valleys.

Table Mountain forms the northern extremity of a mountain range that lies between Cape Town and the Cape of Good Hope. Flanked in the northeast by the Devil's Peak, which rises to 3,200ft (975m), and in the northwest by the Lion's Head, which descends from a height of 2,100ft (640m) to the 1,100-ft (335-m) high Signal Hill (Lion's Rump), Table Mountain is made up of layers of sandstone and granite resting on shale and an older granite base. The jagged escarpment of the mountain, as it stretches out against the sky, is popularly referred to as the Twelve Apostles.

Table Mountain has its very own cloud cover, responsible for the lush vegetation found on the plateau. Formed by winds blowing in from the southeast, the spectacular "tablecloth" is a thin layer of clouds that settles neatly on top of the flat summit. The clouds formed during this extraordinary phenomenon, however, do not reach the lower slopes of the mountain. Rainfall brought in winter by the northwesterly winds is also greater at the summit, and caught by five mountain reservoirs.

## STAR ATTRACTION

The French astronomer Abbé Nicolas Louis de Lacaille conducted important observations of the southern sky from the Table Mountain. When he introduced a new constellation in 1763, he named it *Mons Mensae*, which translates from Latin as "table mountain." Though the constellation lacks bright stars—its brightest star, the *Alpha Mensae*, is barely visible at a magnitude of 5.09—it contains a portion of the Large Magellanic Cloud. Known as Mensa (the Table) today, the star cluster bestows Table Mountain the unique distinction of being a natural feature after which a constellation has been named.

*Aerial view of Robben Island and Table Mountain*

Table Mountain

## BIODIVERSITY HOTSPOT

Owing to its incredibly rich biodiversity, the Table Mountain area has been declared a national park. Formed as the Cape Peninsula National Park in the 1990s and renamed Table Mountain National Park in 1998, the park stretches for 37 miles (60km) from Signal Hill in the north to Cape Point in the south. With its beautiful valleys, bays, beaches, cliffs, and sandy flats, in addition to its remarkable flora and fauna, the park has immense natural, historical, and scenic significance. With more than 1,500 plant species, Table Mountain forms the heart of the Cape Floral Kingdom. One of the six floral kingdoms in the world, the Cape Floral Kingdom is a Natural World Heritage Site.

The gullies and gorges of the Table Mountain provide shelter to indigenous Afromontane forests; fynbos (fine bush), disa orchids, silver trees, and 250 species of daisies also form part of the abundant vegetation. The ecosystem of the mountain also supports a large number of animals, including antelopes such as klipspringer and grysbok, Himalayan tahr, reptiles such as the venomous Cape Cobra, and endangered amphibians like the Table Mountain Ghost Frog.

The plateau is also popular among hikers, with most choosing the easiest route to the top via the Platteklip, or "flat stone," Gorge. Formed by the erosion of rock by heavy rains, this is the deepest ravine that splits the cliff face. This was the route used by the Portuguese explorer Admiral Antonio de Saldanha for the first recorded climb of the mountain in 1503. Today, there are more than 350 routes that lead to the summit. Less adventurous visitors can take the Table Mountain Aerial Cableway (built in 1929) to the top.

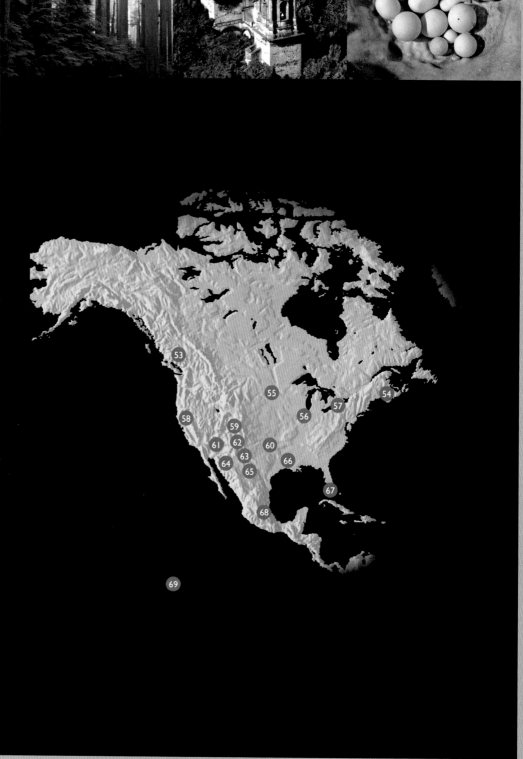

# North America

**T**he sweeping North American territories of Canada, British Columbia, Greenland, United States of America, and Hawaii are part of the Earth's western hemisphere that also includes Central America, the West Indies and South America. Surrounded by the Atlantic Ocean to the west and the Pacific Ocean, to the east, the North American continent also includes the Hudson and Baffin bays, the Gulf of Alaska, California and Mexico, and the Labrador Sea.

Canada and British Columbia and the water world stretching into the Atlantic Ocean has the highest peaks in North America, the largest ice fields outside the polar caps, and some of the most ecologically interesting islands. Some 370 years ago, for example, the coast of Gaspe Peninsula facing Baie des Chaleurs was a tropical estuary—the craggy peaks of the Appalachians lined the horizon and trees covered the land, providing a home to giant spiders and scorpions, while its waters were home to a variety of armored and lobe-finned fish. Off Vancouver, the SGang Gwaay Island, part of the Queen Charlotte Islands known today for its birds, species of moss and ferns, migrating whales and sea lions, was until the 19th century home to the 300 member strong Haida community who subsisted on hunting until wiped out by disease.

In the United States of America, the Great American Desert, stretching from Oregon to central Mexico, encompassing the Mojave, Sonoran, Great Basin and Chihuahuan, is the depository of 2 billion years of geological history. Its Yosemite Valley in the Sierra Nevada is a glacially carved valley and its Great Lakes create the largest expanse of freshwater in the world. Further south, the Hawaiian waters—stretching 360sq miles (932sq km) in the southeastern portion of Big Island— are home to yet another spectacular feature, sea volcanoes. Two of which—Mauna Loa and the Kilauea—awe the world with annual eruptions. Mauna Volcano, considered to be the highest in the world—measured from the seabed—at 56,000 ft (17,169m), is twice the height of Everest.

- The explorer Tom Wilson was the first non-native to see the now-famous Lake Louise in 1882. He gave it the name Emerald Lake, which was later changed to honor Queen Victoria's daughter Princess Louise.

- Mount Robson, the highest peak in the Canadian Rockies, can be seen clearly only for about 14 days a year. The bad weather close to its summit makes it a very challenging climb for mountaineers.

**Canadian Rockies,** Canada

## CHINAMAN'S PEAK

Ha Ling Peak in the Kananaskis Provincial Park in the Canadian Rockies was named after a Chinese cook who in 1886 won a bet with his co-workers by climbing the peak, planting a flag and descending in five and a half hours. The peak was named Chinaman's Peak to honor his feat, and then renamed Ha Ling after the man himself in 1997.

# Canadian Rockies

Bordered by undulating prairies to the east and the innumerable subsidiary ranges of the Columbia Mountains to the west, the Canadian Rockies extend from the forests of central Mexico through to the US–Canada border, forming a natural boundary of sorts between the provinces of British Columbia and Alberta.

About 75 million years ago, the collision of tectonic plates forced the bed of what was probably an inland sea to buckle and rise until it formed the framework of the mountains that we see today. The process of glaciation began with the onset of the Ice Age about 35,000 years ago when massive glaciers covered the entire Rockies. These rivers of ice scrubbed the mountains clean of vegetation and molded its valleys and gorges, polishing the rocks and sculpting them into various extraordinarily

shaped formations. As the earth grew warmer and the glaciers melted, the debris frozen in the ice was deposited on the rocks to form lateral moraines. Lakes were formed where the deposits were large enough to choke the natural drainage. In time, the flood of water ate through the debris and rocks, forming deep gorges and channels.

The only remnants of the Ice Age today are the glacial fields scattered across the continental divide, the most impressive of those being the Columbia Icefield, spread over 126sq miles (325sq km). Lake Louise is the most famous of the moraine lakes of the Canadian Rockies, while the credit for being the tallest peak goes to Mount Robson, with a towering height of 12,970ft (3,954m).

The Canadian Rockies come in various shapes and sizes. "Castellate" mountains, comprising horizontal layers of rocks, are so named because they often have vertical

towers that resemble castle turrets—Banff's Castle Mountains, for example. "Dogtooth" mountains, such as Mount Louis, were formed by severe erosion that left behind hard base rock layers which jut out into the sky in sharp points. A ridge of near-vertical rock layers similar to the dogtooth variety and resembling a saw blade is called a "sawtooth" mountian. Mount Assiniboine, often compared to the famous Matterhorn in Europe, was formed when glaciers scoured four sides of the summit to create a square-topped peak instead of a pinnacle.

Rocks thrusting upwards at angles of 50 or 60 degrees create peaks—Mount Rundle, for instance—which have one smooth sweeping face and one sharp steep face with dipping layers. Anticlinal and synclinal peaks are also common—the former is created when rocks are compressed to form smooth domes without cracking; the latter are formed in the troughs of depressions. The oddest peaks are the "complex" mountains. With their complicated combinations of up-folds and down-folds, these mountains result in structures that defy classification.

*Mount Robson above Yellowhead Highway*

## PEAKS OF THE CANADIAN ROCKIES

The wilderness of the Canadian Rockies houses five national parks—the Waterton, Banff, Jasper, Kootenay, and the Yoho. These, excluding the Waterton which lies along the international boundary further south, interlock and were together declared the Canadian Rocky Mountain Parks World Heritage Site by UNESCO in 1984. The site also includes three adjoining British Columbia provincial parks. All these parks have been established with the intention of protecting and preserving the diverse wildlife of the region and their natural habitat. One of the pioneers in the push for preservation measures was J. B. Harkin, the first Commissioner of Dominion Parks in 1930.

*Mount Assiniboine at dawn*

- The name Gaspé is said to be derived from a Micmac Indian word which means "land's end."
- The Percé Rock contains 150 species of fossils including brachiopods, trilobites, Percé dalminites, marine worms, and corals.

# Percé Rock and Gaspé Peninsula

A rugged extension of the Appalachian mountain chain, the Gaspé Peninsula is situated in the eastern Quebec province of Canada. It runs from the east towards the northeast for 150 miles (240km), from the Matapédia River into the Gulf of St. Lawrence. The St. Lawrence River forms the northern boundary for the peninsula, and it is bounded in the south by Chaleur Bay and New Brunswick. One of the most picturesque areas of Canada, the peninsula encompasses a diverse and majestic landscape of mountains, valleys, rivers, bays, and coastlines.

Elevations in the northern parts of the Gaspé Peninsula are higher than in the southern coast, with Mont Jacques-Cartier rising to a height of 4,198ft (1,280m) amid the forest-covered Monts Chic-Choc (Shickshock Mountains) in the north central area. The peninsula is drained by a number of spectacular rivers including the Cascapédia, Saint-Jean, York, Grande, and du Grand Pabos. The forests, beaches, cliffs, and meadows of Gaspé provide sanctuary to an immense variety of flora and fauna.

Percé Rock (or Rocher-Percé) is a sheer, gigantic monolith that rises out of the Gulf of St. Lawrence just off the outer tip of the Gaspé Peninsula, 465 miles (750km) east of Quebec City. Attached to the shoreline at one time, this peninsular rock island is connected to the mainland by a sand and gravel bar, which is visible only at low tide. This spectacular block of ochre-colored limestone is believed to be 375 million years old.

The Percé Rock is 1,437ft (438m) long, 295ft (90m) wide, and touches 290ft (88m) at its highest point. The name Rocher-Percé translates as "pierced rock" and has

## CONSERVATION IN THE GASPÉ PENINSULA

Large sections of the Gaspé Peninsula are within conservation areas. Major protected areas on the peninsula include the Gaspésian Provincial Park which occupies 313sq miles (802sq km), and the Forillon National Park, which encompasses 93sq miles (240sq km) at the northeastern tip of the peninsula. The Bonaventure Island and Percé Island National Park form the largest gannet seabird colony in North America. The Miguasha Provincial Park was inscribed as a UNESCO World Heritage Site in 1999.

## EROSION OF PERCÉ ROCK

The mammoth Percé Rock is said to weigh in at a staggering 551 million tons. However, because of erosion by the sea, it loses about 330 tons of rock every year, and is likely to disappear completely in 16,000 years at the present rate of erosion. The massive rock had earlier had another hole carved into it by the sea; but constant erosion coupled with a lightning strike in 1845 severed the arch and left behind an isolated column of rock a little way from the main body. This obelisk measures 148ft (45m) in height.

*Hikers at low-tide crossing to the Pierced Rock (Rocher-Percé). Percé Rock is a major tourist attraction in Quebec, with picturesque views of the rock from both Percé and nearby Bonaventure Island*

its origin in the huge hole that has been carved into the rock by the waters of the sea. This 33ft (10m) wide and 60ft (18m) high gap that pierces the calcite veined mass of rock makes it one of the largest natural arches in the world.

Although the Frenchman Jacques Cartier first landed in Gaspé Bay in 1534 and claimed the land for the king of France, the original inhabitants of the Gaspé Peninsula were native people who spoke the language. Only a few of the foreigners ended up settling permanently in the area. The peninsula was inhabited by the Micmac people at the beginning of the 17th century, when Samuel de Champlain sailed along the coasts of Gaspé. Converted to Christianity by the French missionaries, the Micmacs have continued to live in the area since then.

Today, most of the population of Percé Rock and the Gaspé Peninsula resides along the coast, within a few miles of the Gulf of St. Lawrence, with the exception of the copper-mining town of Murdochville. The principal areas of settlement are Matane, Gaspé, Percé, Chandler, and New Carlisle. The peninsula—with its forests and fish-filled clear streams—is excellent for hunting and fishing and thus beneficial for both the local and sporting interests of its community. Other economic activities in the area are lumbering, production of pulp for papermaking, and some mining of lead, copper, and zinc.

- Established by the US Congress on March 1, 1872, Yellowstone National Park is the oldest national park in the world.

- The park holds more than 200 geysers; some erupting to heights greater than 100ft (30m).

# Yellowstone National Park

The oldest and most popular national park in the United States, Yellowstone National Park contains the greatest concentration of geothermal features in the world. Designated a UNESCO World Heritage Site in 1978, the park encompasses 3,472sq miles (8,987sq km) of rugged mountains, spectacular deep valleys, and broad volcanic plateaus.

Several noteworthy geologic features are scattered across the surface of Yellowstone Park. The most striking among these are a black obsidian (volcanic-glass) mountain, eroded basaltic lava flows, fossil forests, and occasional odd structures carved out by the erosive action of wind and water. The most famous and popular of Yellowstone's attractions, however, remain the 10,000 or so hot springs and geysers that bubble underground and burst onto the surface in the form of geysers, mud cauldrons, hot pools of myriad hues, steam vents, fumaroles, and hot rivers.

Yellowstone's extraordinary geothermal activity can be attributed to the unusual thinness of the earth's crust in the area. This, combined with the intrusions of magma at depths of 4 to 10 miles (6.5 to 16km) and a very steep subsurface temperature gradient serves to heat the precipitation water—that percolates through cracks and fissures on the surface—to very high temperatures, until it boils and expands. This superheated water is thrust out under pressure through the hard and strong rhyolite, silica-bearing rock at the surface.

## OLD FAITHFUL

Though not the highest, Old Faithful is the most famous geyser in North America. Located at the head of the Upper Geyser Basin, this 200 to 300-year-old geyser was so named by the Washburn-Langford-Doane Expedition in 1870 because of its apparently "faithful" eruptions every 63 to 70 minutes. On closer observation, however, the interval has been recorded as varying between 33 and 120 minutes. The geyser's eruptions are accompanied by billowing hot steam, and on clear and windless days, its fountain-like eruption column has been known to reach 170ft (52m). The average height of the eruptions, however, is approximately 130ft (40m), and the column stands for about 4 minutes.

*A group of American bison rest near the Old Faithful geyser*

*A bighorn lamb on the alpine slope of Mount Washburn, Yellowstone National Park'*

### CONNECTING YELLOWSTONE

Lieutenant William Clark, who sailed down the Yellowstone River in 1806, was the first person to explore the area. The first trading post on Yellowstone was established by a native American trader called Manuel Lisa, accompanied by a trapper called John Colter, at the mouth of the Bighorn River in 1807. Today, more than 500 miles (800km) of roads and 1,000 miles (1,600km) of trails spread throughout the entire park. Established in 1972, the 80-mile (130-km) scenic John D. Rockefeller Jr. Memorial Parkway today connects Yellowstone to the Grand Teton National Park in the south.

Yellowstone National Park is headquartered at the Old Faithful and Mammoth Hot Springs, and several of the most famous geysers and hot springs are located between the two.

Included among these is the Giantess, which is situated close to the Old Faithful and erupts at intervals of every six to eight months. There is also the Fountain Paint Pot—located in the Lower Geyser Basin, it consists of fumaroles, pink plopping mud geysers, and a blue hot spring pool. The Minerva—located at Mammoth Hot Springs—is a multi-colored terrace with hot water cascades.

Yellowstone is also famous for its many lakes and rivers. The huge Yellowstone Lake, the largest mountain lake in North America, occupies a caldera formed by an eruption 600,000 years ago. Fishing and boating are among the most popular sports. The Yellowstone River traverses a magnificent, brilliantly colored gorge and has two majestic waterfalls along its course.

Forests cover most of the park. Though the lodgepole pine accounts for the majority of the trees found in the area, other species of conifers, cottonwoods, and aspens also abound. The warm months see a profusion of wildflower blossoms.

The wildlife prowling the jungles of Yellowstone is typical of the Rocky Mountains, and consists of elk, bighorn sheep, deer, moose, bison (buffalo), coyotes, and black and grizzly bears. Reintroduced into the park in 1995, 13 packs of wolves now make Yellowstone their home. Bird species in the park number hundreds; several of these species are waterfowl, including the rare trumpeter swan. The fish-filled lakes and streams of Yellowstone draw many anglers, with the trout being the most popular catch.

Devils Tower, USA

- The name Devils Tower is derived from the American-Indian term "The Bad God's Tower." It was called this for the first time by Colonel Richard Irving Dodge in his 1879 book, *The Black Hills*.
- The idea of preserving the tower as a national or state park was first brought up in 1892, but it was not until 14 years later, on September 24, 1906, that it was declared a National Monument by President Theodore Roosevelt.

# Devils Tower

Long before explorers wandered into the West, the Indian tribes of the northern plains, looked at the Devils Tower rising above the surrounding grassland and the ponderosa pine forest with awe. They called it "Grizzly Bear's Lodge" and believed its existence was holy. To this date, various Native American plains tribes including the Sioux, Cheyenne, and Kiowa, worship regularly at the Tower.

Rising 867ft (264m) from its base, 1,267ft (386m) above the Belle Fourche River, and 5,117ft (1,560m) above sea level, Devils Tower is a prominent landmark in northeastern Wyoming. Geological estimates put its age at approximately 50 million years, though erosion probably uncovered the rock formations only one or two million years ago. Its slightly dome-shaped summit is roughly 200ft by 400ft (61m by 122m). Chipmunks, mice, rats, and occasionally snakes are found on top. The area in which the tower stands was once home to prairie dogs, gray wolf,

*A prairie dog eats grass at Devils Tower National Monument*

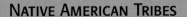

## NATIVE AMERICAN TRIBES

According to the National Park Service, over 20 tribes have cultural affiliation with the Devils Tower. They include the Arapaho, Lakota (Sioux), Blackfeet, Crow, Cheyenne, Kiowa, Eastern and Southern Shoshone, and Oglala Lakota to name a few. These tribes have been known to have offered prayers and to hold vision quests and funerals here. The Arapaho called Devils Tower by the name "Bear's Tipi," the Cheyenne know it as "Bear's Lodge" and "Bear's Peak," and the Kiowa refer to it as "Tree Rock." The Sioux traditionally held their sacred Sun Dance at Devils Tower (around summer solstice) and used to refer to the Belle Fourche River as the Sun Dance River.

black bear, and the grizzly bear. This might well be the reason why the American Indians identified the Tower with bears and their lairs. A favorite with climbers, the Devils Tower every year observes a voluntary closure in June, to allow Indians to worship at the site. Various tribes have over the years objected to the recreational climbing at Devils Tower and this voluntary closure is the administration's attempt to encourage and respect the American Indian culture.

The exact process of how this rock was formed is unknown, though a majority of geologists contend that is was once part of a shallow sandstone seabed during the Triassic period (195 to 225 million years ago). This red sandstone and maroon siltstone can still be seen along the edges of the Belle Fourche River flowing by the tower. It was shaped by a molten rock forced upward from deep within the earth. Debate continues, however, as to whether molten rock tore through the earth's crust or cooled underground. The distinctive furrowed columns are a result of contractions that occurred during the cooling of the rock. The Tower slowly emerged after years of water and wind erosion exposed it. While most of its outer sandstone layer and shales wore off, its harder ingenious core survived.

Today, as rain pounds its furrows, cracks, and surviving sedimentary surface, more and more of the tower will become exposed and eventually erode completely. Pieces of it continue to break off and fall from its steep walls, as do occasionally entire columns, which can be seen lying in a pile of rubble at its base. As this process of weathering continues, Devils Tower will eventually collapse completely—but it is likely to be around for a good million years yet.

## SCALING THE TOWER

The first major non-American Indian event held here was on July 4, 1893 and it included the successful scaling of the mountain by William Rogers, a local rancher. According to a handbill circulated for the occasion, people were invited to witness the first climb and were promised, "plenty to eat and drink on the grounds" with "lots of hay and grain for horses" and "dancing day and night." Rogers climbed the Rock with the help of a 350-ft (107-m) wooden ladder that was held in place with oak, ash, and willow pegs driven into the vertical crack found between the two columns on the southeast side of the giant formation. It is estimated that some 1,000 people, who arrived here by horseback, wagon, and buckboard, witnessed the event.

*Silhouette of man hiking up one of the steep paths at Devils Tower*

- The name Niagara is said to have been derived from the Iroquois Indian word *Onguiaahra* meaning "the strait."

- The flow over the American section of the Niagara Falls was halted for several months in 1969 in order to remove rubble and rocks from the riverbed in an attempt to improve its appearance. The plan was eventually shelved due to unforseen expenses.

# Niagara Falls

The air is enveloped in a blanket of mist and spray where the dark green waters of Niagara Falls thunder into the frothing cauldron at its base. The second largest waterfall in the world after Victoria Falls, Niagara is the collective name given to three waterfalls—Horseshoe or Canadian Falls, American Falls, and the much smaller Bridal Veil Falls. Estimated to have been formed only around 10,000 years ago during the last Ice Age, the falls are relatively young in geological terms. Since then, however, they have shifted about 7 miles (11km) from their spot of origin. This shift was caused by the swiftly flowing waters of the Niagara River, eroding the soft shale and sandstone and causing them to cave in. As a result the river gradually retreated, leaving in its wake a deep gorge.

Approximately 500 years ago, the river encountered an obstacle that caused it to split into two channels, forming an island between them, now called Goat Island. Thus, American Falls lies on the east, while Horseshoe Falls is to its west on the Canadian side of the border. Of the two waterfalls, Horseshoe—named so because of its 2,600ft (792m) long horseshoe-shaped arc—is the more overwhelming. It is 185ft (56m) high, and more than 600,000 gallons (2.27 million liters) of water pour over the edge every second. The almost straight brink of American Falls, on the other hand, is 1,000ft (305m)

*An aerial view of Niagara Falls*

## CANADA'S THUNDERING WATERFALLS

Canada is home to many other spectacular waterfalls. At Virginia Falls, in the Northwest Territories, the South Nahanni River thunders over a precipice almost twice the height of Niagara. This little-known river descends 3,000ft (915m) over a distance of 370 miles (595km) in a series of tumbling rapids and deep gorges. Hunlen Falls and Helmcken Falls are both in British Columbia. At Helmcken Falls, the Murtle River cascades over a cliff to a spray-filled basin 450ft (137m) below. Hunlen Falls are seven times the height of the Niagara and drop in a curtain of spray 1,200ft (366m) to the rocks below.

The Maid of the Mist *carrying tourists into the Niagara Falls spray*

## OVER THE FALLS

Some people have taken the sheer power and size of Niagara Falls as an irresistible personal challenge. Several adventurers have gone over the falls, in a variety of different vessels, including barrels, boats, and sealed capsules.

One of the most famous death-defying escapades took place on June 30, 1859, when Jean Francois Gravelet, better known as Charles Blondin, crossed the falls on a tightrope. The rope was 1,100ft (335m) long, and suspended 160ft (49m) above the falls. Evidently Blondin found the whole experience a bit too tame: a year later he made the crossing again, but this time with his agent on his back!

long, and the fall height is 190ft (58m)—but the actual fall is only 70ft (21m) because of rock piled up at the base—and about 150,000 gallons (568,000 liters) of water pass over the brink of the escarpment every second. Today, about 50 percent of the Niagara waters is diverted and harnessed to generate electricity. The Belgian Franciscan friar, Father Louis Hennepin, is credited as being the first European to discover Niagara Falls; his description of 1678 was instrumental in bringing the falls to the world's attention. Today, the falls attract more than 12 million visitors annually. Bridges and parks on either side of the river provide great vantage points for viewing the stunning falls. Rainbow Bridge, named because of the rainbows perennially shimmering in the spray, offers visitors a glorious view. The oldest and most famous tourist attraction at Niagara Falls is the Maid of the Mist boat cruise. The cruise, named after a mythical Onguiaahra character, has been operating since 1846 and has been carrying passengers to the whirlpools at the foot of the falls. Cruise boats operate from both the United States and Canadian sides of the stunning falls.

Niagara Falls have also featured in Hollywood movies, most notably in the 1953 movie Niagara starring Marilyn Monroe, Superman II in 1980, and Teenage Mutant Ninja Turtles shot in 1987. The falls have also been the subject of an IMAX movie.

- The survival of the mighty coast redwood is largely dependent on fog, which is responsible for one-fourth of the precipitation in the area.
- The giant sequoia (*Sequoiadendron giganteum*) found in the Redwood National Park is generally considered to be the largest living organism in the world.

**Redwood National Park**, USA

# Redwood National Park

O ccupying the northwestern corner of California, the Redwood National Park contains magnificent forests of sequoia redwood trees that cover the coastal mountain region bordering the Pacific Ocean north of San Francisco. Formerly established in 1968, the boundaries of the park were redefined in 1978, and it was inscribed as a UNESCO World Heritage Site in 1980. Home to some of the tallest and most impressive trees in the world, the 172sq mile (445sq km) Redwood National Park showcases 40 miles (64km) of the picturesque Pacific coastline. The park also encompasses land belonging to the Jedediah Smith Redwoods, the Del Norte Coast Redwoods, and the Prairie Creek Redwoods state parks.

## THE SEQUOIA SEMPERVIRENS

The fast-growing coast redwood is among the longest-lived species in the world. Individual trees have an average lifespan of about 600 years and are also the tallest trees in the world. A redwood called "Tall Tree" was identified in the Tall Trees Grove near Redwood Creek in 1963. Measuring 367.8ft (112.1m) in height, when the top broke off later, its diameter was calculated at 14ft (4m). Though commercial logging has largely reduced the population of these magnificant trees, protected from fire by their thick sapless bark they can live to more than 2,000 years.

*Couple standing on a giant sequoia stump in the Redwood National Park*

*Rhododendrons in the Redwood National Park*

More than one-third of the national park's area is covered with old growth or virgin groves of ancient redwoods. The two species that dominate the old growth redwood groves are the coast redwood (*Sequoia sempervirens*) and Douglas-fir (*Pseudotsuga menziesii*). Ideal growing conditions for the coast redwood are found in the sheltered valleys and alluvial flats alongside creeks and streams in the Redwood National Park. As a result, many of these trees reach heights greater than 300ft (92m). The trees are protected from the injurious salty spray and bitter salt-laden winds from the coast by a natural buffer formed by the dunes and communities of scrub plants that grow on the beach. The growth of these trees, however, is stunted by water stress on drier and windier slopes and ridges, and their height is often restricted to 200ft (61m) or less.

Further inland and at a greater altitude, the growth of redwoods is hampered by hot and dry climatic conditions, with the redwood forests making way for mixed evergreen forests of Douglas firs. Other trees that populate the area include hardwoods such as tanoak, madrone, big-leaf maple, California bay or laurel, and red alder. The most common plants that make up the undergrowth of the redwood forests are the redwood sorrel and the sword fern, accompanied by rhododendron, azalea, salal, huckleberry, and other shrubs.

The Redwood National Park is watered by three large river systems—the Smith River, the Klamath River, and the Redwood Creek. Renowned for their sheer beauty and the opportunity that they provide for fishing salmon and steelhead, the rivers have carved out deep gorges in the forest and mountainous terrain of the park. Beginning in the Siskiyou Mountains, the Smith River—named after the explorer Jedediah Smith, who crossed this area in 1828—flows through the northern section of the park and is one of the longest free-flowing river systems in California. The Redwood Creek flows through the southern section of the park and travels northwest along the Grogan Fault, while the Klamath River traversing the middle of the park is the largest river of the North Coast.

The rivers of Redwood National Park provide substantial natural habitats along their banks and estuaries. A wide range of animals, including moose, elk, black bear, beaver, white-tailed deer, and mule deer, thrive and abound in the park's forests.

## EXPLOITING THE FOREST GIANTS

The redwood and giant sequoia produce high-quality timber, prized as a multi-purpose wood suitable for a range of uses including house-building, furniture-making, and rail sleepers. They are straight-growing, with few knots and a fine grain, making them light but strong. A combination of natural oils and resins makes them almost rot-proof and resistant to termite attacks.

In the latter half of the 19th century these trees were heavily exploited, and were nearly wiped out. Though felling of these trees continues, the US National Parks Service has stepped up its efforts to annex remaining tracts of forest to the existing protected areas.

- Carved out by the Virgin River, the Zion Canyon is only about 15 miles (24km) long, and yet reaches depths of 2,500ft (762m) in places.

- Located deep within the Zion National Park, the Kolob Arch is one of the largest free-standing arches in the world.

**Zion National Park,** USA

# Zion National Park

The Great White Throne

Slicing through the rocks of the Washington, Iron, and Kane counties of southwestern Utah, the Zion Canyon is the chief attraction of the Zion National Park. Situated at the edge of the Colorado Plateau, the park encompasses a picturesque region of distinctly colored canyons.

Largely a flat basin close to sea level, Zion evolved approximately 240 million years ago. A small stream headed southward meandered its way across the soft young rocks of a plateau. As the land rose, the stream began to cut itself a path, scouring the underlying rock with particles of grit and sand that eroded further upstream. The result of this was Zion Canyon, a winding gorge slicing through the Navajo sandstone to the older, underlying Kaibab limestone.

The idea of a sanctuary was first discussed in 1909, with the creation of the Mukuntuweap National Monument. More of the wilderness surrounding the canyon was included in the protected zone in 1919 and the Zion National Park was thus established, occupying an area of 148sq miles (383sq km). The park was expanded in 1956, to include 229sq miles (593sq km) of land.

## ZION'S SETTLERS

The earliest inhabitants of Zion were hunter-gatherers who arrived approximately 12,000 years ago, when mammoths and giant sloths roamed the area. After these species became extinct, the hunters turned their attention to smaller animals, and eventually took up farming as a means of subsistence around 2,600 years ago. The tribe, now known as the Anasazi, abandoned the area about 800 years ago after which the Paiute people settled there. Mormons arrived at the canyon in 1858 and gave the park its present name, Zion, meaning "refuge" in Hebrew. In some of the larger caves of the canyon, archeologists have also discovered artifacts from the Pueblo people.

Spectacular rock formations—including towering cliffs, forbidding domes, and deep chasms—make up the landscape of the Zion National Park, ranging in color from deep glowing red to a delicate rose-pink. The Weeping Rock, where water from springs seeps out of the rock surface and drops like tears from the overhang, is among the park's many famous features. While the great sandstone slab of Checkerboard Mesa looms over the road, its surface intricately carved into squares by wind and water, the flat-topped Great White Throne is an imposing monolith rising 2,394ft (730m) above the canyon floor. A natural arch spans two cliff faces in Verkin Canyon. The West Temple, which rises to a height of 3,800ft (1,158m) from the base of the canyon, marks the highest point in the park. A group of jagged sandstone peaks, ranging along the west wall of the canyon, is collectively dubbed the Towers of the Virgin. The Grand Staircase, the Hanging Garden, the Emerald Pool, and the natural amphitheater of the Temple of Sinawava are the other striking features of the Zion.

The topography of the Zion National Park includes forested highlands and lowland deserts, and it includes over 900 varieties of plants. The park provides sanctuary to 75 species of mammals, 291 species of birds, and 44 types of reptiles and amphibians, including a species of desert tortoise. Eight species of fish are found in waters of the Virgin River which flows through the park. The Virgin Spinedace, the Peregrine falcon, and the Zion snail are among the rarest and most remarkable creatures that inhabit this park.

## AMERICA'S NATURAL BEAUTY

An area of about 120,300sq miles (310,000sq km), which includes around 320 different sites, falls under the care of the US National Park Service, which covers historical sites as well as sites of unrivaled natural wonder. These include battlefields (such as Saratoga and Gettysburg), early trading posts and archeological sites where evidence of Indian settlements have been discovered.

The first national park, founded in 1872—and which remains one of the most popular in America—is the Yellowstone National Park. Since then many other sites have been recognized for their fundamental reflection of America's rich historical and geological heritage, and their protection has been guaranteed by their designation as national parks or national monuments.

*The Emerald Pools*

- Monument Valley earned worldwide fame from its inclusion in western movie classics such as *Stagecoach*, *She Wore A Yellow Ribbon*, and *Cheyenne Autumn*.
- The climate of this region has changed negligibly in the last 700 years. Periods of heavy rain continue to alternate with those of drought.

## FORAYS INTO MONUMENT VALLEY

After early attempts by Spanish and Mexican explorers to control the area, the Navajos fled to the Navajo Mountain. In the early 1860s, however, they were rounded up by the legendary Kit Carson and relocated to a reservation. They returned to the area in 1868, only to find themselves competing against prospectors of silver. President Chester Arthur added this area to the Navajo Reservation in 1884, but the search for silver did not stop. In the year 1906, a trading post was established at Oljeto by John Wetherill and Clyde Colville. Established as a trading post by Harry Goulding in the 1920s, the small town of Goulding provides a comprehensive range of facilities for visitors today.

*White Mesa Arch, Arizona*

# Monument Valley

**M**yriad mesas, sandstone buttes, spires, and monoliths projecting from the land make up the dramatic landscape of Monument Valley in the Colorado Plateau. Straddling the border of southeastern Utah and northeastern Arizona, Monument Valley is a Navajo Nation Tribal Park that contains some of the most striking geological formations in the southwestern United States. Contrary to what the latter half of its name suggests, Monument Valley is a wide and flat land from which crumbling formations—the remains of layers of sandstone that once covered the entire region—raise their heads high into the air.

Seated atop the crest of the wide anticline of Monument Upwarp, Monument Valley is composed of beautiful layers of sandstone, siltstone, and shale of various hues.

Large quantities of rocky sediments were deposited in the region when it was a vast lowland basin millions of years ago, during the Eocene epoch of the Cenozoic era. Several millennia later, this area too, underwent the processes of uplifting and folding along with the rest of the Colorado plateau; it twisted and broke to reveal the soft rocks that had been buried beneath the surface.

The erosive action of wind and water over the last 50 million years has created the magnificent spires and buttes of sandstone that we see today. While iron oxide gives the sands and rocks of Monument Valley a reddish tinge, black streaks of desert varnish are caused by the presence of manganese dioxide. Though Monument Valley is home to the famous purple sage of western lore, few trees, except for a rare juniper at the edges of

## THE NAVAJO PEOPLE

Of all the Native American groups that live in the United States, the Navajo is among the largest in terms of population. Believed to have migrated to the United States from Canada between 900 and 1200, the Navajo, are found mostly in northwestern New Mexico, southeastern Utah, and Arizona. Toward the end of the 20th century their population was approximately 170,000. The Navajo speak an Apachean language which belongs to the Athabascan family. Since the supposed period of migration, however, the resemblance between these two groups has been lessened because of the subsequent influence of the Pueblo Indians on the Navajos.

*Elderly Navajo woman weaving carpets,*
*Monument Valley, Utah*

the valley, grow on these soils because of the extreme dryness and lack of moisture. Cliffrose, rabbitbrush, and snakewood can be seen in the rare moist patches of the valley. The scarcity of adequate habitats coupled with the presence of Navajo residents account for the absence of an abundant wildlife.

Today the Navajo Nation Tribal Park spreads across 115sq miles (298sq km), and has been the site of human habitation for thousands of years. The area was occupied by Ice Age Paleo-Indian hunters between 12,000 and 6,000BC. Between then and the Christian era, archaic hunter-gatherers populated the area, followed by the ancient Anasazi people who arrived at the beginning of the Christian era, and then disappeared around AD1300; they left behind

beautiful petroglyphs and pictographs that have been well preserved. The area was then frequented by the Paiute, who ascribed many legends and supernatural tales to it and called the valley "The Treeless Area Amid the Rocks."

The Navajo people who make their home within the park have been preserving their heritage, language, art forms, and traditional way of life for centuries, maintaining a careful relationship of harmony and respect with the land. Guided tours through the tribal park provide a complete experience to visitors, who are told stories and legends associated with this stunning land as it unfolds in front of them. The stark and desolate beauty of Monument Valley is thus complemented by the warm, rich heritage of the Navajo people.

• Fed mostly by snowmelt, peak flow for the Yosemite Falls usually occurs in late May, and by August it often becomes dry. It begins flowing again a few months later, after the winter snows arrive.

• The Half Dome at the head of the Yosemite Valley has a broad sculpted base and rises almost 5,000ft (1,525m) above the valley floor.

# Yosemite National Park

Few places in the world can have as many spectacular features concentrated in one small area as Yosemite Valley, a 7.5-mile (12-km) long natural masterpiece of staggering beauty and diversity nestling in the heart of the Sierra Nevada mountain range of California. Yosemite was first designated a state park in 1864; the boundaries were redefined and additional land incorporated in 1890 to make it a national park. Comprising 1,189sq miles (3,080sq km) it includes groves of giant sequoias, some of them thousands of years old, the meandering Merced River, the stunning Yosemite Valley, and the Yosemite Falls, as well as sheer rock walls, giant buttresses, and imposing peaks. The Yosemite National Park is home to some of the most picturesque and breathtaking scenic landscapes in the United States and became a UNESCO World Heritage Site in 1984.

## JOHN MUIR AND YOSEMITE'S CONSERVATION

The renowned naturalist John Muir is credited with the task which eventually resulted in the establishment of national parks such as the Yosemite and Sequoia. His first visit to the Yosemite Valley was in 1868, after which his interest in glaciers and forests led him to states such as Alaska, Nevada, and Washington. Eight years after his first visit to the Yosemite Valley, Muir advocated a forest conservation policy which led to the establishment of Yosemite as a national park; the conservation efforts initiated by President Theodore Roosevelt were greatly influenced by him. Muir's most significant contribution was the formulation of the idea of Yosemite's glacial origin—a theory that has now found universal acceptance.

*Bank of the Merced River*

The astounding valley landscape of Yosemite was created as a result of glaciation. The granite bedrock of the area was gouged and molded into steep cliffs, bare summits, rounded domes, and gigantic monoliths during the last Ice Age. The flat floor of the Yosemite Valley has evolved from the slow sedimentation of a large lake fed by melt water from ancient glaciers. The process of geological evolution still continues, and the lakes of the valley continue to silt up. The Yosemite Valley floor lies at an elevation of about 4,000ft (1,220m) above sea level.

Today, the Yosemite Valley is filled with blossoming meadows and surrounded by spectacular waterfalls. The most dramatic of these waterfalls is the Yosemite Falls, which is formed by creeks tumbling into the valley from the overhanging edges of tributary valleys. While the Upper Yosemite Falls has a drop height of 1,430ft (436m), the Lower Falls drop down 320ft (98m). Together, the falls have a combined height of 2,425ft (739m) from the crest of the Upper Falls to the base of the Lower, and form one of the tallest and most exquisite cataracts in the world. Other remarkable waterfalls located within the Yosemite National Park include the Bridalveil and Ribbon falls on the western slopes of the Sierra Nevada.

Rock formations within the Yosemite National Park are simply magnificent. El Capitan, a granite buttress that rises about 3,604ft (1,098m) from the floor of the valley, is the most popular site in the park. Other impressive rocks in the park include the Three Brothers, North Dome, Glacier Point, Sentinel Dome, and Cloud's Rest—all of them ranging from 2,800 to 6,000ft (610 to 1,829m) in height.

While the lower reaches of the park are characterized by scattered deciduous and coniferous trees, the higher elevations have a denser growth of conifers, mountain hemlock, and lodgepole pine. However, the Yosemite National Park's most enduring and attractive trees are the magnificent giant sequoias. Mule deer, black bear, chipmunks, squirrels, and various other creatures make up the animal life within the park.

## ROCK CLIMBING IN YOSEMITE

Yosemite Valley offers all types of climbing surfaces: crack, chimneys, faces, overhangs, artificial aid, high angle, low angle—whatever a climber could desire, including Sentinel Rock, Royal Arches, and El Capitan, one of the largest granite faces in the world. Yosemite became the focus for rock-climbing in the US in the 1950s and 1960s, when Royal Robbins, Yvon Chouinard, and Warren Harding first made ascents on climbs that had previously been thought impossible. Robbins, Jerry Galwas, and Mike Sherrick were the first climbers to conquer the sheer 2000-ft (610-m), northwest face of Half Dome in 1957; and Harding, Wayne Merry, and George Whitwore made the first ascent of the Nose Route of El Capitan the following year.

*Loose rope walking above the Yosemite*

- Lava Falls, one of the largest rapids in the Grand Canyon with a 37-ft (11-m) drop, is also the fastest stretch of navigable water in North America.

- The Grand Canyon Skywalk is a horseshoe-shape glass bridge that enables tourists to look down at the Colorado River 4,000ft (1,220m) below.

**The Grand Canyon,** USA

# The
# Grand Canyon

A spectacular complex of waterfalls, caverns, towers, ledges, and ravines, the Grand Canyon landscape appears to change constantly with the play of sunlight—the shadows shift through the day and the rocks lighten to pale pink and blue-grey, then darken to purple-brown and black as the rays of the sun peek through clouds and slant across the massive gorge.

The word "grand" does little to convey the raw beauty of the Grand Canyon. The canyon is 277 miles (446km) long and 10 miles (16km) across; it extends 18 miles (29km) at its widest point, and dips down to 6,000ft (1,829m) at its deepest. Statistics, however, are inadequate for conveying the majesty and grandeur of this dramatic landscape, which has been fashioned by

## THE GRAND CANYON DISCOVERED

Native Americans knew about the Grand Canyon for thousands of years before it was discovered by Europeans. The caves and caverns in the park are rich in archeological remains, and include rock paintings, pots, and wooden figures. In 1540 a small group of Spanish adventurers arrived looking for gold, but finding none they moved on.

An expedition was mounted in 1857 to travel down the canyon by boat, but it had to proceed on foot when the boats were wrecked almost before the trip had started. The most famous expedition was led by Major John Wesley Powell in 1869. Powell, a Civil War veteran and college professor, took nine frontiersmen with him to map the huge canyon, but his account of the journey remained unpublished for more than 20 years.

## ROOSEVELT VISITS THE GRAND CANYON

One of the early visitors to the Grand Canyon was President Theodore Roosevelt, who first came in 1903, and made it a national monument in 1908.

Roosevelt was influenced by the writings of the conservation campaigner John Muir, and pursued policies aimed at protecting vast areas of American wilderness and maintaining the balance of their delicate ecology. Even at the turn of the 20th century, Roosevelt was aware of the delicate ecology of the area. He commented that the wisest course was for Americans to "leave it as it is. You cannot improve on it. The ages have been at work on it and man can only mar it."

*Point Sublime after sunset, North Rim, Grand Canyon National Park*

continuous carving for over 6 million years. At that time, what is now the canyon was simply a huge plain through which the Colorado River meandered. Then movements in the earth's surface caused the land to rise and the river began to cut a channel through the rocks. Today, the Grand Canyon bears the imprint of almost 2 billion years of North America's geological history.

The red terrain appears almost Martian at first glance—dusty depths walled with limestone and studded with fossils and ferrous mudflats. Though it might seem desolate and inhospitable now, before its designation as a national park in 1919, this land was home to various civilizations for at least 10,000 years. From around AD700 until AD1150 the Anasazi people lived here, farming and hunting for a living. Though they were driven out by drought, the pottery and the rundown granaries that they left behind have weathered the ravages of time and tell tales of the ancient culture. Painted pictographs by other tribes and split-twig figurines have been found throughout the canyon, too. Even before

that, Paleo-American hunters roamed these gorges, tracking animals such as the giant ground sloth.

Before it was finally christened the Grand Canyon, the site was known by various names given by the Native American tribes residing in the area. To the Hopi tribe, it was *Ongtukpa*, their ancestral home; the Southern Paiute considered it their holy land, *Puaxant Tuvip*; for the Western Apache tribes it was simply *Ge da'cho* or "edge of the big cliff."

Today, as one of the most visited natural wonders of the world, the Grand Canyon attracts about 5 million visitors every year. But tourists tend to visit only the better-known areas of the canyon and it is possible to find many secluded nooks and valleys, undisturbed by the hordes of visitors. The Grand Canyon is also home to surprisingly lush areas of flora—the Fern Glen Canyon, with its extraordinary microclimate, is one such spot where flowers and plants flourish in the middle of the desert. Calm green pools of water can be found at the base of the walls of the North Canyon Walsh.

- Other famous rock formations around Sedona include Bell Rock, Courthouse Butte, Snoopy, and Coffeepot Rock
- One of the best views of Cathedral Rock can be had from Oak Creek in the canyon of the same name. The road winding through this breathtaking canyon is Arizona's first officially designated scenic highway.

**Cathedral Rock,** Arizona

# Cathedral Rock

Cathedral Rock in Red Rock State Park, near Sedona, Arizona, is one of the world's most famous red rock formations. Glowing ochre, orange, red, gold, and gray with the play of the light, it rises high among the famed stratified red rock cliffs of Arizona, created by sedimentation and erosion over a period of 350 million years, from what was once a wetland area. Some parts of the red rock range are an extension of the Mogollon Rim, the southern edge of the Colorado Plateau, which is home to the world-renowned Grand Canyon.

Towering 900ft (274m) over Oak Creek, Cathedral Rock—a monolithic masterpiece sculpted in sandstone—takes its name from the startling similarity of its appearance to a cathedral. Topped by twin spires with a saddle in between, it offers spectacular vistas of the endless formations of red rock country: the buttes, bluffs, mesas, pinnacles, spires, canyons, and creeks are spread out on all sides. Some of the better-known formations you can spot from the saddle include Courthouse Rock, The Nuns, Lee Mountain, and Twin Buttes.

There is a legend attached to the stone fingers of Cathedral Rock, involving a constantly bickering man and wife who disregard the Great Spirit's decree to live in harmony and therefore end up being etched in stone for eternity as a lesson to the rest of humanity. Legends apart, the red cliffs around Cathedral Rock were home to Native Americans who considered certain spots sacred and magical. Hundreds of years later, New Age followers believe that the region has many vortex centers emanating electromagnetic energy; one of these vortices is Cathedral Rock, which is thought to be a "feminine energy" site.

## BLAST FROM THE PAST

Sedona, Oak Tree Canyon, and Cathedral Rock are part of the Verde Valley, located in north central Arizona. Millions of years ago, in Precambrian times, this area was a submarine volcanic environment. Plate action led to a fault in the region, which in turn showed up in volcanic activity and caused the formation of hot springs. These hot springs threw up deposits of gold, silver, and copper, and were responsible not only for the mineral deposits in the area, but also for the famously colored mountains.

*A section of Sedona's famous red rocks*

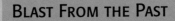

## MOVIE MAGIC

The beauty of the red rock range around Sedona was first seen on the big screen in an adaptation of Zane Grey's book, *The Call of the Canyon* in 1923. For the next 30 years, dozens of westerns were shot in these stunning locales, including *The Rounders, Apache, Leave her to Heaven,* and *Johnny Guitar.*

These prehistoric rocks shelter within their environs, a variety of animals, everything from the dangerous cougar, bobcat, rattlesnake, mountain bear, and coyote, to the harmless deer, elk, badger, chipmunk, and squirrel. More than 200 species of bird can be found in the neighboring canyons, including hawks and bald eagles that can be seen circling the skies above. The plant life is correspondingly rich and beautiful; when it rains, the ground is transformed into a carpet of wildflowers, while throughout the year, trees like sycamore, ash, walnut, cottonwood, scrub oak, and mountain mahogany jostle for space.

The climbing route to Cathedral Rock is nationally feted, though the top 300ft (91m) are considered too dangerous for any but experienced climbers, as the sandstone here is brittle and crumbles easily. However, this has hardly been a deterrent to the five million tourists who visit Sedona and Cathedral Rock annually.

- The area of Death Valley 282ft (86m) below sea level and about 4.75 miles (7.64 km) west of Badwater, forms the single lowest point in the western hemisphere.

- Death Valley was declared a national monument in 1933. and established as a national park only in 1994.

**Death Valley,** USA

# Death Valley

The lowest, hottest, and driest fraction of the North American continent makes up the bleak landscape of Death Valley. This structural depression in Inyo County, southeastern California is bounded by the Panamint Range to the west and the mountains of the Amargosa Range to the east. The valley is inclined roughly north to south and runs for approximately 140 miles (225km); its width ranges from 5 to 16 miles (8 to 26km). Though it is geologically a part of the southwestern part of the Great Basin, Death Valley actually lies near the undefined boundary between the Great Basin and the Mojave deserts.

Death Valley closely resembles other structural basins in the region, but its uniqueness is defined by its great depth. Part of the valley floor is made up of salt pans, sections of which constitute the lowest land areas in the Americas. About 550sq miles (1,425sq km) of the floor of Death Valley is situated below sea level.

## BALLARAT

Named after an Australian gold camp and located at the base of the Panamint Mountain Range to the west of Death Valley proper, Ballarat came into being in 1897. The town's gold mines produced 16,535 tons of gold ore till 1903. One of the town's early residents, an Australian immigrant, George Riggins, named the town. Within a year of its establishment, the town had approximately 400 residents who lived in settlements made of adobe bricks. However, once the Radcliffe Mines ceased operations after 1903, the town lost much of its attraction. Apart from the gold mine, the town was also made famous by legendary figures such as Frank "Shorty" Harris and "Seldom" Seen Slim. Privately owned today, the ghost town of Ballarat offers tourists the chance to view the ruins of old adobe buildings.

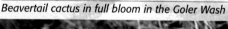

*Beavertail cactus in full bloom in the Goler Wash*

## AMARGOSA RANGE

The Amargosa Range consists of a group of mountains that occupy the stretch of eastern California and southern Nevada in the United States. Covering a distance of 110 miles (180 km) from Grapevine Peak to the Amargosa River, it forms a barrier between the Death Valley and the Amargosa Desert. The range comprises of three subdivisions—the ranges of Grapevine, Funeral, and Black. The area surrounding the range is drained by the Amargosa River. Zabriskie Point, a well-known feature of the Death Valley National Park, is found here. The two relatively well-known peaks in this range are the Grapevine Peak at 8,705ft (2,653m), and Dante's View at 5,475ft (1,669m); the latter provides clear views of Death Valley and the Panamint Range which lies beyond.

*A creosote bush survives in this harsh climate as wind creates patterns in the sand—Mesquite Sand Dunes, Amargosa Mountains*

The geological history of the creation of Death Valley involves various kinds of fault activity at different periods of time. Crustal sinking and volcanic activity have also played a role in the formation of this vast desolate land. Essentially, the rift valley was formed by the sinking of a huge expanse of rock along parallel fault lines in between the mountain ranges to its east and west. This sinking started approximately 30 million years ago, during the middle Tertiary period. As the valley sank, it was filled continuously by eroded sediments from the surrounding mountain ranges. Today, at the centre of the valley—the bedrock is believed to be buried under 9,000ft (2,745m) of sediments—tilting and sinking of the valley floor continues.

The floor of Death Valley is legendary for its arid conditions and extreme temperatures. Ground temperatures as high as 190°F (88°C) have been recorded in the area, and summer temperatures often exceed 120°F (49°C). Most of the rainfall is blocked by the mountains in the west, and the heat combines with the low humidity to make the area very dry and inhospitable. The salt pan that covers much of the valley floor is the remains of a shallow lake that existed in the area a few thousand years ago. Most of the surface water in Death Valley today is contained in the saline ponds and marshes that surround the pan.

Despite the dry and desert-like conditions, there is no dearth of life in the Death Valley. Hardy and salt-tolerant species of picklewood and saltgrass are found around the springs and at the edges of the salt pan. Creosote bushes, desert holly, cacti, desert wildflowers, and mesquite are also found in some areas. Animal life is varied as well, with rabbits, many species of rodents, coyotes, bobcats, wild burros, and the bighorn sheep making Death Valley their home.

• The Meteor Crater, also known as the Barringer Crater, was the first to be officially recognized out of the 160 terrestrial impact craters identified to date.

• The Meteor Crater was discovered with more than 30 tons of meteoritic iron strewn around the site for 8 to 10 miles (13 to 16km).

# Meteor Crater

Located 35 miles (56km) east of Flagstaff in the northern Arizona desert, yawns the giant mouth of the Meteor Crater. Approximately 50,000 years ago, during the Pleistocene epoch, a meteorite slammed into the earth, resulting in a crater, 4,000ft (1,200m) in diameter and about 600ft (180m) deep, with its rim jutting up 120–200ft (36–60m) from the surrounding plain.

Scientists believed that an iron-nickel meteorite, possibly weighing over 300,000 tons, struck our planet causing an explosion that generated a thousand times the destructive energy of the Hiroshima atomic bomb.

As the extraterrestrial object hit the earth's surface at a speed of 12 miles (19km) per second, the intense heat generated caused the iron in the meteorite, along with some rocks in the vicinity, to vaporize. More than a few million tons of limestone and sandstone were displaced to form the cavity. The heat and pressure transformed the graphite in the meteorite and the rocks in the vicinity into miniscule diamonds. The shock of the impact is believed to have triggered off an earthquake measuring around 5.5 on the Richter scale.

*A view of the crater from the observation platform*

## LIVING ON

Unlike other impact craters, the Meteor Crater has remained largely unchanged by the action of the elements. The crater walls have only been slightly modified by erosion, and remnants from the original debris cloud can still to be found today. The rim stands tall around the crater, and the carpet of detritus ejected during the initial impact is still present at the site.

*Geothermal volcanic mud pots*

## CRATER LEGACY

The Barringer family entered into an agreement with a corporation called the Bar-T-Bar Ranch Company in 1941. The company formed Meteor Crater Enterprises Inc, 14 years later, and entered into a long-term lease with the Barringers. Today, the company continues to own the land, and along with its purpose of studying the crater, furthers the cause of science and academics, providing grants, scholarships, and instituting special awards.

Although the Pueblo people—the native inhabitants of the area—were aware of the existence of the crater, it wasn't until the late 19th century that scientists turned their attention to it, and it was only in the 20th century that the crater's origin was scientifically explained. A man named Franklin, a scout for General Custer, was the first person to write a report on the crater in 1871, and for many years it was known as Franklin's Hole. Thereafter, it was mistaken by settlers for an extinct volcano, part of the Hopi Buttes volcanic field nearby and rechristened Coon Butte. It was in 1902 that the mining engineer Daniel M. Barringer came across the crater, and certain that it was an impact crater, decided that a venture for mining iron—or even the entire meteorite—from the site would be very lucrative.

Barringer then set up the Standard Iron Company, and proceeded to secure mining rights from the government. Over the next 27 years this venture cost Barringer and his company over $600,000, a fortune in those days. Even though they dug as deep as 1,374ft (419m) into the earth's crust no significant deposit was found. Barringer was forced to abandon the mission in 1929, due to lack of funds and the fact that it was a futile excercise. He, however, did manage to convince most of the scientific community about the impact origin of the crater. It was in the 1960s that Eugene M. Shoemaker carried out further research and confirmed Barringer's hypothesis. The crater today is owned by the Barringer family, and is known as the Barringer Crater in his honor. Meteor Crater is one of Arizona's most popular tourist attractions.

Scientists are studying extremophile microbes in the Lechuguilla Cave—in the Carlsbad Caverns National Park—in the hope of generating a possible cure for cancer.

Bones of Ice Age animals such as jaguars, camels, lions, and giant sloths have been discovered in the area surrounding the entrance of caves in Carlsbad Caverns National Park.

e Carlsbad Caverns, USA

# The Carlsbad Caverns

### BATS

Carlsbad Caverns are home to more than 1 million Mexican freetail bats. Bat Cave, near the natural entrance to the caverns, is their favored roost. The winged mammals fly out every evening in a thick whirlwind, and then return to the caves before daybreak. These creatures are primarily responsible for the deposits of guano that are found in the caves. This section of Carlsbad is now open only to researchers.

Comprising colossal subterranean caverns and astounding cave formations, the Carlsbad Caverns lie beneath the surface of the Chihuahuan desert, near the base of the Guadalupe mountains of southeastern New Mexico and west Texas, and form one of the longest cave systems in North America. More than 80 recognized caves make up the Carlsbad Caverns National Park; these caves are famous not only for their overwhelming size but also for the beauty and diversity of their incredible natural limestone structures.

Stalagmites, Carlsbad Caverns

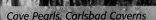
*Cave Pearls, Carlsbad Caverns*

## ANCIENT ARTIFACTS

Several caves of the Carlsbad Caverns bear pictographs left by Archaic hunters and gatherers who are believed to have settled in the area in 6,000BC. The Painted Grotto, the Upper Painted Grotto, and Slaughter Canyon contain profuse and remarkable examples of such rock art. Shards of pottery dating between AD800 and AD154 have also been discovered at several archeological sites within the Carlsbad Caverns National Park.

The deepest of the three main levels of Carlsbad's labyrinthine chambers is 1,024ft (312m) below the surface. The Caverns were originally formed under water. The creation of the caves can be traced back 250 million years to the Captain Reef—a Permian fossil reef—composed of the remains of sponges, algae, seashells, and calcite precipitated directly from the water. After the evaporation of the sea, the reef remained buried under layers of salt and gypsum, and was only uncovered after millions of years of erosion and similar processes.

Once the reef emerged above ground, the percolation and seepage of acidic rainwater through its cracks led to the dissolution of the calcite minerals and hastened the process of the formation of the great limestone chambers. The action of sulphuric acid upon limestone is believed to be the cause of the stalactites, stalagmites, and the various other extraordinary formations that we now see within the caverns. The formation of these remarkable structures started thousands of years ago, and is an ongoing process.

Human occupation of the Carlsbad Caverns area dates back to 12,000BC, with the arrival of the Palaeo-Indian people. In the late 19th century, guano mining from the caves became a thriving industry. The first extensive exploration of the caverns is credited to Jim White, who first entered the caves in 1898. Over the next 20 years, he conducted guided tours through the caverns. It was only in 1918 that Ray Davis published photographs of the stunning Carlsbad Caverns, leading to a surge in tourist activity. On October 25, 1923, the Carlsbad Caverns was declared a National Monument in the interests of conservation. It was then granted National Park status on May 14, 1930. Inscribed as a UNESCO World Heritage Site in 1995, the park is visited by tens of thousands of tourists every year.

Notable formations of the Carlsbad Caverns National Park include the Lechuguilla Cave—the deepest and third longest cave in North America, and the fifth longest in the world. Big Room—possibly formed by a partial caving in of the roof—is the largest cave chamber on the continent. There is also the Papoose Room, Ogle Cave, and the Giant Dome stalagmite. Some of the more unusual calcite shapes in Carlsbad are soda straws (hollow stalactites), cave pearls (made out of layers of calcite building up around sand grains or other tiny objects), and helictites (strange twisted shapes that appear to defy gravity). Other rare formations include delicate needle-like structures made out of aragonite.

The Carlsbad Caverns National Park also encompasses a wilderness area on the surface that provides sanctuary to a host of native plants and wildlife, including golden eagles, red-tailed hawks, elks, and cougars.

NORTH AMERICA The Carlsbad Caverns

- The first oil wells in Florida were situated at Sunniland, a village in the Everglades, 40 miles (64km) southeast of Fort Myers.

- The Everglades farming district is often referred to as the Vegetable Kingdom since it is the major supplier of garden vegetables for the northern markets.

**Everglades,** Florida

# Everglades

**A** dense network of habitats with great diversity of flora and fauna characterize the Everglades in southern Florida. Spread over an area of almost 4,000sq miles (10,000sq km), this region of sawgrass marshes forms the largest expanse of subtropical rainforest in continental America. Formed almost 5,000 years ago, the Everglades occupy a shallow limestone basin, and are watered by Lake Okeechobee, the third largest freshwater lake in the United States, after Lakes Michigan and Iliamna, situated at the northern edge of the glades. The water from the lake seeps into the underlying limestone, forming a series of aquifers that feed these wetlands.

The Everglades are crisscrossed with small lakes and channels on which water lilies and bladderworts bloom. Bladderworts are specially adapted for thriving in these waters, which are low in nutrient content. The plants have small air bladders that trap insects and larvae, which are then absorbed to obtain the essential nutrients. Small low islands or hammocks are scattered across the open patches of water; cypresses, live oaks, palms, and saw palmettos are among the shrubs and tropical plants that grow in abundance on the organic

## THE FLORIDA MANATEE

Among the animals taking advantage of the abundant fish in the Everglades' coastal waters are 12 species of turtle, including giant loggerhead turtles and green turtles. The Florida manatee is a gentle, plant-eating mammal and is a member of the group of animals known as *Sirenia*, which were once believed by sailors to be mermaids.

Manatees feed on the seagrass beds in the shallow waters fringing the mangrove forests. These harmless creatures face a threat from marina developments, which decrease their feeding area and bring with them pollution and the increased danger of death or injury from boats.

*A manatee or sea cow floating at the water's surface*

soils. Formed where the underlying limestone rises above the water table, the hammocks also serve as home to many species of plants such as orchids, cacti, and ferns. Impenetrable forests of sawgrass—speckled with minute sharp teeth and growing up to 13ft (4m) in height—remain the predominant form of vegetation in the glades. A strip of red mangroves fringes the freshwater swamps toward the coast, forming North America's only forested marine wetland.

Encompassing 2,380sq miles (6,105sq km) in the southwestern section of the glades, the Everglades National Park was established in 1947 to conserve the unique ecosystem of the glades. More than 1,000 seed-bearing plants—including 25 varieties of orchid and 120 species of trees—populate the glades. Over 320 species of birds, including the wood stork, the reddish egret, and the southern race of the bald eagle nest in the area; the coastal mangrove region provides shelter to anhingas, roseate spoonbills, pelicans, wood ibis, and herons. The coastal waters host more than 150 species of fish, which serve as food for the swamp's predators such as the American alligator, the American crocodile, the rare Florida panther, and otters.

The Native Americans called the glades *pa-hay-okee*—meaning "grassy waters"—and navigated the vast expanse of the marshland as they hunted and fished. Despite such activity, the ecosystem remained intact until the arrival of non-native settlers in the middle of the 16th century. Unbalanced industrialization in the name of progress caused destructive draining of the swamps and alteration of the water flow, leading to a drastic reduction in water supply and consequently the animal population—while an estimated 1.5 million birds nested in the Everglades in the 1930s, only about 50,000 remain today. The opportunity to explore the world's largest freshwater swamp, as well as activities such as sport fishing, however, continues to lure thousands of visitors to the Everglades every year.

## THE AMERICAN ALLIGATOR

The larger of the two living species of alligators (the other is the Chinese alligator), the American alligator is the most famous of the Everglades predators. Endemic to southeastern United States, these reptiles have a diet that consists of turtles, frogs, birds, small mammals, snakes, and fish. These creatures are known to live in freshwater lakes, rivers, and swamps and only rarely in brackish water. Relentlessly hunted for its hide, the American alligator was labeled an endangered species in 1967; but conservation efforts led to a great increase in its numbers, and they were removed from the list in 1987. It is illegal, however, to feed any alligator in the Everglades, and they are protected from over-hunting by the US Fish and Wildlife Service. The largest ever alligator found in Florida measured 17ft (5.3m) in length.

*The American alligator, the Everglades main predator*

- Paricutín is located 12 miles (20km) west-northwest of Uruapan and just north of the Tancítaro Peak volcano.

- At the end of the first year of Paricutín's eruption, its cone stood 1,475ft (450 m) higher than the base elevation of 7,480ft (2,280m) above sea level; in 1952, the peak had reached an elevation of 9,210ft (2,808m).

# Paricutín

One of the youngest volcanoes in the world, the Paricutín is located in the state of Michoacán in the central western part of Mexico. In the early 1940s, three of the largest cities in Mexico—Puebla, Guadalajara, and Mexico City—occupied this area. Situated some 200 miles (323km) west of the capital city, the area around Paricutín was mostly a serene and peaceful backwater populated by the native Tarascan Indians. The gently undulating landscape of the Paricutín region was considered one of the loveliest in the country. Though hundreds of cinder cones dotted the small valleys in the area, it had experienced negligible volcanic activity in earlier times. The only recorded eruption had occurred centuries before—the explosion of the Jorullo on September 8, 1759.

The Jorullo and Paricutín volcanoes are part of the larger Trans-Mexican Volcanic Belt, which extends almost 700 miles (1,129km) from east to west across the central-southern Mexico. According to geologists, prehistoric eruptive activity had deposited a layer of volcanic rocks almost 6,000ft (1,829m) thick, resulting in the creation of a high and fertile plateau. Moisture-laden winds from the Pacific Ocean nourish this plateau in the summer months; the consequent bountifulness of farming land has in turn made this belt the most populated region in Mexico.

Tourist guide sitting on solidified lava in front of a buried church in the Paricutín region

## CINDER CONES

Cinder cones are relatively small volcanic landforms created when lava solidifies into cinder-sized fragments after ejection and forms a mountain around the crater. While some cinder cones are formed during the course of a single eruption, many are a result of multiple eruptions. However, if volcanic activity continues for thousands of years, the cinder cones tend to develop into stratovolcanoes. The cinder cone of Paricutín is a basaltic scoria that was formed as a result of a nearly continuous chain of eruptions, which is for all purposes considered one single eruption.

## RETROSPECTIVE MYTHS

Though the Tarascan people had no myths or legends associated with the volcanoes, the Paricutín eruption prompted a rather curious phenomenon. Events that had occurred a few years before the eruption were recognized as "omens," or heralds of the eruption in retrospect. The destruction of a wooden cross on a hillside in 1941, a plague of locusts in 1942, and a series of earthquakes the following year—all these events were later thought to have been announcing the imminent explosion.

*A Tarascan Indian woman weaving on a backstrap loom*

Though Paricutín is only one of the 1,400 vents that are to be found in the Michoacán-Guanajuato monogenetic field—Jorullo, too, lies in this field—what makes this small volcano extraordinary is that it is one of the rare volcanoes that have been under observation right from the time of its birth. On February 19, 1943, the day before the eruption, almost 300 earthquakes shook the entire area. On February 20, the day the eruption began, Dionisio Pulido, a farmer, saw the earth being torn apart to form a huge fissure from which clouds of smoke were emerging in the middle of a cornfield—this fumarole marked the birth of the Paricutín volcano.

The Paricutín eruption was strombolian in nature, characterized by short explosive discharges of lava. By February 22, news of the eruption had spread, and the scientists who would go on to document every moment of Paricutín's life had arrived at the scene. By then, a 164-ft (50-m) high scoria cone had already been formed by the eruptions. Within a week, the cone had grown to 328ft (100m), and ash and small fragments of lava were raining down on the nearby villages. Soon, eruption columns several feet high were being seen and the volcano would explode occasionally with canon-like blasts. By August 1944, the villages of Paricutín and San Juan had been evacuated just in time, before they were buried entirely under lava and ash. The eruption finally came to an end with a blaze of activity in 1952, nine years after it had started.

Miraculously, the Paricutín eruption did not result in any direct casualties, although it caused widespread damage to land and livestock. Today, lava covers almost 10 square miles (25sq km) surrounding the towering cone, and only a couple of church towers rise above the rugged sea of frozen lava.

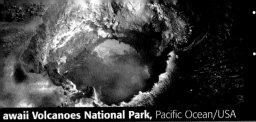
- The 450-feet (137-m) long Thurston Lava Tube was formed when molten lava continued to flow from the Kilauea even after the lava stream's outer crust had cooled and hardened.

- Imminent eruptions of the volcanoes are signaled by changes in the local electromagnetic fields; magma heated above1,112°F (600°C) loses its natural magnetism, indicating that a large body of molten rock has developed within the volcano.

# Hawaii Volcanoes National Park

Stretching across 377sq miles (976sq km) in the southeast of Big Island and encompassing two of the most active volcanoes in the world—Mauna Loa and Kilauea—the Hawaii Volcanoes National Park is one of the most fascinating geological sites on earth. Established in 1916, it was originally called the Hawaii National Park, and was given its present name in 1961. The area was declared an International Biosphere Reserve in 1980, and inscribed as a UNESCO World Heritage Site in 1987. The park offers its visitors an unmatched experience—the chance to watch the eruptions and lava flow from the volcanoes from close yet safe quarters.

The English explorer and navigator James Cook's arrival in Hawaii in 1778 and 1799 drew the world's attention to the Big Island. Standing at 13,677ft (4,169m) above sea level in the south central part of Big Island, Mauna Loa is the world's largest volcano. A shield volcano with a summit caldera which is 600ft (183m) deep, Mauna Loa has erupted 33 times since its first well-documented eruption in 1843. Archibald Menzies, a Scottish botanist, became the first non-native person to reach the summit of Mauna Loa in 1794. Mauna Loa's most recent eruption was in 1984.

## BEATING EVEREST

Though the height of Mauna Loa is stated as 13,677ft (4,169m), that figure is only the elevation of the volcano above sea level. The flanks of the mountain reach down an additional 16,400ft (5,000m) below the sea to the ocean bed. Because of the upward thrust of the lava, the central portion of the volcano has carved out a further depression of 26,240ft (8,000m) in the shape of an inverted cone below the ocean floor. Thus, if all three segments are considered, the true height of Mauna Loa—from its true base to its summit—crosses a staggering 56,000ft (17,169m), approximately twice the height of the Everest.

*Hot lava flows from a volcano, Hawaii Volcanoes National Park*

## HAWAIIAN VOLCANO OBSERVATORY

Founded in 1912 by the pioneering volcanologist Thomas Jagger, the Hawaiian Volcano Observatory was set up on the rim of the Kilauea caldera. Now under the control of the US Geological Survey, the observatory maintains a volcanic geological monitoring program. Due to their active nature, Mauna Loa and Kilauea form the focus of much of the observatory's research. Although it contributes greatly in the understanding of volcanic and seismic processes, the most important function that the observatory carries out is the identification of potential eruption and large-scale earthquake sites in order to facilitate emergency responses.

*Aerial view of a lava cone in a volcano*

Kilauea, at 4,078ft (1,243m) above sea level, is Hawaii's youngest volcano. Living well up to its name, which means "spewing" or "much spreading," Kilauea is believed to be the home of Pele, the goddess of Hawaii's volcanoes. The volcano has been erupting and spewing a continuous stream of lava, primarily from the volcano's east rift zone, for 24 years—since its last eruption in 1983, the volcano has been gobbling up existing parts of the island and creating new chunks of land. The Halemaumau crater and the Puu Oo and Kupaianaha are the best-known of Kilauea's vents.

More than 70 million years of volcanism, and evolution, have contributed to the creation of the Big Island. A constant process of destruction and creation has bestowed this land with eternal transience. Craters, cinder cones, spatter ramparts, fumaroles, calderas, lava tubes, black sand beaches, and thermal areas are just some of the volcanic features to be found on the island. Notable among these is the Kau Desert, a region of extraordinary lava formations, and also the Mauna Loa Trail, which winds from the peak of the Kilauea to that of the Mauna Loa.

The Hawaii Volcanoes National Park encloses an astounding volcanic area with a unique ecosystem. A treefern forest—a dense tropical area—that receives almost 100in (254cm) of annual rainfall, represents a substantial percentage of the indigenous flora. A species of bat is the only notable native mammalian inhabitant of the area; most bird species found on this island are endemic and many are endangered.

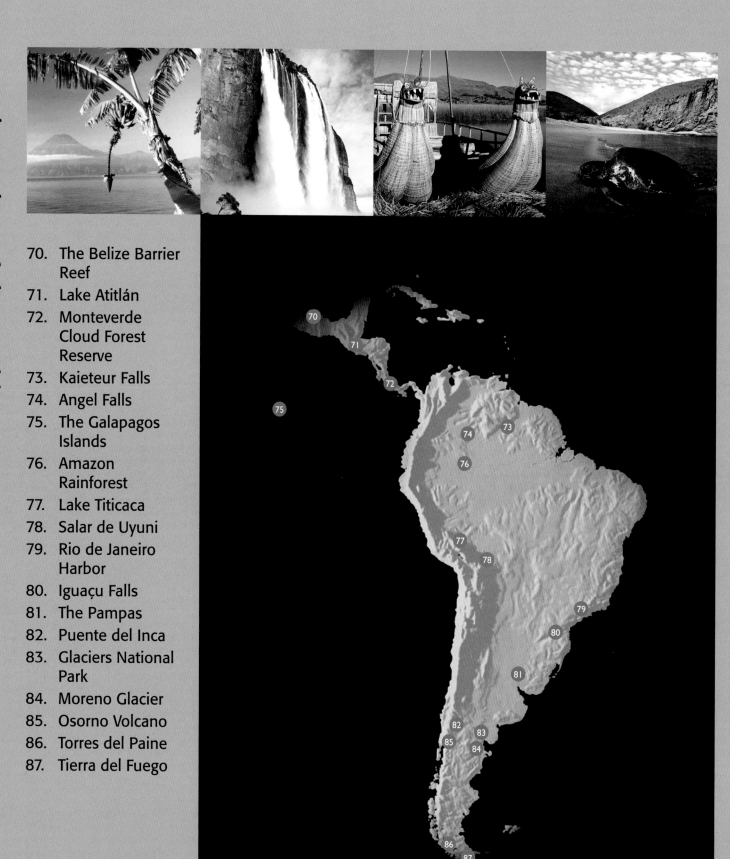

# Central & South America

Including the southern-most tip of North America, Mexico and the South American continent, Central and South America is defined by two major features: the Caribbean Plate that gave birth to various mountain ranges and geologically active sites (volcanic eruptions and earthquakes still occur here) and the incredible diversity of the Andes and the Amazon rainforest.

When writer and philosopher Aldous Huxley first saw the panoramic Lake Atitlan with its three volcanoes—San Pedro, Atitlan and Toliman—in the Guatemala Highlands, he was elated. "It's the most beautiful lake in the world!" he said. Few, who have visited this area and explored the Mayan country would dispute his remark. Charles Darwin had something similar to say, when he landed in the 5-million-year-old Galapagos Islands west of Eucador, claiming he had never expected the islands to be inhabited by so many different species—all the reptiles (including marine iguanas), half the birds, a third of the plants and a quarter of the fish are only found in this one location. It's this shock and awe that continues to inspire travelers, scientists, and naturalists that visit this incredible region.

It was ninety million years ago that the South America continent was born during massive tectonic movements that also pushed up the Andes mountain range. At about the same time, the Amazon River began to carve its way through a 2.5-million-sq mile, (6.5-million-sq km) basin—covering nearly 30 percent of the South American continent—and gave birth to the great Amazon Rainforest. While most of the Amazon Rainforest falls in Brazil, the countries of Bolivia, Peru and Guyana are as exciting—the oldest known remains of South America's culture can be found in Peru's 20,000-year-old Pikimachay Cave, and Kaieteur Falls in Guyana is magnificent.

**The Belize Barrier Reef,** The Caribbean

- The Belize Barrier Reef has come under severe threat from oceanic pollution in recent years. Hurricanes and global warming, and the resultant rise in ocean temperatures, has led to acute coral bleaching and consequently endangered the marine population.

- The South Gallows Reef was named after a spot on the caye where gallows to hang criminals once stood. Originally they had been erected in Belize City, but were later moved here because the sight of public executions disturbed the citizens.

*Schooling Sunshinefish*

## THE BELIZE BARRIER REEF RESERVE SYSTEM

The Belize Barrier Reef Reserve System, the largest barrier reef in the northern hemisphere, consists of seven sites—Bacalar Chico National Park and Marine Reserve, Blue Hole Natural Monument, Half Moon Caye Natural Monument, South Water Caye Marine Reserve, Glover's Reef Marine Reserve, Laughing Bird Caye National Park, and the Sapodilla Cayes Marine Reserve. The Half Moon Caye was designated a natural monument in 1982 and became the first marine protected area in Belize and Central America.

# The Belize Barrier Reef

It was in 1842 that Charles Darwin came upon the turquoise waters of Belize after exploring many exotic lands and sailing around the world. "This is the most wonderful reef in the West Indies," he said while describing this beautiful stretch of the Caribbean in his work on the origin of coral reefs.

More than a century and a half after his visit, and despite the perceptible threat of oceanic pollution, the beauty of this stunning underground tropical forest that spans nearly 180 miles (290km) on the Atlantic–Caribbean coast of Belize, remains more or less unaffected. Even today, you can feast your eyes on innumerable varieties of brightly colored fish zigzagging in and out of the reef's millions of nooks and crannies, watch at close distance the magnificent whale sharks during diving expeditions, or spot turtles—the loggerhead, the green, and the hawksbill—glide slowly past in the tranquil waters.

The Belize Barrier Reef is believed to have been formed during the Ice Age. Second longest in the world, it is also one of the richest reefs in terms of its biodiversity. Three of the four coral atolls are said to be found here—Lighthouse Reef, Turneffe Islands, and Glover's Reef. More than 450 caves, islets, and islands across the length of the reef hide an incredible host of marine treasures.

Around 65 species of coral and over 300 species of fish have been identified on the Belize Barrier Reef, with scientists claiming discovery of still new species from time to time—remarkable figures, considering that the Caribbean as a whole boasts 70 species of coral and 500 species of fish. These statistics were partly responsible for UNESCO conferring World Heritage status upon seven areas of the reef in Belize in 1996; destruction or deterioration of this marine habitat, UNESCO felt, would impoverish the world as a whole.

Shortly after that, another biodiversity hotspot was discovered at the reef, in the semi-enclosed lagoons of what is popularly known as the Pelican Caye—a group of cayes overgrown with mangroves. Scientists today believe almost 90 percent of the reef and its inhabitants are yet to be discovered.

Archeologists studying Mayan ruins in Belize say that they have reason to believe that the people of that ancient civilization harvested the reef regularly. The reef's waters are "harvested" even today, but with conservation in mind. Tourism serves as the reef's greatest resource, with 250,000 visitors generating over $100 million each year.

## THE BLUE HOLE

The Blue Hole is almost perfectly circular, with a diameter of over 1,000ft (305m) and a depth of 400ft (122m). Formed during the Ice Age, this magnificent limestone cavern was flooded by rising in sea levels. The legendary explorer and diver Jacques Yves Cousteau charted the depths of this cavern in 1971 and declared it one of the 10 best scuba diving spots in the world.

*The Blue Hole*

- Lake Atitlán gets its name from the Mayan word *Atitlan*, which means "the place where the rainbow gets its colors."

- The forests aurrounding Lake Atitlán act as one of the last remaining habitats for the Quetzal, the national bird of Guatemala.

**Lake Atitlán,** Guatemala

# Lake Atitlán

Nestling in the central highlands of Guatemala, 5,128ft (1,563m) above sea level, Atitlán is a lake of extraordinary natural beauty. Often called the most beautiful lake in the world—most notably by the author Aldous Huxley—Atitlán is surrounded by jagged mountains. Little villages dot the shores of the rippling lake with its vivid blue waters.

Lake Atitlán is volcanic in origin, and was formed by the Los Chocoyos eruption that took place approximately 85,000 years ago. This tremendous eruption ejected more than 72cu miles (300cu km) of ash and lava, and created a huge caldera that later filled water to form the lake that we see today. In 1976, Guatemala was wracked by an earthquake that measured 7.5 on the Richter scale. The massive tremors fractured the bed of the lake and led to subsurface drainage that caused the level of water to drop by 6.6ft (2m) within a month.

Three younger cone-shaped strato-volcanoes—Atitlán, Toliman, and San Pedro—form the spectacular backdrop for this caldera lake. San Pedro, at 9,900ft (3,020m), is the oldest of the trio. It became extinct about 40,000 years ago, around the time that Toliman, measuring 10,360ft (3,158m) today, started growing. Atitlán emerged only around 10,000 years ago. Standing tall at 11,600ft (3,535m), Atitlán last erupted in 1853 and is still considered active.

## SAN BUENAVENTURA DE ATITLÁN NATURE RESERVE

This nature reserve on the shores of Lake Atitlán occupies nearly half the valley of San Buenaventura in Panajachel. Encompassing vast tracks of native forests, the reserve is dedicated to the conservation of the natural environment of the Lake Atitlán basin. The reserve encloses a Butterfly Preserve that provides refuge to hundreds of species of butterflies and moths and has a laboratory for the breeding and study of pupae and chrysalis. The nature reserve has also been instrumental in planting thousands of trees within its boundaries.

*View of Lake Atitlán*

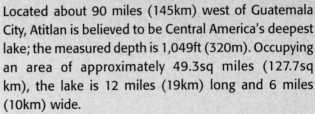

Located about 90 miles (145km) west of Guatemala City, Atitlan is believed to be Central America's deepest lake; the measured depth is 1,049ft (320m). Occupying an area of approximately 49.3sq miles (127.7sq km), the lake is 12 miles (19km) long and 6 miles (10km) wide.

While the volcanic soils that nourish a lush plant life cover the steep escarpments of Lake Atitlán, the fertile basin of the lake supports extensive cultivation of coffee and a variety of farm crops, most notably corn. The region also produces fruits and vegetables such as strawberries, avocados, the pitahaya fruit, tomatoes, cucumbers, beans, and garlic.

The small villages and towns that ring Lake Atitlán are predominantly Mayan in their culture and traditions. The Tz'utujil and Kaqchikel make up the majority of the population of the Atitlán area. Famous for its shrine to the deity Maximón, Santiago de Atitlán on the south shore is the largest of the lakeside communities. Panajachel, on the opposite side, is a small town with a booming tourism industry that caters to the needs of visitors to the lake. San Pedro la Laguna, San Marcos, and Santa Cruz la Laguna are other towns on the shores of the lake that act as quiet retreats for travelers.

The villages provide tourists with the perfect opportunity to absorb the gentle and relaxed lifestyle of the Mayans and to buy native handicrafts. There are also attractions such as lively nightspots and language schools, and the surrounding mountains provide the avid and adventurous traveler with ample opportunities for climbing or simply walking and exploring the wonderful landscape. The lake also serves as an excellent location for a wide variety of water sports such as fishing, water skiing, and boating.

*Indigenous people tying bundles of onions on the banks of the lake*

## BASS TROUBLE

The Atitlán basin, though declared a national park in 1955, used to be virtually unknown to the world. An attempt to boost tourism and the economy in general was undertaken by introducing a new fish, the black bass, into the lake. The move backfired resulting in an ecological disaster when the voracious feeder wiped out most of the lake's local species of fish. This in turn accelerated the extinction of the Atitlán giant grebe, a rare bird that would feed on the small native population of fish.

- Tropical forests cover only 5 percent of the earth's surface, yet they contain almost half of the plant and animal species that inhabit the planet.

- Despite measures taken to protect the species from extinction, the harlequin frog has almost vanished from the Monteverde Cloud Forest Reserve.

**Monteverde Cloud Forest Reserve,** Costa Rica

# Monteverde Cloud Forest Reserve

A journey through the Monteverde Cloud Forest Reserve is like walking through an exquisite canopy of green. A profusion of verdant greenery greets the eye in every direction. While the exposed ridges bear spectacularly dwarfed elfin forests that have been shaped by the winds, the protected valleys of the preserve have a prolific growth of tall majestic trees, with orchids, ferns, mosses, bromeliads, and vines trailing across them and decorating the entire forest.

Situated in the Tilaran Mountain Range in the Puntarenas province of northwestern Costa Rica, 3.7 miles (6km) east of the town of Santa Elena, the Monteverde Cloud Forest Reserve derives its name—which translates into "green mountain"—from the lush vegetation of the area. The mountain chain lies on the extreme northwestern edge of a volcanic range that runs across Costa Rica, and reaches average elevations of almost 5,000ft (1,524m) above sea level; the forest reserve encompasses over 19sq miles (50sq km) of cloud and rain forests on the slopes of this range.

The dense forests of Monteverde extend on both sides of the Continental Divide that separates the Atlantic and Pacific Oceans. The Cerro Los Amigos, at an altitude of 6,042ft (1,842m), is the highest point in the forest reserve, while the Valley of Peñas Blancas, with an elevation of 2,624ft (800m), is the lowest point within the reserve. Monteverde is made up of primarily basaltic and andesitic

## SANTA ELENA CLOUD FOREST RESERVE

One of the first community-managed reserves in Costa Rica, the Santa Elena Cloud Forest Reserve on the slopes of the Tilaran Mountains was officially opened in March 1992. It operates on the unique philosophy that the long-term sustainability of the sanctuary is the concern of the entire community. Proceeds from entrance fees, tours, and the sale of souvenirs are either invested in the management of the reserve, or used to fund educational programs in a local school. Together with the Children's Eternal Rainforest, the Arenal Conservation Area, and the Monteverde Cloud Forest Preserve, Santa Elena Cloud Forest Reserve constitutes 108sq miles (280sq km) of area under contiguous conservation. Conservation efforts concentrate heavily on establishing forest corridors to lower altitudes since many of the species protected by the reserves require large areas to breed and forage.

*A tourist taking a canopy ride through the magical cloud forest*

An Olinga crouching on a branch in the Monteverde Cloud Forest

rocks. The soil with its sandy and loamy texture, is of volcanic origin. While the low-lying areas of Monteverde have poor drainage and tend to contain swampy forests, the majority of the reserve is criss-crossed by swift clear streams that run down the mountain slopes, creating innumerable beautiful rapids and waterfalls; deep ravines and gorges have also been carved out by these streams.

Cloud forests tend to receive far less rainfall than rainforests. Their high altitude ensures conditions of far greater humidity, thus, they are actually cloudier than the rainforests. The Monteverde Cloud Forest Reserve is shrouded by a veil of mist at all times, supporting a luxuriant and abundant flora and fauna of incredible diversity.

Eight distinct biological zones can be identified within the preserve, which is home to more than 2,500 species of plants and trees, 100 species of mammals, almost 1,200 types of reptiles and amphibians, more than 400 kinds of birds, 500 species of butterflies, and thousands of varities of insects. Fortunate visitors exploring the forests can often catch a glimpse of the jaguar, puma, monkeys, ocelot, Baird's tapir, bellbirds, and the famous but elusive Resplendent Quetzal.

## THE QUAKERS

The Monteverde Cloud Forest Reserve is home to the Quaker community of Costa Rica. Made up of people who migrated to Costa Rica from the United States in the 1950s because of their refusal to register for the war draft of 1949, the Quaker community espouses a philosophy of peace and harmony. The community has been instrumental in spurring conservation efforts in the area. They raised money with the help of organizations such as the World Wildlife Fund and Nature Conservancy, and started buying off large sections of the cloud forest in 1972. This initial effort is what resulted in the formation of the Monteverde Cloud Forest Reserve.

- Kaieteur Falls ranks 122nd on the list of tallest single-drop waterfalls in the world.
- A large terrestrial bromeliad plant, called Brocchinia micrantha, is found in the Kaieteur area; it serves as the exclusive home for the golden rocket frog, or *Colostethus beebei*.

**Kaieteur Falls,** Guyana

# Kaieteur Falls

One of the most spectacular waterfalls in the world, Kaieteur Falls forms a cataract on the Potaro River in west-central Guyana. Situated in one of the most diverse rainforests on the planet, the falls are the primary attraction of the Kaieteur National Park which was established in 1930.

Following a sheer plunge of 741ft (226m) over the brink of a sandstone plateau, the waterfall has carved out a gorge 5 miles (8km) long, and forms a short series of cascades that descend another 81ft (25m), making the total height of the fall a staggering 823ft (251m). The average width of this perennial waterfall is 370ft (113m).

Almost five times as high as Niagara Falls on the United States–Canada border, and more than twice the height of Victoria Falls in Africa, Kaieteur's magnificence stems from its combination of great height as well as volume—on an average, approximately 23,400cu ft (663cu m) of water tumbles over the over the edge of the Pakaraima plateau every second. The only waterfall that comes close to matching the immense volume of water discharged by Kaieteur is the Jog Falls, located in the southern state of Karnataka in India.

Charles Barrington Brown—one of the two British geologists appointed as government surveyors to the colony of British Guiana (Guyana)—was the first European to discover Kaieteur Falls. Along with his partner James Sawkins, Barrington Brown was engaged in the task of surveying and mapping the region. It was on one such expedition that Brown chanced upon Kaieteur Falls in April, 1870.

## KAIE'S FALLS

One of the most popular tales associated with Kaieteur Falls is that of the Patamona chieftain Kaie, after whom the falls have been named. According to folklore, Kaie canoed over the edge of the waterfalls and offered his life as sacrifice to the great spirit Makonaima in order to ensure that his tribe was protected from annihilation by the bloodthirsty Caribs. The word *teur* means "waterfall."

*The majestic Kaieteur Falls, Guyana*

*Pataro River near Kaieteur Falls*

Myth and legend surround the gargantuan Kaieteur Falls, its spray creating an illusion of permanent mist at its bottom. The rainforests surrounding the falls are reputed to have provided the author Sir Arthur Conan Doyle with the inspiration for his well-known novel *The Lost World*. This region of incredible beauty has only recently begun realizing its tourism potential.

The Kaieteur National Park was one of the first areas to be so designated in South America. Today, the park occupies an area of about 242sq miles (627sq km). Thanks to the low population density of the area, the rainforests have remained relatively untouched and pristine. In recent years, with increasing awareness of the need for conservation, efforts to maintain the natural ecosystem and to properly administer the park have gained momentum. Attempts have also been made to include the park in the UNESCO World Heritage List.

Apart from encompassing an impressive white-sand forest, the park also forms a natural habitat for many species of animal, particularly amphibians and reptiles. Many of the species of plant and animal found in the national park are endemic, and sometimes endangered. The main threats posed to the area today are by humans—most significant being the problem of the illegal mining of diamonds and gold, which inevitably results in deforestation and pollution.

- Angel Falls, the world's tallest waterfall, is almost 20 times the height of Niagara Falls.
- The fractured red sandstone peak of Auyán Tepuí reaches a height of 8,250ft (2,515m)

**Angel Falls,** Venezuela

# Angel Falls

The Rio Churún, a tributary of the Caroní River, makes its way slowly across the Auyán Tepuí, a high plateau that overlooks the jungles of southeastern Venezuela. Swollen with waters from torrential tropical downpours, the river gathers pace down a short incline at the northern edge of the plateau, near the borders with Guyana and Brazil, and then plunges over the cliff as the majestic Salto Angel, or Angel Falls. From a distance, the thin white line at the cliff edge appears to gradually broaden into a blur of spray, until the water drops out of sight into the jungle below.

Angel Falls, with a total fall height of 3,212ft (979m), is the tallest cataract in the world. About 500ft (150m) wide at the base, the waterfall has an average width of 350ft (107m); the magnificent waterfall first drops 2,648ft (807m) along the precipice, barely touching the steep face of the Auyán Tepuí; then after meeting with an obstruction, it drops a further 564ft (172m) into a frothing cauldron of foam.

Thought to have been called Churún Merú by the local Pemón people, the actual Pemón name for Angel Falls is Kerepakupai-merú, which translates to "waterfall of the deepest place." In actual fact, the Churún Merú is another waterfall that occurs further up along a canyon

*A sky diver jumping from the edge of the Auyán Tepuí*

## THE PEMÓN

The forests and savannas of Canaima National Park have been inhabited by various Carib tribes—collectively known as the Pemón—for almost 10,000 years. Two archeological sites, containing handmade tools considered to be around 9,000 years old, have been discovered in the park. Today, about 10,000 Pemón people live in the area in dispersed communities of 40 to100 members each. These people to this day continue to follow the  traditional way of life, and subsist on hunting, gathering, farming, and trading artifacts.

The magnificent Salto Angel, Jimmy Angel's accidental discovery

## FINDING THE FALLS

The first documented sighting of Angel Falls was in 1910, when Ernesto Sánchez la Cruz reported his discovery; however, it was an American bush pilot Jimmy Angel who brought the breathtaking falls to the attention of the world. Angel was seeking gold in 1933 when he noted the falls in his logbook. After crash landing his plane he emerged from the dense jungles with the knowledge of what the local indigenous peoples had guarded for several hundred years: the Kerepakupai Merú, the world's highest waterfalls.

that bisects Auyán Tepuí, and is just about half the height of Angel Falls. Angel Falls or Salto Angel is named after the American pilot Jimmy Angel whose plane crash-landed nearby.

Angel Falls is located within the Canaima National Park in the state of Bolivar, Venezuela. Established in 1962, it is the second largest national park in the country. Spread over an area of 11,700sq miles (30,000sq km), the national park encompasses a spectacular landscape of sheer cliffs and amazing waterfalls. Almost 65 percent of the park is covered by tepuis, or table mountain formations—Auyán Tepuí is one such mesa, or flat-topped mountain. The Canaima National Park is also home to a wide range of flora, and several endemic species grow on the tepuis. Out of the 900 plant species found on the Auyán Tepuí, 10 percent are endemic to the region. The fauna of the park, too, is rich, consisting of 118 mammals, 550 birds, 72 reptiles, and 55 amphibians. The park was inscribed as a UNESCO World Heritage Site in 1994.

For a long time the entire area was virtually inaccessible to civilization, and could only be reached by the most resolute adventurers. Today, however, it is possible to reach the waterfall and view it from close range in either motorized dugout canoes or in light aircrafts. However, because of the dense thicket of forest that encircles it, Angel Falls is best viewed from the air. The area has also become a favored destination among the more adventurous visitors who arrive here to hang-glide or paraglide off the edge of the plateau.

**The Galapagos Islands,** Ecuador

- Lonesome George, estimated to be between 60 and 90 years old, is the last-known survivor of the Pinta Island tortoises. The Charles Darwin Research Stations' most famous resident, his death could mark the extinction of one more species from the planet.

- A service at Post Office Bay on the isle of Floreana—a major tourist attraction today—started more than 200 years ago. A wooden barrel was placed there, in which pirates and navigators would leave their mail to be collected and delivered by homeward-bound ships.

# The Galapagos Islands

Acknowledging the debt that his revolutionary theories of biological adaptation, natural selection, and evolution owed to the diverse mix of animals found in the Galapagos Islands, Charles Darwin said, "I never dreamed that islands, about 50 or 60 miles apart, formed of precisely the same rocks, placed under a quite similar climate, rising to a nearly equal height, would have been differently tenanted." An astounding range of flora and fauna thus characterizes the Galapagos Islands, which are located about 600 miles (1,000km) to the west of Ecuador in South America.

Consisting of 13 major and 6 smaller islands, the Galapagos are of volcanic origin, with the oldest estimated to have been formed 5 million years ago and the youngest around 2 million years ago. With over 50 eruptions having taken place in the past 200 years, the islands continue to evolve with volcanic activity destroying as well as creating land and isles. When British naturalist Charles Darwin

## DARWIN'S FINCHES

Galapagos finches are descended from common ancestral stock which arrived by chance from South America. They found a large number of vacant niches in various habitats throughout the islands, and have evolved into 13 species of distinguishable size, shape of bill, plumage, song, diet, and habits.

This adaptive radiation is best illustrated by the differences in the beaks of the various species. Some have the typical seed-eating bill; others, that feed on cacti, have developed a long, pointed bill; and yet more have a small tit-like bill for feeding primarily on insects.

The woodpecker finch has developed not only a specialized bill, but also a complex behavior pattern which includes the ability to use a cactus spine to prize larvae out of cracks and crevices.

visited the islands in 1835 on the HMS *Beagle*, the new pahoehoe lava—basaltic lava cooled down to form a smooth, billowy, or ropey surface—on Santiago Island had not even started forming.

Though Darwin is the first person to have scientifically studied Galapagos, archeologists have found evidence of other voyagers anchoring there. Floreana Island's first recorded human settler was an Irish crew member aboard an English vessel, which anchored there in 1807. Not much is known about his reasons for settling there or how he survived on the island. However, today about 20,000 people inhabit the Galapagos Islands.

The islands were accidentally chanced upon for the first time by Tomás de Berlanga, the Bishop of Panama, in 1535 when he was sailing for Peru but was carried to the Galapagos Islands by strong currents. Though historians contend that the Incas may have arrived here long before Berlanga, there is no evidence to support this theory.

The islands are populated by more than 5,000 species of plants and animals, including 1,900 that are not found anywhere else in the world—among them the marine iguana, Galapagos penguin, and a variety of finches, although the most famous inhabitants remain the giant tortoises. Spanish voyagers in the 16th century called these islands Galapagos—an old Spanish word for a type of saddle that the tortoises apparently resembled. In 1570, the cartographer Abraham Ortelius plotted the Galapagos, calling them the Insulae de los Galapagos or Islands of the Tortoises. After their annexation by Ecuador, the islands were given the official name Archipelago de Colon, or Archipelago of Columbus, in 1892.

Today, the Galapagos Islands are under the jurisdiction of Ecuador and are maintained as part of its national park system. Galapagos was one of the first natural sites in the world to make it to UNESCO's World Heritage List in 1978. Almost 95 percent of the islands' area is designated as reserve land.

## ISLAND REPTILES

The Galapagos Islands are the only place on earth where you can find marine iguanas. These lizards feed exclusively on seaweed, and have adapted to their marine way of life by developing partially webbed feet. Seven different species of marine iguana, each showing marked variations, have evolved on the different islands. On six of the islands, there is also a species of land iguana peculiar to the Galapagos.

The islands are also famous for another reptile, the giant tortoise. Mature individuals can weigh 300lb to 400lb (135kg to 180kg). Fifteen distinctive species have evolved to adapt to niches for which there are no other competitors—despite this, four species are now extinct and a fifth is now represented by a single male.

*Marine iguanas, Santa Cruz Island*

- There are more fish species in the Amazon river system than in the entire Atlantic Ocean.
- 70 percent of the plant species identified by the US National Cancer Institute as holding anti-cancer properties come from rainforests.

**Amazon Rainforest,** Brazil

*Military Macaw in fruiting palm tree*

## RAINFOREST PROTECTION

Since 1970s more than 230,000sq miles (600,000sq km) of Amazon Rainforest—roughly the size of France—has been destroyed. The good news is that South America's rainforests are in better shape than their African counterpart. This is largely because of the consistent pressure from environmentalists and increasingly ecologically minded governments. In December 2006, for instance, Brazil set aside some 57,915sq miles (148,500sq km) of northern Amazon—an area of land bigger than the United Kingdom—as a protected area, making it the largest protected rainforest area in the world.

# Amazon Rainforest

The richest biological incubator on the earth, the Amazon Rainforest has for long been the symbol of our planet's amazingly lush and pulsating biosphere. The dense woods take their name from the River Amazon, which winds through its forests to meet the Atlantic Ocean, and is home to millions of plant and animal species, as well as many indigenous people.

The Amazon Basin over which the rainforests grows (it was half its current size some 8,000 years ago) stretches for more than 2.3 million sq miles (5.9 million sq km) and includes most of Brazil and parts of French Guiana, Suriname, Guyana, Venezuela, Colombia, Ecuador, Peru, and Bolivia.

The Amazon Rainforest is made up of a mosaic of ecosystems that include deciduous forests and savannahs in addition to the rainforests. There was a time when the Amazon River flowed westward, believed to be part of the proto-Congo (Zaire) river system of the co-joined continents of Africa and South America, known as Gondwana. The rise of the Andes and the linkage of the Brazilian and Guyana bedrock blocked the river and caused the Amazon to become a vast inland sea. Gradually, the inland sea worked its way through the east, giving birth to the fantastic Amazon forests.

The biosphere of the Amazon is characterized by unique vegetation. Its canopy includes trees that reach

## TRANS-AMAZON HIGHWAY

Stretching some 3,286 miles (5,300km) across the Amazon region, the Trans-Amazon Highway, construction of which began in 1970s, links the city of Recife in the east to the Peruvian Andes in the west. Running on an east to west axis of the rainforest, it is crossed by north to south roads, some of which are paved. The Trans-Amazon Highway is part of an ambitious Amazon development plan by the Brazilian government. Environmentalists worry that the highway will encourage illegal logging, ranching, and mining, and endanger whatever is left of the "lungs of the world."

*Burning of tropical rainforest, Amazon Basin*

100ft to130ft (30m to 40m) above the forest floor. Below the canopy are multiple leaf and branch trees, collectively known as "understory." The lowest part of the understory is called the shrub layer and includes shrubby plants and tea saplings. This amazing topography supports the greatest diversity of living organisms in the world. Although the world's rainforests cover less than 2 percent of the earth's surface, they house an estimated 80 percent of all life on the planet. The number of creatures that inhabit tropical rainforests—an estimated 5 to 50 million species—is so great that is it is almost incomprehensible.

The Central Amazon Conservation Complex (CACC) is the largest protected area, over 23,400sq miles (60,000sq km), and the Jaú National Park is the largest national park—8,860sq miles (2,272,00sq km) in the Amazon Basin. The CACC supports varoius ecosystems, igapó forests, lakes, and channels, home to the largest array of electric fish in the world. The site protects key threatened species, including the giant arapaima fish, the Amazonian manatee, the black caiman, and two species of dolphins. The Jaú National Park protects the hydrological basin of the river, the oldest and the most recent sedimentary formation of the Amazon Basin, and an impressive range of fauna, with many species associated with blackwater river systems. It is also home to many endangered species such as the woolly spider monkey, giant anteater, South American river turtle, and giant armadillo.

Lake Titicaca is 120 miles (190km) long and measures 50 miles (80km) at its widest point. The lake is divided into two parts by a narrow strait called Tiquina.

The only fish native to Lake Titicaca are two species of killifish and one of catfish. The trout was introduced into the lake in 1939. Its shallow portions are also inhabited by a species of frog that can grow up to a foot in length.

**Lake Titicaca,** Bolivia/Peru

# Lake Titicaca

A lake of exceptional beauty and effulgence, Lake Titicaca straddles the border of Bolivia to the east and Peru to the west. It is the world's largest tropical lake, and at an altitude of 12,500ft (3,810m), the highest commercially navigable lake in the world. The second largest lake in South America after Lake Maracaibo, Titicaca has a surface area of approximately 3,200sq miles (8,300sq km).

Lake Titicaca is watered by more than 25 rivers of which the largest one, Ramis, drains almost 40 percent of the entire Titicaca basin. The lake is also fed by rainfall and melted water from glaciers on the sierras that border the Altiplano, or highlands. Although it is drained by the Desaguadero River, Titicaca loses most of its water through evaporation. Many densely populated islands dot the surface of the lake; the largest among these is the Isla de Titicaca, or Isla del Sol. The average depth of Titicaca varies between 460ft and 600ft (140m and 180m), depending on the volume of water present in the lake; the greatest depth of the lake has been recorded at 920ft (280m), near the Isla Soto in the northeastern corner of the lake. Great waves often ruffle the surface of this immense body of water.

## LAKE BALLIVIÁN

Lake Ballivián was situated on the Bolivia-Peru border during the Pleistocene Epoch. The surface of this ancient lake was at least 330ft (100m) above Titicaca's present surface. This huge lake then drained and evaporated over time, leaving behind two smaller lakes—Lake Titicaca and Minchin (predecessor to the present day Lake Poopó) in the northern and southern regions of its basin respectively.

*A view of Lake Titicaca*

## THE UROS AND THE TOTORA

The islands of Titicaca are created and recreated constantly from *totora*—a reed-like papyrus which has a dense growth in the marshy shallow sections of the lake. Protected within the Bay of Puno, these floating islands provide shelter to about 2,000 Uros, the descendants of an ancient tribe. They use the reeds to build their homes, and their famous boats, or *balsas*—made out of bundles of dried totora— resemble the papyrus craft of the ancient Egyptians. The totora is sometimes eaten as well. The Uro people protect the reeds from fire by lighting them only on a layer of stone. The Uros islands thus derive their name from these people, who subsist on fishing, weaving, and tourism.

*A traditional twin-keeled boat, Floating Islands*

Geologists are divided in their opinion on the origin of this massive lake. While a small school argues in favor of a volcanic origin, stating that the lake was originally a crater, others contend that it is the remnant of an ancient river system that flowed all the way to the Pacific Ocean. However, the most popular opinion is that the lake was created by glacial activity.

In the Aymará language, *titi* means "puma," and *caca* means "eternal city." Titicaca also translates as "rock puma" in the Bolivian tongue, and the shape of the lake is thought to resemble a puma punching a rabbit. An integral part of the development of the Inca civilization, Titicaca is surrounded by myth. According to legend, the Incas were born out of this lake. The children of the sun god, Manco Capac, and his sister-consort, Mama Ocllo, are believed to have emerged from the lake and founded the Inca dynasty. The Incas consider the lake and its waters sacred even today.

The lake and its islands are also held sacred by the Aymará Indians. Tiahuanaco, a cluster of ruins on the Bolivian side of Titicaca, showcases many aspects of this ancient civilization which predates that of the Incas. The Aymará people still live in the Titicaca basin, and sustain themselves by cultivating barley, grains, and potatoes on stepped terraces. A field of barley found near Titicaca, growing at a height of 15,420ft (4,700m) above the sea level, marks the highest cultivated plot in the world.

The naval wing of Bolivia, an otherwise landlocked country, conducts its maneuvers on Lake Titicaca. A steamer first plied the lake in 1862; today, scores of vessels travel between Puno on the Peruvian shore to the small Bolivian port of Guaqui.

**Salar de Uyuni**, Bolivia

# Salar de Uyuni

An enormous white sea of salt, the Salar de Uyuni lies in the Department of Potosí in southwestern Bolivia. This arid and windswept expanse of salt is located on the Altiplano, close to the crest of the Andes, at an elevation of 11,995ft (3,656m) above sea level. Occupying approximately 4,085sq miles (10,582sq km), the Uyuni Salt Flat is the largest salt-encrusted waste land in Bolivia.

Stretching away almost endlessly until it blends into the horizon, this blinding ocean of white is separated from the smaller Coipasa Salt Flat in the north by a range of hills. Saltworks are located on the shores of Salar de Uyuni—at Salinas de Garci Mendoza in the north, at Llica on the northwestern edge, and Calcha at the southern end. It is estimated that the Salar de Uyuni contains around 10 billion tons of salt; of this vast quantity, less than 25,000 tons of salt is extracted every year.

### UYUNI

Standing 12,024ft (3,665m) above sea level, the town of Uyuni is located to the east of the vast Salar de Uyuni. The town was founded in 1890, and flourished as a market and mining center and a railroad junction under its Syrian and Slav colonists. The silver mines of Pulacayo and Huanchaca are situated just northeast of the town. A branch of Bolivia's chief north–south railroad line runs from Uyuni toward the Pacific Ocean, and provides the country with access to the port facilities of Antofagasta in Chile.

*The busy market place in Uyuni*

Salt being harvested in the great salt flat of Salar de Uyuni

## SALAR DE COIPASA

Salar de Coipasa, or the Coipasa Salt Flat, also lies on the bleak Altiplano area of southwestern Bolivia. Situated about 100sq miles (160sq km) to the southwest of the city of Oruro, near the Chilean border, Salar de Coipasa is located at an elevation of 12,073ft (3,680m) above sea level. Occupying approximately 856sq miles (2,218sq km), Coipasa is the second-largest salt flat in Bolivia. The dormant Coipasa Volcano, with a total elevation of 16,149 ft (4,925m), rises nearly 4,165ft (1,260m) above the floor of the salt flat.

The Uyuni Salt Flat is the crystalline residue of a gigantic saltwater lake that occupied the area roughly 40,000 years ago. Known as Lago Minchin today, most of the waters from this prehistoric lake evaporated in the blazing Andean heat over the years, leaving behind two modern lakes—Lake Poopó and Lake Uru Uru, and two salt deserts—Salar de Uyuni and the much smaller Coipasa.

The thick layers of Quaternary lake sediment of Uyuni actually serve as a record of thousands of years of wet and dry periods on the Altiplano. Thus, researchers of palaeoclimatic changes focus on and continue to explore and investigate the Salar de Uyuni. The presence of coral within limestone underneath an ancient lakeshore terrace is one of the interesting discoveries made by such research.

Waterless oases can sometimes be found breaking the monotony of the Salar landscape as it reflects the glaring Andean sun. In the middle of the salt desert lies La Isla del Pescado, or the Island of Fish; the only sign of life for miles around, the island derives its name from the piscine shape it appears to possess. The Incuahasi Island is a fossil coral reef, from which cacti often rise as high as 30ft (9m).

Despite the incredible barrenness of the Salar de Uyuni landscape, an area of great geological activity lurks to its west along the Bolivian-Chilean border. The landscape is dotted with peaks of major late Cenozoic volcanoes, cresting above vibrantly colored lakes of brine and large oddly shaped boulders sculpted by the wind; a large number of geysers, mudpots, and hot springs attest to the geothermal activity of the region, in stark contrast to the frigid climate of the area. The extreme environmental conditions of Salar de Uyuni and its surroundings are being studied by NASA in an effort to understand the origin of early life on earth and other planets. The stunning beauty and surrealism of the Salar landscape has made it a major tourist attraction today.

- Rio de Janeiro has the world's largest natural deep-water harbor and the only replanted urban forest in the world.

- Rio de Janeiro boasts 50 miles (80km) of beaches, the most famous of which is the Copacabana, immortalized in a 1970s pop hit single and a Broadway musical of the same name by the singer-songwriter Barry Manilow

**Rio de Janeiro Harbor,** Brazil

# Rio de Janeiro Harbor

The Harbor of Rio de Janeiro occupies one of the most stunning sites in the world. Situated on the east coast of Brazil, it encompasses the vast Guanabara Bay, which includes 42 islands, 53 beaches, and 4,000sq km of watershed. The Guanabara Bay faces the Atlantic Ocean to its south and is surrounded by the rising granite hills of Rio de Janeiro on its southwest shore and Niterói on its southeast.

The bay is about 19 miles (31km) long with a maximum width of 18 miles (29km). It has a mile-wide (1.6km) entrance that is flanked on the east by the Papagaio Peak and the Santa Cruz fortress, and on the west by the fantastically shaped Sugar Loaf Mountain and the São João fortress.

The first Europeans to reach Brazil were the Portuguese explorers in 1502. As they glided towards the entrance of the Guanabara Bay, with its backdrop of sheer rock, they were convinced that the bay was a river and named the harbor Rio de Janeiro, or the "River of January," in honor of the month in which they arrived.

The Tamoio people, the original inhabitants of the area, had long before named the bay, Guanabara (arm of the sea). A great bay that looked like a river was not the only nomenclature the Portuguese settlers invented, calling the smaller bay of Botafago a "lake." The Tamoi themselves named the bay's eastern edge Niterói (hidden waters). The strangely shaped mountain was named Pão de Açúcar since it evoked the famous sugarloaves of Madeira Island, and the highest mountain on the Rio de Janeiro coast was called Corcovado (hunchback). Today, both pre-European and Portuguese names are used interchangeably.

## PÃO DE AÇÚCAR

Pão de Açúcar, or Sugar Loaf Mountain, retains some vestiges of the Atlantic forest containing native species that have disappeared from other areas of the Brazilian coast. Visited by climbers, mountaineers, and ecologists, the mountain is also home to many rare species of plants, such as the orchid *Laelia lobata*. It is found only in two places—at Sugar Loaf and Pedra da Gávea (Gávea Rock), both in Rio de Janeiro.

*A view of Rio's harbor and Sugar Loaf Mountain*

The Guanavvbara Bay has since then shrunk, and the coastal mountains that were once carpeted with Atlantic rainforest (Mata Atlântica) and other native species of vegetation, such as semi-arid forests and tree and scrub woodlands, have all but disappeared with the exception of a few green pockets. Landfills have twice altered Guanabara Bay's contours. In the 1920s and then again in 1960s, small hills that were once home to Rio's earliest settlers were sluiced through to create land for an airport, a six-lane highway, parkland, and beaches, as well as the city's modern art museum.

Rio de Janeiro is also home to the Parque Nacional da Tijuca, the world's largest urban forest replanted by man. Covering some 12sq miles (32sq km), Tijuca is home to hundreds of species of plants and wildlife found only in Atlantic rainforests and was declared a UNESCO Biosphere Reserve in 1991. Until the 18th century the original forest spread over the region remained largely intact. As Rio de Janeiro grew into a colonial capital, the ensuing expansion decimated most of the lower forests that were used for the city's construction. Between the 18th and 19th centuries, the introduction of coffee plantations and the creation of the imperial city of Tijuca, destroyed the forest on the higher reaches of the city. By the mid-19th century, the realization of the environmental loss led Emperor D. Pedro II to appoint Major Gomes Archer to start reforestation efforts. Most of the forest that exists here today was grown from the seeds obtained from the Paineiras forest and later from nursing beds prepared in Tijuca itself.

## ISLAND OF PAQUETÁ

The tropical island of Paquetá, situated in the heart of Guanabara Bay, is home to the only Brazilian baobabs found in the Americas—an African tree that residents call Maria Gorda meaning "Fat Mary." Paqueta is close to the Pedra da Moreninha (Moreninha Rock) and the Parque Darke de Mattos (Darke de Mattos Park) known for their scenic sunsets over the bay. All motorized vehicles are banned from the island; only bicycles and horse-drawn carriages are allowed on the roads.

The statue of Christ the Redeemer, on the summit of Corcovado, towers over the Tijuca National Park, one of the world's largest urban forests

- The Iguaçu Falls were formed as a result of volcanic activity that shook the earth about 100 million years ago.

- The Spanish explorer Álvar Núñez Cabeza de Vaca is credited as being the first European to discover the Iguaçu Falls in 1541.

**Iguaçu Falls,** Brazil/Argentina

# Iguaçu Falls

Following a meandering course across the Paraná Plateau, the River Iguaçu tumbles over its edge in a magnificent crescent arc. The Iguaçu Falls are a constellation of as many as 275 separate cascades, with their heights varying between 200ft and 270ft (60m and 82m). The horseshoe-shaped rim of the waterfall, which stretches from Paraná in Brazil to the Misiones province in Argentina, is 1.7 miles (2.7km) long. The precise border between the two countries is marked by a narrow semi-circular chasm called La Garganta del Diablo, meaning "devil's throat" in Spanish; sprays rise approximately 500ft (150m) into the air from the bottom of this cascade.

The name of the waterfall derives from a Guaraní word meaning "great water;" it is made up of two words in the local tongue—*y* stands for "water" and *guasu* means "great." While Argentineans use the Spanish name of the waterfall, Cataratas del Iguazú, The Brazilian use the Portuguese version, Cataratas do Iguaçu. Both versions—Iguazú and Iguaçu—are accepted universally.

The River Iguaçu has its source in Serra do Mar, close to the Atlantic coast. It then travels around 820 miles (1,323km) westward, cutting across southern Brazil and gaining in strength and volume as tributaries join

*Iguaçu Falls*

## THE WORLD'S LARGEST DAM

The Paraná River, the fifth largest in the world, flows with great force, and a huge dam has been built to harness its powers and produce hydroelectric power. Itaipu, on the border between Paraguay and Brazil, was the site selected. Once the construction work had been completed, sluice gates closed for 40 days to allow the reservoir to fill, creating a new lake 100 miles (161km) long, and covering an area of 600sq miles (1,554sq km). After 14 years of work, during which million of tons of concrete were poured, the world's largest dam and hydroelectric scheme was completed in 1988. Its generators have a capacity of 12,600 megawatts—sufficient to power the whole of Paraguay and the industrial cities of Rio de Janeiro and São Paulo in Brazil.

## SALTO DOS SETE QUEDAS

On the Alto Paraná River, about 100 miles (160km) upstream of the confluence with the Iguaçu, is the Salto dos Sete Quedas or Guairá.

This waterfall, which has an average height of only 110ft (34m), may seem an unlikely contender for the world's greatest fall, but when measured on its average annual flow of water it outstrips all others.

The lip of the Salto dos Sete Quesdas is 3 miles (5km) wide and the estimated flow of water is 470,000cu ft (13,300cu m) per second. At this rate of flow, the falls could fill the dome of St. Paul's Cathedral in London in less than a second.

*Iguaçu River and Falls amid sub-tropical forest*

it along the way—its path punctuated by a series of 70 cataracts. The grandest of its falls occurs after the River Paraná joins forces with it. Leaping off the Paraná Plateau in the guise of the Iguaçu Falls, it discharges 1.4 million gal (6.5 million liters) of water every second, and then rushes onward to meet the sea. The smaller cataracts of the Iguaçu Falls are broken by rocks and ledges which disperse the waters into clouds of mist and spray; sunshine on the mist often results in the formation of exquisite rainbows.

The sprays from the waterfall, rising as high as 328ft (100m), nourish the vast tropical vegetation around it. The rock outcrops that surround the falls are covered with dense foliage that includes species of palm, bamboo, and downy tree ferns. Wild tropical flowers, such as begonias, bromeliads, and orchids, splash the landscape with vivid colors. The contiguous jungle that borders the waterfall is protected by the Iguazú National Park (established in 1934) on the Argentinean side and the Iguaçu National Park (established in 1939) on the Brazilian side. Sharing the waterfall between them, these national parks are home to more than 400 bird species, including the startlingly colorful macaw, 100 species of exotic butterfly, and a host of mammals such as jaguars, iguanas, ocelots, and peccaries. The Iguazú National Park and the Iguaçu National Park were designated UNESCO World Heritage Sites in 1984 and 1986 respectively.

- The Pampas—*La Pampa* in Spanish—get their name from a Quechua Indian word which means "flat surface."
- Violent gales and storms common in the Buenos Aires region of the Pampas are called *pamperos*.

**The Pampas,** Argentina

# The Pampas

Lushly vegetated and well-watered silted stretches set against patches of barren land and salty streams make up the great plains of the Argentine Pampas. Spread over an area of 295,000sq miles (760,000sq km), this vast plain extends westward across central Argentina from the Atlantic coast to the Andean foothills. Bounded by the Gran Chaco in the north and Patagonia in the south, the plain slopes gently from the northwest to the southeast—from an elevation of 1,640ft (500m) above sea level at Mendoza to only 66ft (20m) at Buenos Aires.

Two distinct zones can be identified in the Pampas. The drier zone occurs to the west, and occupies most of the La Pampa province. This part of the Pampas is characterized by large saline areas and sandy deserts; the water, too, is somewhat brackish. However, the humid Pampas in the east form the economic heartland of the Argentine nation. Including part of the Buenos Aires province, this region of the Pampas has temperate climes, and is the most populated area of the country. Fine sand, clay, and silt are washed down by great rivers flowing into the Atlantic, and blown into the area by stormy winds from the west. Warm air from the tropical north often meets the cool southern winds, creating disturbances that result in violent gales and heavy rains. Consequently, this area experiences high precipitation and is exceedingly fertile.

*An aerial view of agricultural fields in the Pampas. This region is also referred to as the "bread basket of Argentina"*

## THE PAMPAS IN ART

Famous for their natural bounty and beauty, the Pampas have been featured in numerous artistic pieces. They have served as the backdrop in much of Argentina's gaucho literature, including remarkable works such as *El Gaucho Martín Fierro* written by José Hernández in 1872, and Ricardo Güiraldes's 1926 novel *Don Segundo Sombra*. A fairly large segment of Argentinian musical folklore draws its inspiration from the Pampas as its theme.

## THE PAMPEAN CLIMATE

Climate in the Pampas varies between hot summers in the north to relatively cooler summers in the south. Buenos Aires, at the northern edge of the Pampas, experiences a climate akin to that of southeastern United States, with hot and humid summers and cool and mild winters; the southern areas of the Pampas are distinguished by cool summers and cold fronts advancing northward from Patagonia, accompanied by occasional snow and frosts during the winters. Rainfall, too, varies across the plain, with the humid east experiencing a mean annual rainfall of 39in (99cm).

The flat plains of the Pampas are a grassland biome. Trees occupied most of the area centuries ago; since then however, human intervention has caused much of the larger species of plants to be replaced with different species of grass like the Pampas grass, bunchgrass, and mesquite. The undulating plain is thus covered with many varieties of grass, interspersed with groves of exotic pines, oaks, eucalyptus, and poplars. The Pampas also see a profusion of plants such as cattails, water lilies, and reeds; usually found in wetland areas, these plants have adapted to the windy climate of the Pampas. The Pampas merge with the Patagonian steppe in the south; the tussock grasses intermingle with scattered bushes and spiny plants heading southward. Large sections of the Pampas have also been converted to cultivated croplands.

A variety of animals proliferate in the Pampas, among them the Geoffrey's cat, the maned wolf, and the llama-like guanaco, as well as the flightless South American bird, the greater rhea. Seed-eating birds such as the great pampas finch, the long-tailed reed finch, and the double-collared seedeater are also found in abundance.

One of the richest and most fertile lands of the world, the Pampas have been providing sustenance to both man and beast for centuries. The gently rolling grassy plains provide visitors with some of the most serene and scenic landscapes of the South American continent.

*A section of the Llalqui Pampa desert, Chile*

**Puente del Inca,** Argentina

# Puente del Inca

**P**uente del Inca is a natural stone bridge which crosses the Cuevas River in a town of the same name. It is located in the Andes Mountains of Argentina, not far from the border with Chile, at a height of 8,921ft (2720m) above sea level. Puente del Inca translates as "bridge of the Incas." However, it was not built by the Incas, or for that matter, by man. A creation of nature, it is a finely arched stone bridge, which forms a path 80ft (24m) above the river. An imposing sight, it is covered in snow in the winter and remains stained yellow and green by the mineral deposits of the thermals springs that flow under it for the rest of the year. The bridge is 150ft (46m) long, about 70ft (21m) wide and nearly 30ft (9m) thick, and has been further strengthened by calcareous deposits from sulphur springs at its base.

Scientists believe that erosion by the Cuevas River and the sediments from the sulphur springs played an important role in creating this stone bridge. According to another theory, the bridge was formed in the Ice Age, as a result of petrifaction of rock over ice. Charles Darwin, one of the most famous visitors to this wonder, wrote in *The Voyage Of The Beagle*: "the Incas Bridge consists of a crust of stratified shingle cemented together by the deposits of the neighboring hot springs. It appears, as if the stream had scooped out a channel on one side, leaving an overhanging ledge, which was met by earth and stones falling down from the opposite cliff."

Either way, the hot springs below the Puente del Inca play a major role in the making of this spectacle. There are five thermal mineral springs on the right edge of the bridge, which bubble to the surface at different

## AROUND AND ABOUT

Puente del Inca is best known as a stopover on climbing expeditions en route to Aconcagua in the Andes. Standing at 22,825ft (6,959m), Aconcagua is the highest peak in the world outside the Himalayas. Both are located in the province of Mendoza, which has earned renown for its wines.

## CURE ALL

Minerals in thermal springs are known to cure many maladies including gout, rheumatism, and stomach infections. The waters here contain high levels of sodium, sulphates, bicarbonates, and chlorates, which make the water a great tonic. Sulphur is known to help cure skin diseases.

*The hot springs of Puente del Inca*

temperatures ranging from a hot 98.6°F (36°C) to a tepid 57.2°F (14°C). These springs are thought to be superior to the more famous ones at Vichy because of their greater carbonic acid component. In 1925, a luxury spa was built just under the bridge to take advantage of the spring waters. Unfortunately, 40 years later a great avalanche destroyed it completely.

There are several legends attached to the Puente del Inca. According to one, a fleeing Inca king came to a dead end at the Cuevas River. Unable to cross, he began praying to the gods to show him a way. The gods, deciding to be benevolent, laid down this stone bridge for him, allowing him to escape his assassins. Another legend has an army of brave Inca warriors laying themselves down to form a human bridge for their chief to cross the river, only to be turned to stone when he crossed. The most believable story has the bridge being used by Inca warriors to cross over to Chile.

- Although the area is devoid of human habitation today, it is believed that prehistoric hunter-gatherers lived here at one time; at least 14 sites of archeological importance have been discovered within the park.

- Occupying almost half of the Glaciers National Park, the Southern Patagonian Ice Field is, at 5,460sq miles (14,000sq km), the largest ice mantle outside Antarctica. It encompasses 47 important glaciers, of which 13 drain into the Atlantic basin.

# Glaciers National Park

A stunning vista of glittering glaciers and snow-clad peaks greet the eye at the Parque Nacional Los Glaciares (or the Glaciers National Park) in Argentine Patagonia. Spread out over 1,722sq miles (4,459sq km), this national park is located in the Santa Cruz province of Argentina, along the Chilean border.

The snow-clad portion of the Andean Cordillera, portions of the Patagonian Ice Field, and a relatively ice-free section to the east make up this astounding natural park. There is a dramatic variation in altitude within the park; while the Lago Argentino and Lago Viedma—glacial troughs formed at the end of the Pleistocene Epoch—measure only 820ft (250m) above the sea level, Cerro Fitzroy rises to an imposing height of 11,236ft (3,405m). Speckled with ice caps, ice fields, glacial lakes, and towering mountains, this national park showcases one of South America's most spectacular landscapes.

Roughly divided into two parts, the northern section of the national park comprises Lake Viedma, the Viedma Glacier, and a handful of smaller glaciers. This section is also distinguished by the famous Cerro Fitzroy mountain, and the magnificent Cerro Torre which—with its pinnacles rising to a height of 10,236ft (3,102m)—matches in sheer majesty, the Torres del Paine in Chile.

The southern portion contains three major glaciers—the Perito Moreno, the Upsala and the Spegazzini, all of which drain into the Lago Argentino. Also fed by glaciers such as the Mayo, Agassiz, Onelli, and Ameghino, Lago Argentino is 15,000 years old, and Argentina's largest lake, with an area of 572sq miles (1,466sq km). The Upsala, 37 miles

## CERRO CHALTÉN

The Cerro Torre and Cerro Fitzroy mountains rise tall above the park. Called Cerro Chaltén—meaning "smoking mountain"—in the Tehuelche dialect, Mount Fitzroy was given its current name by the Moreno Expedition led by Perito Moreno in 1877, in honor of the famous captain of the HMS Beagle, which charted the channels of Tierra del Fuego and the Santa Cruz River. The local name stems from a rare aerolic phenomenon—because of which the summit always appears to be shrouded in smoky clouds. First scaled by the Frenchmen Lionel Terray and Guido Magnone in 1952, the mountain today poses an almost irresistible challenge for many climbers.

*Mount (Cerro) Torre*

## CLIMATE OF LOS GLACIARES

Annual mean temperature in the Glaciers National Park is 45.5°F (7.5°C), and the climate is thus classified as temperate. Average maximum and minimum temperatures recorded within the park hover around 53.6°F (12.0°C) and 37.9° F (3.3°C) respectively. Most of the rainfall occurs in the months of April and May. While westerly windstorms disturb the area during late spring and summer, the winters are usually marked by snowfall.

*Perito Moreno Glacier*

(60km) in length and 6 miles (10km) in breadth, is the largest glacier in South America. While tourists can travel to the Perito Moreno by land, boat excursions through waters of the lake dotted with icebergs take them to the otherwise inaccessible Upsala and Spegazzini, and the Bahia Onelli. Both the glacial lakes—Argentino and Viedma—drain into the Atlantic basin through the Santa Cruz River.

While sub-Antarctic Patagonian forests and the Patagonian steppe characterize the eastern section of the park, the ice-covered western portion is devoid of vegetation. The forested regions include species such as cypress, winter's bark, and the southern bark. The steppe region is characterized by extensive tussock grasslands interspersed with bushes and shrubs. One

hundred species of birds have been identified within the Glaciers National Park. Other animals such as guanacos, southern Andean Huemul, Argentine gray fox, and the Austral hog-nosed skunk are also found in the park. Two species of fish have been introduced into the Argentino and Viedma lakes.

Established as a national park on April 28, 1945, the Los Glaciares area was first protected in 1937. The actual boundaries of the area to be incorporated within the sanctuary were only decided in 1971. The need for conservation of this pristine natural habitat of such incredible beauty—with its skyrocketing granite peaks, silvery lakes, lagoons, and the plant and animal species which exist within it—prompted the UNESCO to designate it a Natural World Heritage Site in 1981.

**Perito Moreno Glacier,** Argentina

# Perito Moreno Glacier

One of only three advancing Patagonian glaciers, the majestic Perito Moreno Glacier is situated within the Glaciers National Park in the southwestern part of Santa Cruz province in Argentina, 51 miles (82km) from the town of El Calafate. The front face of the glacier, when approached from the famous Lago Argentino (the largest Lake in Argentina), appears as a massive, jagged, and twisted mass of ice that looms menacingly over its surroundings.

Among the several outlets of the Southern Patagonian Ice Field, the glacier extends for about 50 miles (80km) through the Patagonian region before terminating at the Lago Argentino in a 2-mile (3-km) wide and 165-ft (50-m) high bluish wall of ice. The snout gets its distinctive blue color from the oxygen that remains trapped in the snow.

The Perito Moreno is often called the "Crusher" or "Crushing Glacier." The epithet, bestowed on it by tourists, is largely a result of the spectacular show that occurs during the process of calving. The glacier makes explosive cracking sounds as the snout constantly fractures and casts off huge boulders of ice which tumble down and crash into the icy waters of the Lago Argentino below.

Once they fall into the lake, these ice floes of various shapes and sizes, ranging in color from white to sapphire blue, remain adrift until they melt completely into the waters of the lake. The spectacle attracts flocks of visitors, particularly during the height of summer, which is when the crushes are at their flamboyant best.

Sometimes the gigantic blocks of ice have been known to detach from the glacier and fall into the narrow Témpanos Channel, resulting in its subsequent blockage.

## LAKE PERITO MORENO

A medium-sized lake with a narrow neck that divides it into two distinct sections—the Eastern Lake and the Western Lake—makes up the Perito Moreno lake in the Bariloche region of Argentine Patagonia. Occupying an area of approximately 4.5sq miles (11.8sq km), the lake has a maximum length and width of 4 miles (6.7km) and 1.7 miles (2.9km) respectively. Several streams, including the Casa de Piedra and Goye, drain into this beautiful lake. The entire shoreline of the Eastern Lake can be traversed easily by foot, but the Western Lake is almost inaccessible from the coast. Some points along the shores provide excellent opportunities for fishing, particularly the area around the Angostura stream, which joins it to Lake Nahuel Huapi.

*Boat on the breathtakingly beautiful Lake Argentino, Glaciers National Park*

The waters then dam up in the Rico arm of Lake Argentino, with a dramatic increase in the water level. An increase of 82ft (25m) was recorded in 1988, and the maximum increase has been estimated as 98ft (30m). Eventually, the water pressure becomes so high that it breaks through the wall of ice, and normal drainage levels are restored through the Témpanos Channel. This phenomenon recurs every few years.

The Perito Moreno Glacier and its surroundings were officially designated as the Perito Moreno National Park in 1937, with the aim of conserving the glacier, two important lake systems, and the flora and fauna of the area. Covering 444sq miles (1,150sq km) in northwestern Santa Cruz, the park encompasses an area of high, rugged mountains, intersected by deep valleys. Three distinct zones of vegetation can be identified within the boundaries of the park—the Patagonian steppe in the east, comprising coironales (tussock grasses) and twisted mata; a transitional zone of short vegetation; and the forests of lenga around the Nansen and Azara lakes. The fauna within the park includes a large number of guanacos, choiques, huemul, and the endemic pilquín or orange chinchillón. The avifauna comprises both aquatic and high-altitude birds. The cultural heritage of the park includes seven caverns decorated with ancient rock art at Casa de Piedra Hill.

*Perito Moreno Glacier*

## FRANCISCO "PERITO" MORENO

The mammoth Perito Moreno Glacier has been named after the well-known Argentine scientist and explorer Dr. Francisco Pascasio Moreno, better known to the world as Perito Moreno; *perito* means "expert." This intrepid explorer traversed across much of Argentina's rugged wildernesses in the late 19th century, studying and researching the natural treasures of the country. He donated an area of land to the Argentine government, which later became the nucleus of the Nahuel Huapi National Park. The glacier was named after him in recognition of his contribution to the cause of conservation of the country's natural heritage.

- Many of Osorno's eruptions have been explosive in nature, and characterized by rapidly moving pyroclastic lava flows and surges.

- Charles Darwin once viewed one of Osorno's midnight eruptions aboard the HMS *Beagle*.

**Osorno Volcano,** Chile

*Lake Nahuel Huapi, Bariloche in the Osorno Volcano area*

## Ascending Osorno

Puerto Kloker, Ensenada, and Petrohué are the points from which Osorno can be ascended. The snow does not settle on the slopes until about 6,569ft (2,000m), and bluish cracks in the snow can be observed on the southeastern slope. Mountaineering and trekking activities are concentrated on this stretch, and many sportsmen hit the slopes of the Osorno Volcano every year. Ascents usually take around 6 hours, and are carried out in the company of local guides. Tourists can also reach the top of the summit via cable cars, and then trek down to the base.

# Osorno Volcano

Towering over the large Todos los Santos and Llanquihue lakes, the graceful snow-clad peak of the Osorno Volcano rises steeply into the sky. A symmetrical, almost perfect cone, the Osorno Volcano is one of the most famous and beautiful landmarks in Chile. Situated about 37 miles (60km) northwest of the city of Puerto Varas in the south of the country, Volcán Osorno has a summit elevation of 8,730ft (2,661m) above sea level, and is thus visible from every point in the Osorno district, even from some points on the Chiloé Island.

The peak of this majestic volcano often remains obscured from view by the perennially overcast weather conditions which are typical of this region. However, the sight that is revealed when the clouds part and the mist clears is absolutely stunning. The slopes of the mountain are covered with verdant vegetation and topped by a permanent cap of pristine white snow that remains intact all the year round. The same cloud cover is also responsible for the abundant rainfall that the area receives. Squalls roll in off the South Pacific coast, bringing with them rain clouds—it rains for more than 200 days a year in the Osorno Volcano area.

Boats at Petrohué, Todos Los Santos lake in the Vicente Pérez Rosales National Park

The Osorno Volcano was formed on top of an eroded stratovolcano called La Picada. Believed to be approximately 250,000 years old, La Picada has a mostly buried caldera that is 3.7 miles (6km) wide, and lies under Osorno on the northeastern side. This ancient volcano is also marked by scoria cones and postglacial maars. One of the most active volcanoes of the southern Chilean Andes, the conical Osorno has two gray domes of dacitic lava on its northwestern and south-southeastern flanks.

Osorno has produced lava flows through fissure vents and scoria cones on its sides—particularly on the western flank—which have on occasion reached the Lago Llanquihue. Osorno has erupted frequently over the past 14,000 years, both from its summit and flank vents, producing fingers of basaltic and andesitic lava that have flowed into the Llanquihue and Todos los Santos lakes and created a series of small coves along the ragged shoreline. Osorno is composed primarily of basaltic and basaltic andesitic lava, covered by rich black soils on the middle and lower slopes, and black volcanic sands at the edges of the lakes.

The abundant rainfall ensures the proliferation of dense forests on the slopes of the volcanoes. Coihues and lengas dominate the stretches between 656ft and 3,280ft (200m and 1,000m) above sea level. Further up, the most ancient species of the forests, the Andean birch, can be found. Between 4,000 and 5,000 years old, this species is protected by regulations governing endangered species of flora. The fauna that these jungles shelter is also diverse, and includes the pudú, chingue (Patagonian skunk), culpeo (Patagonian fox), quique (a kind of ferret), and puma. Bird species that reside in these humid jungles include the hummingbird, kestrel, huet-huet, and a variety of woodpeckers.

Not surprisingly, with its picturesque landscapes and its incredible range of flora and fauna, the Osorno Volcano attracts thousands of visitors every year.

## VICENTE PÉREZ ROSALES NATIONAL PARK

The Osorno Volcano forms the primary attraction of the first national park of Chile. Established in 1926, the Vicente Pérez Rosales National Park today occupies an area of about 969sq miles (2,510sq km). The park is an incredible treasure house of volcanoes, mountains, lakes, and native flora and fauna. Apart from Osorno, other striking natural features within the park include the Todos los Santos lake, the Puntiagudo river valley, the Cayutúe valley, the Tronador Volcano, and the spectacular Petrohué river waterfalls; the latter provides the most magnificent views of Osorno.

**Torres del Paine,** Chile

- Torres del Paine literally means "Towers of Paine." The word *paine* comes from the Tehuelche Indian word meaning "blue."

- A group of five British aristocrats, guided by native horsemen, or *baqueanos*, are believed to have been the first recorded tourists to visit Torres del Paine in 1879.

# Torres del Paine

## LOS CUERNOS DEL PAINE

Rising to a height of 6,300ft (1,920m), the magnificent Cuernos del Paine (Horns of Paine) consists of black granite rocks that have been given their peculiar shape by tectonic and glacial forces. Thousands of visitors arrive every year to climb and trek these impressive peaks. The origin of Cuernos del Paine is also shrouded in legend. One of the most popular myths about this mass of jagged granite is that the evil serpent Cai Cai caused massive floods in the area to kill the warrior inhabitants of Torres del Paine, and when the waters receded, he took the bodies of the greatest warriors and turned them into the stony peaks of the mountain.

*Parque Torres del Paine, seen from Lago Pehoé*

A marvelous panorama of stunning mountain scenery and exquisite blue waters, the Torres del Paine is made up of an astounding range of granite peaks that lie between the Patagonian steppe and the Andes mountains in southern Chile. The landscapes of the Paine Massif are almost surreal in their beauty, with windswept grasses and sheer frozen Andean cliffs that fill this corner of the world with breathtaking forms and vibrant colors.

The name Torres del Paine refers not only to the mountain range but also to the set of three distinctive peaks that are famous the world over, and the national park within which this range is situated. Administered by the Corporación Nacional Forestal of Chile, the Torres del Paine National Park was established in 1959. The Paine Massif, with its wealth of craggy cliffs, sculpted granite peaks, swift rivers and waterfalls, lakes fed by melt water from glaciers, green meadows, and forests, forms the primary attraction of the national park. The most staggering peaks of this mountain range include the Monte Paine Grande, the three spectacular peaks of Torres del Paine—Fortaleza, Escudo, and the distinctive horn-shaped peaks of Los Cuernos del Paine.

*A section of the breathtaking Torres del Paine*

Located at the southern edge of the Patagonian Ice Cap, this mountain range was formed at least 12 million years ago, when sedimentary rocks met hot magma, and the earth's crust crumpled and folded and was thrust upward to form the mountains. After the end of the Ice Age, when the glaciers covering the massif melted, the underlying rocks were carved by the erosive action of wind and water, and fashioned into huge towers of distinct shapes and sizes. Even today, some of the peaks remain permanently covered in ice.

The Paine Massif is located exclusively by the Rio Paine; this river originates at the Dickinson Lake at the northern edge of the park, travels through several lakes within the park, before draining into the Lago del Toro at the park's southern end. Heaped with crushed rocks and sediments from the mountains, the waters of the lakes in the Torres del Paine National Park take on a multitude of hues—from milky white and gray to intense yellows, greens, and blues. Some of the lakes, such as Laguna Azul and Laguna Verde are so named because of their characteristic colors. The Grey Glacier, Grey River, and Grey Lake together form the most extensive water system in the park.

The great diversity of fauna and flora of the area led to 7,128sq miles (18,445sq km) of the Torres del Paine National Park being declared a World Biosphere Reserve by the UNESCO in 1978. Four distinct zones of vegetation can be identified within the park— pre-Andean scrublands that cover the shores of the rivers and the lakes; Magallanes forests; Magallanes tundra, with patches of plants, and pasturelands and short bushes; and high-altitude vegetation which becomes scarcer with increasing elevations. The park also shelters about 106 species of birds, including the rare Coscoroba swan and Darwin-Nandu, 24 species of mammals, and about 570 guanacos.

## WORLD BIOSPHERE RESERVE

Since its inscription as a World Biosphere Reserve, the Torres del Paine National Park has been the focus of both national as well as international researchers. Activities include restoration of lands earlier cleared and overgrazed for rearing domestic animals. Plant succession and the reintroduction of certain rare species into the park, and their probable impact on ecology, are also being researched. The study of many species including the South Andean deer, European hare, condor, eagle, Magellan ostrich and flamingo, are also being planned.

- Chile owns approximately 70 percent of the land of Tierra del Fuego and the rest belongs to Argentina.

- The northern part of Tierra del Fuego became Chile's only oilfield when petroleum reserves were found in Manantiales in 1945.

**Tierra del Fuego,** Chile/Argentina

# Tierra del Fuego

Tierra del Fuego forms part of the hook at the tip of the South American continent, a finger of land reaching towards the vast icy wastes of Antarctica just 600 miles (965km) away. Separated from the South American mainland by the Strait of Magellan, the archipelago is spread over an area of 28,000sq miles (72,520sq km), its southernmost tip forming Cape Horn.

The Isla Grande de Tierra del Fuego forms the central island of the archipelago, with an area of 18,571sq miles (48,100sq km). While a section of this island and a clutch of isles to the west and south of it form part of Chile's Magellan Region, the eastern half of the island falls under the territory of Argentina. Until this division came about in 1881, both Chile and Argentina claimed ownership over the archipelago.

It is thought that Tierra del Fuego might have been part of what was once a land bridge that linked the Antarctic Peninsula to the South American landmass. Geological evidence suggests that this bridge broke off around 25 million years ago. Fossils discovered on the continents suggest that once upon a time Antarctica and South America were both inhabited by similar plants and animals, lending credence to the claim.

## TIERRA DEL FUEGO NATIONAL PARK

Accessible from the city of Ushuaia, the Tierra del Fuego National Park is the southernmost national park in the world. Occupying approximately 243sq miles (630sq km), the park is contained within the Argentine part of the Isla Grande de Tierra del Fuego. It is Argentina's only coastal national park, with a rich and diverse coastal wildlife including seals, walruses, and many sea birds. The park, with its stunning seascapes and beautiful fjords, offers visitors the chance to go fishing and kayaking.

*Tierra del Fuego, Argentina*

## THE LES ECLAIREURS HEADLIGHT

The excellent location of Ushuaia allows visitors to take in the impressive panorama of mountains, forests, and the sea all at the same time. On one of the many promontories along the Beagle Channel in front of the city is the Les Eclaireurs Headlight. A 36-feet (11-m) tall tower painted in red and white stripes, the headlight has a lighting device that works on solar energy. It is often mistakenly called the Headlight of the End of the World, a name that Jules Verne used for the San Juan de Salvamento Headlight at Isla de los Estados.

*Tierra del Fuego as seen from Ushuaia*

In 1520, the Portuguese navigator Fernando Magellan sailed through the strait later named after him and discovered the archipelago. It is believed that Magellan called it Tierra del Fuego, meaning "Land of Fire," because of the fires that he saw along the horizon on his approach. Magellan apparently thought that these were fires lit by the natives as they lay waiting to attack, but modern speculation gravitates towards lightning and other natural sources as the cause. Sir Francis Drake sailed through the strait 58 years after Magellan and saw the cluster of islands that was later named Cape Horn by Dutch explorers.

A complete survey of the islands was not undertaken until the 19th century by Captain Robert Fitzroy who sailed to these islands aboard the HMS *Beagle*. Twenty-two-year old Charles Darwin was the naturalist who acompanied him on his journey.

The inhospitable climate of Tierra del Fuego is classified as subpolar oceanic, characterized by short cool summers and long wet winters; while the northeast sees strong winds and little precipitation, the south and the west suffer wind, fog, and heavy rain, hail, or snowfall most of the year. The permanent snowline is only about 2,297ft (700m) above sea level and the low temperature through the year helps preserve the ancient glaciers.

Six species of tree grow in this hostile climate. Fruits such as the beach strawberry and calafate are also found in the area. The archipelago's fauna includes parrots, seagulls, guanacos, kingfishers, condors, owls, and hummingbirds. The native inhabitants of Tierra del Fuego—known as Fuegians—are primarily members of the Ona (Selk'nam), Haush, Yahgan (Yámana), and Alacaluf (Kawésqar) tribes.

# Australia & Oceania

**A**ustralia is both an island, a country, and one of the world's six continents (seven, if you include Antarctica). But, geographically, this large island is also part of the unbelievably vast waterscape known as Oceania. Besides Australia, Oceania is home to American Samoa, Fiji, Kiribati, New Caledonia, New Zealand, Papua New Guinea, the Solomon Islands, Tuvalu, Vanuatu, and Western Samoa.

Blessed with a wide range of natural attractions both on land and water, Australia boasts a remarkable gamut of coral reefs (along its northern coast) that support a variety of marine life including the dugong and the green turtle; Uluru, like the Devils Tower in America, is a natural wonder (the Anangu tribe consider it the most sacred place in Australia); the Kakadu National Park is home to an archeological and ethnological reserve that has been inhabited continuously for the last 40,000 years; the magical Blue Mountains that rise in Cumberland Plain, and the 135-million-year-old Daintree Rainforest (lest you think it's all desert and water), which houses 430 species of birds and an amazing world of reptiles, especially frogs.

Beyond Australia lie the physically most diverse marine environments on the earth. They are divided into three regions (often overlapping)—the Indo-Pacific Cradle, the Coral Triangle and the TransFly. In the Indo-Pacific Cradle, stretching from Indonesia to Solomon Islands, it's the birds and turtles that predominate; the Coral Triangle spanning Malaysia, Indonesia, the Philippines, Papua New Guinea, the Solomon Islands, Fiji and North Australia is the vast repository of corals (75 percent of all coral species), more than 3,000 species of reef fish and migrating populations of sharks and giant manta rays; and the TransFly region contains pockets of grassland, wetland and monsoon forest, where 80 species of birds not found anywhere else in the world reside.

**Kakadu National Park,** Australia

- Kakadu is the only national park in the world to encompass an entire river system within its boundaries—the South Alligator River catchment area.

- The English explorer Phillip Parker King made several forays into Kakadu between 1818 and 1822, and named the Alligator River, mistaking the large number of aggressive saltwater crocodiles for freshwater alligators.

## LIVING DINOSAURS

Saltwater crocodiles, which have roamed the planet since the age of the dinosaurs, have changed little in millions of years. Males are typically around 16 ft (5m) in length—the largest on record was said to be 29ft (8.8m). These creatures have been known to bring down animals as large as the water buffalo, with jaws more powerful than the great white shark or the tiger.

# akadu ational Park

Rugged escarpments, gorges that plummet down, lush green wetlands, meandering rivers, and cascading waterfalls are among the stunning spectacles that welcome you to the Kakadu National Park in Australia. Spread across an area of 7,724sq miles (20,005sq km) in the Northern Territory, Kakadu is Australia's largest national park. The Park was included in the UNESCO World Heritage Site list in three stages from 1981 to 1992—it is one of the very few sites in the world to be recognized for its cultural as well as its natural heritage.

The climate at Kakadu is primarily monsoonal. During the wet season, areas within the park have been known to record 60in (154cm) of rain in less than 100 days. Consequently, the area is also called the Big Wet by Australians. The extensive wetlands, formed as a result of such copious rainfall, help sustain an array of bird and animal life, and have been declared a Ramsar site. Landforms within the park include hills, savannah woodlands, plateaus, estuaries, rainforests, floodplains, billabongs, tidal flats, and coastal beaches—together, they provide habitat to a diverse range of flora and fauna.

Over 10,000 kinds of insects, 289 species of birds, 132 types of reptile, more than 60 species of mammals, 55 species of freshwater fish, and 25 frog species call the park their home, as do more than 1,600 different varieties of plants, many of them rare and endemic.

The oldest rock formations in the park are estimated by archeologists to be approximately half as old as the earth—the oldest rocks found within its range are a compound of sedimentary rocks estimated to be at least 2,500 million years old. The depression known as the Pine Creek Geosyncline exhibits the largest deposits of these rocks. The younger rocks of the region are of the igneous variety.

Drawing its name from the Gagudju language, Kakadu has one of the highest concentrations of Aboriginal rock art in the world. The earliest inhabitants of the park, the Aborigines first set foot in Australia, in the Arnhem Land Plateau adjoining Kakadu, during the Ice Age. The rich natural resources of Kakadu are believed to have supported human habitation for at least 25,000 years, and possibly even earlier, for 40,000 to 60,000 years. The theory garnered support when Mike Smith and Rhys Jones, researchers from the Australian National University, found evidence of Aboriginal residence in the Park dating back more than 50,000 years after conducting carbon dating tests.

The Aboriginal art sites make for a fascinating timeline of survival and evolution. The site provides an exceptional record of human history and interaction with nature spanning tens of thousands of years. The artwork at these sites—almost 15,000 of them are believed to be scattered throughout Kakadu—range from paintings which depict the early Aborigines hunting wild animals with spears to more recent "contact" images of Macassans and Europeans. The paintings also highlight Aboriginal legends about the Creation Time, or Dreamtime. A number of these sites are still considered potent and sacred among Aboriginal communities. The park today is jointly managed by its traditional Aboriginal owners and the government of the Northern Territory.

*Aboriginal pictographs on rock, Kakadu National Park*

*Termite mounds*

## THE SIX SEASONS OF KAKADU

Although people tend to refer only to the wet and dry seasons in Kakadu, Aboriginal legend identifies six distinct seasons: Gudjewg (monsoon season), from January to end of March; Banggerreng (storm season), in April; Yegge (cooler but still humid), from May to middle of June; Wurrgeng (cold season), from mid-June to mid-August; Gurrung (hot dry season), from mid-August to mid-October; Gunumeleng (pre-monsoon storm season), from mid-October to end of December.

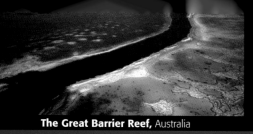

• The flora and fauna of the Great Barrier Reef is going to change dramatically if current estimates of climate change prove to be accurate. The recent high water temperatures have caused the corals to lose their color in a process called "coral bleaching," and the Great Barrier Reef is no exception.

• Corals owe their spectacular colors to the different species of algae that grow on them. Corals are colorful only while they are alive, and all dead corals are essentially white.

**The Great Barrier Reef,** Australia

# The
# Great Barrier Reef

Flourishing in the clear, tropical coastal waters off northeastern Australia, the stunningly beautiful Great Barrier Reef is actually a scattered labyrinth of around 2,900 exquisite reefs and more than 1,000 islands. In today's world, where human action is largely responsible for the destruction of many of natures' treasures, the relative purity of this much-visited yet well-protected reef makes it an even more extraordinary and priceless natural reserve.

The largest coral reef system in the world, the Great Barrier Reef stretches for approximately 1,250 miles (2,011 km) along the Australian coast from Lady Elliot Island to the Cape of York, and encompasses one of the world's most diverse tropical ecosystems. The individual reefs vary in size from 0.004sq miles (0.01sq km) to 39sq miles (100sq km), together occupying an area of 134,633sq miles (348,698sq km).

The Great Barrier Reef supports a complex and diverse life system that can only be rivaled by that of a tropical rainforest. It is home to more than 1,500 different fish, 4,000 species of mollusks—including chitons, snails, giant

## CORALS

Coral reefs are made up of individual coral polyps, each living inside a shell of hard calcium carbonate called aragonite. These minute organisms cluster to form colonies in shallow tropical waters where the temperature remains constant between 72°F (22°C) and 82°F (28°C). The clusters of the Great Barrier Reef are so massive that they can be seen from outer space. The magnificent and dense underwater coral forests, with striking formations such as staghorn corals, brain corals, and mushroom corals, are made up of centuries of calcareous remains. The polyps begin growing on the exoskeleton of the previous generation, often forming walls of limestone as high as 328ft (100m).

*The Great Barrier Reef*

## DARK STAR

The crown-of-thorns starfish is the greatest natural predator of living corals. An individual adult of the species is capable of wiping out 64sq ft (6sq m) of living coral in a single year. Proliferation of this species is believed to be the most dangerous natural threat posed to coral reefs. Their effect on coral colonies is potentially devastating because although they can recover from these outbreaks, coral polyps have a slow recovery rate.

*A crown-of-thorns starfish*

clams, and octopus—and more than 400 types of corals. The reef is also home to 30 species of whales, dolphins, dugongs, and porpoises in addition to several varieties of sharks and rays—warm water sharks, manta rays, and stingrays. Six of the seven species of sea turtle, all of which are endangered, depend on the remote islands of the reef for safe nesting grounds. The cays in the reef provide sanctuary to 242 species of bird including reef herons, osprey, pelicans, frigate birds, sea eagles, and shearwaters. A wide selection of sponges, anemones, worms, crustaceans, and echinoderms are also found at the Great Barrier Reef.

Declared a World Heritage Site in 1981, the Great Barrier Reef is of interest not only in terms of its scientific value because of the plethora of life-forms that it supports, but also for its immense cultural importance. Several middens and other archaeological sites of Aboriginal or Torres Strait Islander origin are located in the Great Barrier Reef, some remarkable examples of which can be found on Lizard and Hinchinbrook Islands, and on Stanley, Cliff, and Clack Islands, where there are also some impressive rock paintings.

The earliest documents describing the reef's existence come from a French naval expedition led by Louis-Antoine de Bougainville in 1768. However, it was first sited in 1770 when the British explorer James Cook's ship *The Endeavour* grounded on the reef. The process of mapping channels and passages through this spectacular maze of reefs started with Cook and continued well into the 19th and 20th centuries. The Great Barrier Reef Expedition of 1928–29 was responsible for expanding greatly the extant knowledge of coral physiology and the ecology of reefs. A research station was built on Heron Island in 1951, which to this day carries out scientific and other investigations of the reef.

Threats posed to the Great Barrier Reef include tropical cyclones, global warming, overfishing, rapid coastal development, discharge of untreated sewage into the sea, drilling for petroleum resources, shipping, and large-scale tourism. The Great Barrier Marine Park was set up in 1975 in order to combat these problems. Almost 98 percent of the Great Barrier Reef today is contained within the marine park, making it the largest protected area of ocean in the world.

- The name Bungle Bungle is believed to have originated from "bundle bundle," a variety of grass that grows in the Kimberley region.
- Western Australia's Purnululu National Park encompasses an area of 926sq miles (2,397sq km).

**Bungle Bungle Range,** Australia

# Bungle Bungle Range

It seems inconceivable that one of the most impressive landforms on this planet has become widely known in Australia and across the world only over the last two decades of the 20th century. Rising up to 1,895ft (578m) above sea level, the Bungle Bungle Range is located in the Purnululu National Park in the State of Western Australia. Despite being known to the Aborigines for centuries, it somehow managed to remain unseen by the rest of the world right up until 1980. However, once it was noticed, the impact of its discovery was so widespread and immediate that in 2003 it was conferred the status of a World Heritage Site and recognized as a "superlative natural phenomena."

It is easy to see what makes the range so special. The sight of towers that resemble beehives, their steeply sloping surfaces marked with interchanging horizontal strips of orange and black or gray, is awe-inspiring. Changing colors with the seasons, the elements, and light, the breathtaking beauty of this range is best viewed from the air. Made up of Devonian Age quartz sandstone, the conical towers of this dissected range were formed as a result of 20 million years of uplift and erosion. The colored stripes are a cyanobacterial crust (or algae) and contain deposits of orange silica; the beehive-shaped towers are the most magnificent examples of cone karst in sandstones in the world.

## ROAD TO HEAVEN

Despite remaining unknown up until the 1980s, what is even more surprising is that ground access into the remote Bungles range was achieved much later. Though a route was clearly visible from the air, there were no tracks or trails on the ground. It took the genius of an East Kimberley resident, a "spotter" plane, sacks of flour, lots of patience, and a four-wheel drive to find a trustworthy entry into the wonders of the Bungle Bungle Range. The "spotter" plane, carrying the sacks of flour, flew low over the area. On sighting the most accessible route, the sacks were thrown out, and the dusty-white left behind on the brilliant red earth was picked up by a four-wheel drive.

*A stunning view of the Bungle Bungle Range reflected in a nearby pond*

Contrary to its solid appearance, the sandstone is actually quite fragile. The weight of the overlying rock holds the grains of sand in the sandstone tightly in place. When removed, the stone is easily eroded. The rounded tops of the cones are a sign of the weakness in the stone. This dearth of internal strength has been ruthlessly exploited by flowing water, and, over time, it has eroded the tapering channels, thus dividing the towers.

It is water that most effectively sets off the Bungles. Narrow, meandering gorges lined with Livistona palms provide a dramatic frame to this thick and intricate labyrinth of stone towers, thrusting them into even greater prominence and earning for them the nickname of Australia's "Grand Canyon." Seasonal waterfalls and pools can be found in these sheer gorges, making them an equally attractive tourist draw. Some of the best known gorges in the park are Echidna Chasm, Frog Hole, Mini Palms, Piccaninny Creek, and the Cathedral Gorges. However, the Purnululu Park is closed to visitors from January to March—the wet season—as many of the gorges are filled with raging torrents, which transforms them into treacherous areas.

## WILD THINGS

The Purnululu National Park is lush with bird and animal life. It also hosts a variety of reptiles. Eucalyptus and spinifex monopolize the landscape, though Livistona palms can be found in many of the gorges and waterholes. More than 130 species of birds can be spotted here, including rainbow bee-eaters and flocks of budgerigars. In fact, birds are the most visible of the park's inhabitants.

*A Livistona palm near the entrance of Echidna Chasm in the Bungle Bungle Range*

**Kings Canyon,** Australia

• Kathleen Springs, the exquisite spring-fed waterhole at the mouth of the Kathleen Gorge in Watarrka National Park, is integral to the Aboriginal history of the area.

• The Kings Canyon area is powered by the Kings Canyon Solar Power Station. In operation since December 2003, this project is the largest single installation of its kind in Australia.

# Kings Canyon

Red sandstone walls soar up to the skies and pockets of lush greenery in sheltered gullies interweave to form Kings Canyon in Australia. Part of the sprawling 281sq miles (720sq km) Watarrka National Park in the Northern Territory, Kings Canyon lies at the western end of the George Gill Range, between Alice Springs and the Uluru-Kata Tjuta National Park. Rising up from the Kings Creek valley, the walls of Kings Canyon reach 886ft (270m) at their highest point.

A tourist hotspot today, the canyon is the result of 440 million years of work by the elements. Fossils discovered in areas of the canyon testify to a time when the valley was still under water. The land was formed by the process of sedimentation and cementation, followed by pressure exerted on the earth's crust by the movement of the tectonic plates; wind, rain, and streams that cut through the rock in search of a pathway then carved out the gorge. Weathered sandstone cones in areas within the canyon bear a striking resemblance to the Bungle Bungle in Western Australia. Kings Canyon is a little younger than its southern cousins, Uluru (Ayers Rock) and Kata Tjuta (the Olgas), which were formed almost 550 million years ago.

Among the bounties that Kings Canyon has to offer are the Lost City, a spectacular group of rock formations

## KINGS CANYON RIM WALK

The 3.7-mile (6-km) Kings Canyon Rim Walk is a challenging looped walk that runs along the brim of the canyon. A particularly difficult climb at the beginning of the walk has been named Heartbreak Hill or Heart Attack Hill by the locals because of its steepness. This stretch takes visitors up to the top of the canyon from where they can gaze at the spectacular landscape with its stunning gorges. A detour halfway up the walk leads to the lush Garden of Eden. The last half of the walk leads through the Lost City and then a slow descent brings visitors back to the starting point. The walk is recommended only for people who are physically fit.

*Kings Canyon, Northern Territory*

## WATARRKA NATIONAL PARK

The Watarrka National Park is home to cycads, ferns, and palms, some of which date back to the Jurassic Period. The high rock faces of Kings Canyon protect these from the surrounding desert conditions. More than 600 plant species manage to survive on the water that collects between cracks in the rocks of the canyon. The park also provides shelter to 100 varieties of birds and 60 species of reptiles. The name, Watarrka, is derived from an Aboriginal word for the umbrella bush that thrives in the area.

*Cycads* (Macrozamia macdonnellii), *growing in the MacDonnell Range, Garden of Eden, Kings Canyon*

with beehive domes, and the Garden of Eden, a lush patch veiled by palms and ferns, fed by streams, and decorated with tropical pools that mirror the red sandstone. The rich red color of the canyon rocks is believed to be the result of dust with a high iron content settling on the white sandstone and their subsequent chemical combination. The scenic landscape with its rugged cliffs and gorges also provides refuge to a wide variety of flora and fauna.

The Kings Canyon area has been home to the Luritja people for at least 20,000 years. Many sections of the canyon are considered sacred sites by the Aboriginal people. Dreamtime legends about the canyon are popular even today. The first European to set eyes upon the canyon was Ernest Giles in 1872. An explorer, Giles is also credited with the discovery of many other sites such as Mount Olga and Palm Valley, among others. The 14-mile (22-km) long Giles Track that connects Kings Canyon to Kathleen Springs, is popular with the more adventurous hikers, and has been named in his honor. Other walks in the Kings Canyon include the 1.6-mile (2.6-km) Kathleen Springs Walk and the rather difficult Kings Canyon Rim Walk.

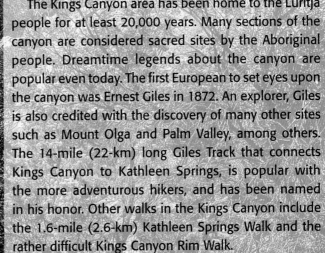

**Uluru (Ayers Rock),** Australia

# Uluru (Ayers Rock)

One of Australia's most famous natural landmarks, Uluru is an enormous tor or isolated mass of weathered rock located in the middle of the continent, very close to the geographical center. Better known to the rest of the world as Ayers Rock, this gigantic monolith—one of the largest in the world—is located within the Uluru-Kata Tjuta National Park near the southwestern corner of the Northern Territory. Approximately 16 miles (24km) northwest of Uluru, is Kata Tjuta, the other attraction of the park.

Towering 1,141ft (348m) above its surroundings, Uluru is about 2.2 miles (3.6km) long and 1.2 miles (1.9km) wide. This colossal oval block of rock occupies about 1.29sq miles (3.33sq km). Erosion of the weaker layers of rock has made the lower slopes jagged, and numerous gullies and basins have been scoured on the top, which have resulted in the formation of the Mutitjulu waterhole. Caves and crevices which have been eroded into the monolith are decorated with cave paintings, which have been assimilated into Aboriginal tales of creation.

## COLORS OF ULURU

Dusty outback roads lead from Alice Springs to motels near Uluru, allowing visitors the chance to experience the fascinating spectacle of the rock changing color with the changing light of morning and evening. As the sun sets, the rock appears to glow with an inner fire as it changes from the dry brown of the day to an intense fiery orange and then blazing red, before turning into a black silhouette against the fading light. The dawn light reveals Uluru in even more beautiful pastel shades. Sunrise and sunset at Uluru are considered among the most surreal and dazzling natural displays that Australia has to offer.

*The brooding mass of Ayers Rock*

## GEOLOGICAL HISTORY

Uluṟu is composed from a coarse-grained sandstone, a sedimentary rock called arkose sandstone. Kata Tjuṯa is a conglomerate of a sedimentary rock, boulders, pebbles, and gravel held together by mud and sand. As a result, it contains many minerals and different types of rock including granite and basalt.

The distinctive red color of Uluṟu is attributed to weathering of the rock. Time and environmental factors such as rainwater and oxygen affect the iron minerals in the rock (imagine how iron looks when it rusts). The weathering of the feldspar minerals inside the sandstone also contributes to the beautiful color. It's also interesting to note that both Uluṟu and Kata Tjuṯa extend for several miles underground.

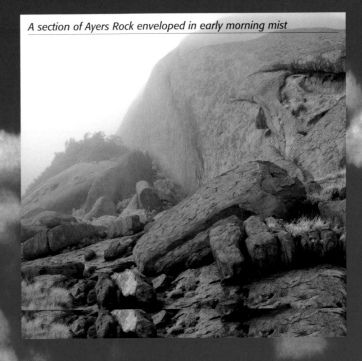

*A section of Ayers Rock enveloped in early morning mist*

The Kata Tjuṯa, meaning "many heads" in the Pitjantjajara language, is a cluster of 36 monoliths. The tallest of these is Mount Olga, which rises to a height of 1,790ft (546m) above the desert plain. Also referred to collectively as "the Olgas," these rocks together occupy about 13.5sq miles (35sq km). The layers of rock at Kata Tjuṯa are almost horizontal, unlike the close to vertical stratification of Uluṟu, and this accounts for the difference in patterns of erosion of the two outcrops.

Both areas have been affected primarily by two kinds of erosion—rain and heat. Despite the desert-like conditions surrounding the area, these rocks receive a plentiful rainfall every year; this precipitation occurs in the form of a few but major storms. During these infrequent rainstorms, raging torrents of water crash down the sides of the rounded rocks, often taking the form of giant cataracts, and wash away the looser chunks of rock in their path. The variations in temperature between extremely hot days and acutely cold nights is responsible for thermal erosion; the rapid and constant processes of expansion and contraction of the rocks eventually cause fragments to break away from the monoliths.

The first European to sight Uluṟu was the Australian explorer Ernest Giles in 1872. The first European to visit the rock and actually climb it was the surveyor Henry Gosse. He named it the Ayers Rock after Sir Henry Ayers, who was then the Chief Secretary of South Australia. However, Uluṟu has been a significant part of the Aboriginal Anangu culture a long time before that. The rock is of immense spiritual significance to them, and so the Anangu consider climbing the rock disrespectful, even though it is not legally prohibited. The 512sq miles (1,326sq km) Uluṟu-Kata Tjuṯa National Park—called the Ayers-Mount Olga National Park until the 1990s—today belongs to its traditional Anangu owners and is administered according to the *Tjukurpa*, a complex word that symbolizes Anangu law, religion, ethics, knowledge, and harmony.

- The remarkably Martian-like topography of the Flinders Ranges in the southern Outback region has led scientists to choose it as the location for a simulation space station.

- Temperatures in the central Outback deserts can be as high as 120°F (50°C) on summer days and as low as 15°F (-10°C) on winter nights. However, temperature variations are less extreme in the outer reaches.

**The Outback,** Australia

# The
# Outback

A vast remote land, broken only by long, lonely stretches of road, the Australian Outback is considered to be one of the last open frontiers in the world today. Though often harsh and unforgiving, this great land is also one of exquisite beauty and diversity. Sprawling across 2.5 million sq miles (6.5 million sq km) of the country, from Darwin at the rim of the Gulf of Carpentaria in the north to the southern tip of the mainland, this dry and dusty desert land is transformed by rain into a sea of color as thousands of wild plants blossom and bloom.

The sheer size and remoteness of this stretch of Australia had in the past deterred people from exploring it at length; however, it is this sense of isolation—the unearthly tranquility and desolation which it offers—that has made this fierce land such a huge tourist attraction today. The wilderness of the Outback was first conquered by pioneers who ventured out of the sheltered pleasures and comfort that the coastal settlements offered in order to carve out a new life in the wild and untamed interior of the country. The Australian Stockman's Hall of Fame and Outback Heritage Centre in Longreach,

*Eastern grey kangaroos*

## THE FLYING DOCTORS

The Royal Flying Doctors Service of Australia is a non-profit organization dedicated to providing health care and medical emergency assistance to all those who live and work in, or travel to the remote regions of Australia. First established in 1928 and developed on a national basis in the following decade, it is the world's first comprehensive aerial medical organization, and provides help to thousands of unprepared outback explorers every year. The Flying Doctors use high-frequency radio networks and telephone communication to trace imperiled travelers, and provide assistance in various emergencies, including cases of snake bite, dehydration, illness, or accident. In addition to on-the-spot medical aid, they also provide valuable safety guidelines for enthusiastic travelers starting out on their journey.

## LITCHFIELD NATIONAL PARK

One of the lesser-known Outback parks, the small Litchfield National Park is located near Darwin. A host of beautiful features adorn this tabletop plateau. The Wangi and Florence falls are the most famous of the park's four waterfalls. Other attractions include the Buley Rockholes (a series of rapids, small cascades and pools); the isolated Greenant Creek, surrounded by tall palm and monsoonal forests; the deep and narrow gorge carved out by the Tolmer Creek; and the strange and fascinating Magnetic Termite Mounds.

*The fascinating Buley Rockholes in Litchfield National Park*

Queensland pays tribute to these brave and unsung heroes of Australia.

The 1,860-miles (3,000-km) long Stuart Highway, running from north to south as it dissects the center of Australia, is the most popular road for people traversing the Outback. Other routes through this difficult and rugged terrain include the Oodnadatta, Birdsville and Tanami tracks, the Gunbarrel Highway, and the "Bomb Roads." Situated halfway down the Stuart Highway is Alice Springs, the capital of the Outback. The Ayers Rock monolith is its most famous tourist destination.

On either side of the Stuart Highway are the hot, dusty Outback deserts—the Tanami in the north, the Simpson Desert in the east, and the Great Victoria, Gibson, and the Great Sandy Desert in the west—terrifying in their barrenness. Other Outback attractions include the Nullarbor Plain—intersected by the Eyre Highway—in the north, spectacular gorges such as the Katherine Gorge, and the jagged and beautiful Kimberley Plateau in the west. The crimson cliffs of the McDonnell Ranges, the underground mining town of Cooper Pedy, the Devils Marbles boulder formations in Tennant Creek, the astonishing Gosse's Bluff impact crater, and the Mount Augustus and Kakadu national parks are also much visited.

Despite its apparent starkness, the Outback is quite fertile, and often amazes travelers with its profusion of plants and trees. The deserts of Australia receive adequate amounts of rainfall and are thus dotted with a great variety of small shrubs and bushes in some areas. The diverse range of animals that populate the Outback form one of its main attractions. Kangaroos, dingoes, wild camels, and many species of lizards form the backbone of the fauna of this region; poisonous snakes, spiders, and the Australian crocodile are among the more deadly of the Outback dwellers.

**The Pinnacles,** Australia

# The
# Pinnacles

Thousands of impressive limestone pillars rising out of a desolate landscape of ever-shifting yellow sands make up the astonishing Pinnacles Desert in Australia. Situated in the heart of the Nambung National Park in Western Australia, these columns of limestone often reach a height of 11ft (3.5m). While some of these pillars resemble domes and tombstones, others appear like giant teeth protruding from the ground, their jagged edges tapering into sharp points.

Though the formation of the Pinnacles took place over thousands of years, they were perhaps exposed only recently in terms of geological time. The denudation of the dunes by bush fires and the removal of loose quartz sands by the south-westerly winds resulted in the revelation of these odd but fascinating structures made of limestone. The discovery of Aboriginal artifacts and the lack of evidence of recent Aboriginal occupation has led archeologists to believe that the Pinnacles were exposed around 6,000 years ago. Covered by the desert's restless and rolling sands, they were re-exposed once again only a few centuries ago.

## DISCOVERING THE PINNACLES

The earliest European records of the Nambung area can be traced back to 1658, when two small hills within the park—called the North and South Hummocks—were marked on Dutch maps. The navigator Philip Parker King also mentioned these hills in his journal in 1820. However, the Pinnacles Desert remained relatively unknown until the late 1960s when the government decided to incorporate the area within the Nambung National Park, established in 1956. Today, however, the park is one of the most famous natural attractions in Australia, and almost 150,000 tourists visit the national park and the desert every year.

*The limestone columns of the Pinnacles Desert*

## PLANTS AND ANIMALS OF THE PINNACLES DESERT

The Pinnacles Desert teems with wildlife. Though most of the creatures stay hidden from the eyes of visitors because of their nocturnal habits, kangaroos and emus sometimes wander across the paths of visitors early in the morning. Not easily frightened, these animals can be viewed from close quarters if visitors are quiet and careful. Reptiles such as the Gould's monitor and the harmless carpet python can also be seen sheltering in the shade of the limestone pillars. The Nambung National Park is also home to a variety of plants and trees. The most common plant species that is found close to the Pinnacles is the parrotbush (*Dryandra sessilis*).

*Emus taking an early morning stroll in the Pinnacles*

The limestone of the Pinnacles Desert is marine in origin—the remnants of sea shells from an earlier epoch, these fragments disintegrated into sands rich in lime particles and were carried to land by the waves of the Indian Ocean. Winds then carried these sands further inland, forming highly fluid dunes. Three old systems of sand dunes can today be seen running parallel to the Western Australian coastline. Characterized by yellow or brownish sands, the Spearwood dune system that makes up the Pinnacles Desert is the oldest of these.

Small amounts of the calcium carbonate present in the dunes were dissolved by the slightly acidic winter rain as it percolated through the grains of sand. In summer, when the waters dried out, the calcium carbonate was precipitated in the lower levels of the dunes. Over time this precipitate cemented around tiny grains of sand. This process was repeated several times, until a hard limestone rock layer was formed. The growth of plants allowed the development of a layer of soil and humus rich in decayed organic matter over the rest of the quartzite sand, increasing the acidity of the soil and accelerating the leaching process; a layer of hard calcrete was formed over the softer limestone beneath.

Over time, plant roots and water created cracks and fissures in the limestone. Further subsurface erosion occurred, until most of the limestone was again dissolved by water, leaving only the hardiest and most resilient columns of limestone. The Pinnacles are thus the eroded remains of this earlier thick bed of limestone.

Even today, unidirectional winds are uncovering more of the limestone spires in the northern part of the desert and hiding those at the southern end. This cyclical process will probably be repeated continuously, granting an evanescent quality to this extraordinary landscape of strange and wonderful shapes. These eerie structures are best viewed at dusk and dawn, when they cast long and extraordinary shadows over the rippling sands.

• Australian pioneer William Cox is credited with laying the first road into the Blue Mountains in 1814. The road, which stretches for 101 miles (163km), was constructed in six months by about 30 convicts supervised by eight guards.

• The Lennox Bridge in the Blue Mountains is the oldest bridge in the Australian mainland. Constructed in 1832, again with the use of convict labor.

**The Blue Mountains,** Australia

# The
# Blue Mountains

According to Aboriginal legends, three sisters of the Katoomba tribe—Meehni, Wimlah, and Gunnedoo—who lived in what is today called the Jamison Valley, fell in love with three brothers of the Nepean tribe. When the girls' parents found out about the affair, they forbade marriage. Angered by the rejection, the boys decided to use force and win the girls in battle. Fearing for the girls' lives, a witch doctor cast a spell on them and turned them into rock, with plans of undoing the spell after the battle ended. Unfortunately, the witch doctor himself was killed, and the girls have remained rocks forever. This is the story of the Three Sisters—standing at 3,024ft (922m), 3,011ft (918m), and 2,972ft (906m)—the most famous of the Blue Mountain rock formations.

The Blue Mountains, a part of the Greater Blue Mountains Area, are located about 62 miles (100km) west of Sydney. Declared a World Heritage Site by UNESCO in 2000, these mountains are actually a series of deeply dissected sandstone plateaus and granite cliffs—some of them around 3,280ft (1,000m) in height—surrounding a plateau. The many gorges that run in between these are in places more than 2,460ft (750m) deep.

*The Weeping Rock Falls*

## NAMES WITH A PAST

The Marked Tree, a few miles west of Katoomba, is so named because it carries the initials of Blaxland, Lawson, and Wentworth; the pioneering explorers had supposedly carved them into the tree after reaching that point in 1813. Today, hundreds of tourists have added their names to the list. The section of highway past the Marked Tree that leads into Medlow Bath is known as Whipcord Hill. The name refers to a penal colony that used to be situated there. Behind it is Pulpit Point, where religious services were held.

Tectonic upheavals about a million years ago, followed by wind and water erosion, are what geologists believe to be the cause of the formation of the Blue Mountains. The eucalyptus trees found on these mountains secrete a volatile oil that combines with droplets of water and suspended particulate matter to form a shimmering haze which gives a blue tinge to the mountains.

The Aborigines have lived in the shadows of the Blue Mountains for more than 20,000 years; the Red Hands Cave, with well-preserved hand stencils on its walls, bears testimony to this. The name Katoomba, an area in the heart of the preserve, is the Aboriginal word for 'shiny, tumbling water.' It refers to the 656ft (200m) waterfall that thunders down the side of the mountains. Prior to 1877, this area was called The Crushers because it was the site for a stone quarry from which ballast was supplied to the railways.

The first Europeans to carve a trail through the ravines were Gregory Blaxland, William Charles Wentworth, and William Lawson. Their success is attributed to lessons learnt from earlier failed expeditions. They walked along the mountain ridges, rather than following the course of the river below. The unfolding vista from this elevated position included rich grazing lands, which were to later stand pastoralists and ranchers in good stead. Today, a string of towns have been named after these pioneers.

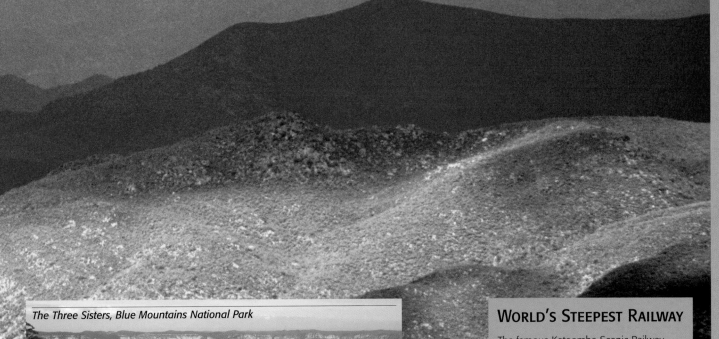

*The Three Sisters, Blue Mountains National Park*

## WORLD'S STEEPEST RAILWAY

The famous Katoomba Scenic Railway descends through sandstone cliffs via a rock tunnel, leading out into a lush green rainforest. It was initially part of the Katoomba mining tramways constructed between 1878 and 1900 for coal and shale-oil mining operations. According to the *Guinness Book of World Records*, it is the steepest funicular railway in the world, with an incline of 52 degrees over a distance of 1,361ft (415m). The railway was opened for tourism shortly before World War II, partly in an attempt to keep it from falling into disrepair, since the Katoomba Colliery had stopped operations and the tramway had been left to gather rust.

...ley of the Giants, Australia

- Styx Valley near Hobart, Australia, is a contender for the title Valley of the Giants. Its swamp gums, are second only to the American redwoods in terms of height.

- At over 400 years old, Grandmother Tingle is the oldest of the trees in the Valley of the Giants.

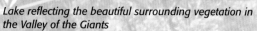

*Lake reflecting the beautiful surrounding vegetation in the Valley of the Giants*

## A DIFFERENT PERSPECTIVE

The Valley of the Giants now boasts a unique path from which to view the enormous trees. The Tree Top Walk was constructed with the purpose of minimizing the impact of humans on the forest. A swaying bridge that winds its way through the canopy of trees and rises to a height of 131ft (40m) offers breathtaking views of the forest. The design of the Tree Top Walk through the Valley of the Giants was inspired by the forest itself, more specifically by the tassel flower and sword grass, plants found in the tingle forests.

# Valley of the Giants

Nestled in a small valley in the southwest of Western Australia is a lush forest with a towering reputation. Made up of some of the world's tallest trees that grow to heights of about 260ft (80m), this is nature at its finest. Found not far from the coast in the Walpole-Nornalup area, the forest, known as the Valley of the Giants, now lies within the Walpole-Nornalup National Park, occupying an area of approximately 78sq miles (200sq km).

The giants of this valley belong to the Eucalyptus family of the tingle (*Eucalyptus brevistylis*), the red tingle (*Eucalyptus jacksonii*) and the yellow tingle (*Eucalyptus guilfoylei*). The forest also consists of marri (*Eucalyptus calophylla*), jarrah (*Eucalyptus marginata*), and karri (*Eucalyptus diversicolor*). Karri trees can reach heights of up to 300ft (90m) and are the tallest trees found in this part of Australia. One of the most distinctive features of the tingle trees, especially the red tingle, is the size of its trunk, which can reach a girth of more than 66ft (20m). Several of them possess a hollowed-out base, making it possible for people to step inside the tree trunk. Reasons for the formation of unusual structures include fire, fungus, or insect attack. Along with their gigantic size, the age of these trees is also worth a mention, with some of them as old as a few hundred years.

Tingle and karri forests found in areas of fertile soil and abundant rainfall constitute a moist evergreen ecoregion that is a hotspot of flora and fauna. Some of these can trace their origins back to the Gondwana period more than 60 million years ago. These include the Gondwanian spider, endemic species of frogs, and freshwater fauna. Other species of animals found in the tingle forests include the quokka, southern brown bandicoot, pygmy possum, chuditch, and the western gray kangaroo. Though the birdlife does not display the richness or the endemism that would be expected in such a forest, birds like the white-tailed black cockatoo,

Western Rosella, red-winged fairy wren, golden whistler, purple-crowned lorikeet, and owlet nightjar, as well as honeyeaters and parrots can be spotted in the valley at different times of the year.

While their majesty and age may well be a misleading factor, tingle tree forests are quite vulnerable to human appreciation. Owning to their shallow root systems, the trees remain dependent on surface nutrients. However, when thousands of people come walking through the forest—the Valley of the Giants is one of the most popular natural attractions in Australia—and wear a path around the tree base, it exposes the roots and makes the tree vulnerable. One of the biggest trees in the Valley of the Giants collapsed two decades ago for this very reason. However, this mishap has prompted the park management to build alternative viewing platforms to accommodate the million or more visitors that come annually to pay homage to these giants.

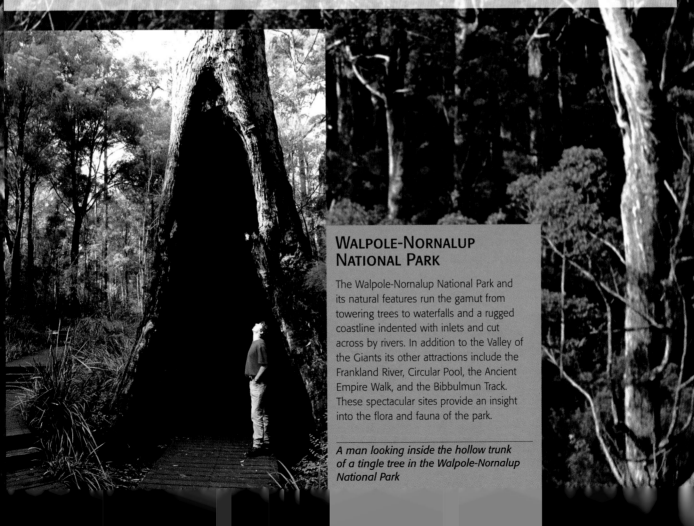

### WALPOLE-NORNALUP NATIONAL PARK

The Walpole-Nornalup National Park and its natural features run the gamut from towering trees to waterfalls and a rugged coastline indented with inlets and cut across by rivers. In addition to the Valley of the Giants its other attractions include the Frankland River, Circular Pool, the Ancient Empire Walk, and the Bibbulmun Track. These spectacular sites provide an insight into the flora and fauna of the park.

*A man looking inside the hollow trunk of a tingle tree in the Walpole-Nornalup National Park*

- The Twelve Apostles Marine National Park is located 4 miles (7km) east of Port Campbell and encompasses approximately 29sq miles (75sq km) of protected area.

- The limestone cliffs near the Twelve Apostles are being eroded at a rate of 0.8in (2cm) per year, and in the future more such stacks are likely to be formed from the rocky headlands.

**Twelve Apostles,** Australia

## SHIPWRECK COAST

The stretch of coast between Cape Otway to Port Fairy in Victoria was christened Shipwreck Coast by European explorers and settlers. The Aboriginal people were well-acquainted with this coast, and used steps cut into the steep cliffs to access marine food sources, but the jagged cliffs and rocks posed a great threat to the European ships. Though they tried to give this dangerous area a wide berth, many ships were dashed against the cliffs along this stretch. The most famous of the shipwrecks is the Loch Ard, which was wrecked in 1878 and caused around 50 casualties. The Twelve Apostles are situated along this perilous stratch.

# Twelve Apostles

Soaring high above the heaving waters of the Southern Ocean, the mighty Twelve Apostles stand guard just off the coast of Victoria. These gigantic stacks of rock are among the most amazing attractions of the Port Campbell National Park, which stretches from Princetown to Peterborough. One of the most-visited natural attractions in Australia, the Twelve Apostles are considered iconic of the natural treasures that the Great Ocean Road has to offer. The backdrop to the impressive figures of the Apostles is framed by magnificent and imposing limestone cliffs that tower almost 230ft (70m) above the seashore. The Apostles are shorter—with the tallest one reaching a height of about 148ft (45m)—but create an even more dramatic visual impact by jutting out without warning from the waves.

The origin of the Twelve Apostles can be traced back 20 million years ago, when the soft limestone cliffs of the Port Campbell coastline were being pummeled by the forces of nature. Created over the years as a result of the deposition of marine skeletons on the ocean floor, the limestone was gradually exposed as the waters of the ocean retreated. The fierce Southern Ocean continued to hew at these rocks with its strong waves, and turbulent winds constantly blasted the cliffs, until finally the limestone began to erode. This process carved caves out of the soft stone; however, erosive action over the years has reduced the caves to arches. Further erosion resulted in the eventual collapse of the arches, leaving behind these isolated rock islands a short distance from the shore.

The untamed ocean also conceals a marvelous seascape beneath the waves. A remarkable labyrinth of caves, arches, canyons, fissures, and gutters have been carved out by the sea. Decorated with colorful seaweeds, ferns, and gardens of sponges, these karst features are populated by numerous sea creatures. The Twelve Apostles Marine National Park protects these underwater reaches for 11 miles (17km) along the coastline. Comprising some of the most spectacular underwater seascapes in Victoria, the undersea habitats shelter many inter-tidal and sub-tidal invertebrate colonies, including a variety of sea spiders, sea slugs, sea snails, and sea stars. Schools of reef fish and the occasional Australian fur seal can also to be found here; weedy sea dragons float gently amid the thick brown fronds of the bull kelp. While breeding colonies of seabirds inhabit the rock stacks, little penguins nest in the caves below the Twelve Apostles.

Besides the Twelve Apostles, a host of wonderful natural features have been carved out along the coast by the sea. These include the Pudding Basin Rock, Island Arch, the Razorback, Muttonbird Island, Thunder Cave, the Blowhole, Bakers Oven, London Bridge, and the Grotto, among others. Extensive viewing platforms and boardwalks have been constructed along the coast to facilitate the viewing of these awe-inspiring vistas. Though the views are magnificent at any time of the day, sunrise and sunset provide particularly stunning visual experiences, thanks to the astounding range of colors to be seen in the blazing sunlight.

## WEEDY SEA DRAGON

Weedy sea dragons are delicate creatures that shelter in kelp forests. Growing to 18in (46cm) in length, their elegant bodies are modified with several leaf-like fins. They are related to seahorses and pipefishes, and just as with those species the eggs are held by the males. During the two months of brooding, tiny pink eggs can be seen attached to their tales. The baby sea dragons are hatched as miniatures of the adults, and can grow to a length of 2.7in (7cm) in three weeks. Recently voted the Marine State Emblem of Victoria, these tiny creatures are found only in the southern Australian waters.

*The weedy sea dragon protects itself by blending in with aquatic plants.*

*Waves crashing against a sea stack arch at Twelve Apostles, Port Campbell National Park*

• The Coromandel enjoys glorious weather all year round; with average temperatures of 80°F (27°C) in summer and 55°F (13°C) in winter.

• Coromandel gets its name from the coast of the same name in southern India, which inspired the names of three Royal British Navy ships; one of these landed on the New Zealand Coast and gave its name to both a town and to the peninsula.

**Coromandel,** New Zealand

## GATEWAY TO THE COROMANDEL

A gold-mining and logging town from the 19th century, Thames is another place whose name can be attributed to Captain Cook; he rowed up the Waihou River and dubbed it the Thames. The Thames Coast Road that runs along the edge of the peninsula is one of the world's most scenic places.

# Coromandel

Located on New Zealand's North Island and comprising a diverse mix of pristine beaches, rainforest, hot pools, coastal scenery, secluded bays, marine wonders, mountains, and volcanic activity, the Coromandel can well be described as having an embarrassment of natural riches. A peninsula on the Island's east coast that extends 68 miles (110km) into the South Pacific Ocean, the Coromandel stretches from Cape Colville in the north to Te Aroha and Katikati in the south. More than 476 miles (145km) of mountains in the Coromandel Range run through the Peninsula, surrounded by 10 towns. This area was home to the Maori for hundreds of years before Captain James Cook's visit in 1769. Besides the naming of Mercury Bay and Cook's Beach, he is also responsible for the turn of events that followed in the peninsula's history. It was due to his report that the Coromandel region was selected for logging, which consequently led to the gold boom.

The Coromandel is famous the world over for the beauty of its beaches, which cover over 1,312 miles (400km) of this spectacular area. Pristine white sand beaches line the Peninsula's east coast, offering everything from challenging surf to gentle seas. The unique Hot Water Beach under which a river of hot water flows, is a reminder of the country's volcanic history. Hot pools can be dug up at low tide which then disappear at high tide.

## THE KAURI

The kauri is one of New Zealand's endemic species of trees found only in the Coromandel ecoregion where the humidity and warmth make for perfect growing conditions. Its abundant presence not only triggered the growth of a logging industry in the 19th century, but its gum was also one of the area's main exports. A combination of the two almost logged it out of existence. It is one of the giants of the world and can grow up to 131ft (40m) in height and live for 2,000 years.

*The giant kauri trees in the Coromandel ecoregion*

*Remains of rock arch at Cathedral Cove near Hahei, Coromandel Peninsula*

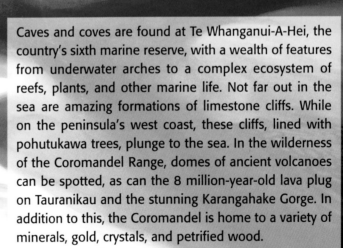

Caves and coves are found at Te Whanganui-A-Hei, the country's sixth marine reserve, with a wealth of features from underwater arches to a complex ecosystem of reefs, plants, and other marine life. Not far out in the sea are amazing formations of limestone cliffs. While on the peninsula's west coast, these cliffs, lined with pohutukawa trees, plunge to the sea. In the wilderness of the Coromandel Range, domes of ancient volcanoes can be spotted, as can the 8 million-year-old lava plug on Tauranikau and the stunning Karangahake Gorge. In addition to this, the Coromandel is home to a variety of minerals, gold, crystals, and petrified wood.

Coromandel's esthetic beauty is further enhanced by its diverse range of flora and fauna. The most famed is the kauri tree, the presence of which turned this area into one of the world's best logging destinations in the 19th century. The cloud forests on the highest peaks of the range are one of the main sites for the massive southern rata trees. Hundreds of years old pohutukawa (Christmas flower) trees, puriri, and large ferns form part of the regenerating native forests. The peninsula is also a natural sanctuary and home to many varieties of birds, including the brown kiwi, kingfisher, harrier hawk, tui, warblers, and finches; up to 74 species of shorebirds have been spotted here.

• *Hangi* is a method of Maori cooking in Rotorua, which involves ingredients being mixed together and placed in pits dug over natural thermal vents to steam and cook.

• The environmental conditions and the warmth of the waters have created a bird spa at the Motutara Point wildlife refuge and sanctuary in Rotorua.

**Rotorua Thermal Area,** New Zealand

# Rotorua Thermal Area

Situated on a volcanic plateau in the heart of the thermal belt of the North Island, New Zealand, Rotorua is famous throughout the world for its astounding geothermal activity—spouting geysers, boiling mud pools, and a phenomenal array of hot springs. More than 1,200 geothermal features dot the surface of Rotorua, including alkaline chloride springs, a host of flats, fumaroles, steaming grounds, gray and white sinter terraces, and hot lakes. Whakarewarewa, Waiotapu, Waimangu, and Tikitere are the chief thermal areas.

Located approximately 1.8 miles (3km) from Rotorua city, Whakarewarewa—which means "uprising of the war party at Waihiao"—near the banks of the Puarenga River, is Rotorua's most famous geothermal site. With its 500 or so hot springs and sinter deposits of many-hued porous silica or mineral encrustations, it is the chief tourist attraction in this area. New Zealand's largest geyser, the Pohutu, which erupts about 15 times a day and climbs to heights of 90ft (27m), is located in Whakarewarewa. Geyser activity in this area was on the decline in the 1980s because of the over-tapping of geothermal resources by bores. Following the government's ban on bores within 0.9 miles (1.5km) of Pohutu, the geothermal aquifer is regaining natural levels and geyser activity is gradually returning to its original state.

## LAKES OF ROTORUA

Lakes form an integral part of the Rotorua landscape. Lake Rotorua (Crater Lake) itself is the largest of a group of lakes, including Rotoiti and Tarawera, which were earlier called the "hot lakes." Lying at an elevation of 920ft (280m) above sea level, Lake Rotorua occupies a huge crater formed by an immense ancient volcanic explosion. The health-spa city of Rotorua is located at the edge of the lake. The volcanic Mokoia Island, which is held sacred by the Arawa Maoris, is in the middle of the lake. The largest lake in New Zealand with an area of about 234sq miles (600sq km), Lake Taupo lies 56 miles (90km) southwest of Rotorua. Created by a violent eruption about 1,800 years ago, this lake fills the crater of the ancient Taupo Volcano.

*The Waiotapu thermal wonderland*

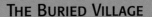

## THE BURIED VILLAGE

Established by a Christian missionary in 1848, the Te Wairoa Village was located in a valley above Lake Tarawera. Abandoned during the land wars of the 1860s, the village was repopulated when it became the staging post to the Pink and White Terraces. However, it was wiped out entirely by the sudden and violent eruption of Mount Tarawera in 1886. Bombarding the village with rock, ash, and boiling mud for over four hours, this eruption was arguably the worst natural disaster to hit New Zealand. Besides Te Wairoa, the Terraces and two smaller villages were destroyed and buried under hot ash and mud.

*The spectacular Pohutu and Prince of Wales geysers*

The chemistry of the waters of Tikitere is quite different from that of the other geothermal sites of Rotorua. While alkali-chloride waters are more common in other North Island areas, the waters of Tikitere are described by scientists as acid-sulphate (shallow waters) or chloride-bicarbonate (deeper waters). Also called Hell's Gate, this area is extremely rich in deposits of elemental sulphur. About 5,000 tons of this bright yellow mineral has been removed through surface diggings. Sulphur lines many of the steam vents; the sulphur beds caught fire in 1881 and burnt down the bathhouses, almost suffocating the people inside.

Located about 20 minutes south of Rotorua is Waimangu (Black Water), famous for its Warbrick Terrace and Emerald Pools. The Warbrick Terrace appears to be composed of liquid rock; a combination of algae, iron oxide, hydroxides, and silicates are responsible for the rich colors of this undulating formation. The Emerald Pools, their lush green color apparently the result of sphagnum moss, are nestled in a crater caused by the 1886 eruption of Mount Tarawera. Inferno Crater and the Frying Pan—a steaming body of water that sizzles—are other attractions in this area. Waiotapu, the Maori word for "sacred waters," is situated about 30 minutes south of Rotorua, and features the spectacular Champagne Pools. Occupying a 900-year-old volcanic crater, this series of enormous hot pools is colored a rich mixture of gold, yellow, and orange.

One of the heartlands of ancient Maori culture, Rotorua has particular spiritual significance to them. The Maori consider themselves *kaitiaki* (guardians) of the geothermal resources; using the mineral waters for bathing, cooking, medicine, dyes, and rituals is an integral part of Maori tradition. As the elaborate names indicate, myth and legend surround many of these geothermal sites.

- The Aranui Cave, part of the greater Waitomo Caves system, is so named after a Maori youth who accidentally discovered it in 1910.
- The famous glowworms apart, the Waitomo Caves are also home to a variety of other insects such as the albino cave ants and giant crickets. The walls of the caves are covered with fungi, including a mushroom-like fungus called the cave flower.

**Waitomo Caves,** New Zealand

# Waitomo Caves

Epitomized by breathtaking stalactites, stalagmites, and incrustations, the Waitomo Caves are an elaborate network of subterranean limestone caverns located in the central North Island of New Zealand, about 50 miles (80km) south of Hamilton. Consisting of about 300 known caves, the Waitomo Caves were formed about 30 million years ago by geological and volcanic activity.

The Waitomo Caves were first explored in 1887 by the English surveyor Fred Mace and the Maori Chief Tane Tinorou, who stumbled upon the caverns as they followed an underground stream. Over the next few years, the two of them explored the caves thoroughly and charted them. Tane Tinorau is credited with the discovery of an easier route of access to the caves while on an individual trip.

Fossilized corals, sea shells, and fish skeletons embedded in the limestone structures testify to the underwater origin of the entire cave system. Whale bones, too, have been found in some of the underground chambers. The caves were created when tectonic plate movements caused the entire Waitomo area to thrust out and rise above the sea. Weak points in the rocks allowed the percolation of water through them; as water passed through the rocks, it left behind calcium deposits, which eventually resulted in the formation of the stalactites, stalagmites and other spectacular features. In some places, the limestone is as thick as 656ft (200m).

## THE GLOWWORMS

Celebrities in their own right, New Zealand's glowworms are not actually worms but the larvae of an insect called the fungus gnat. The glow is created as bait to lure other insects which serve as food. The glowworms' affinity for damp and dark places leads them to nest in places such as the Waitomo Caves. A specially appointed Scientific Advisory Group is responsible for the upkeep and protection of these tiny creatures. The group monitors conditions within the cave such as humidity, level of carbon dioxide, and air temperature. The collated data is then used to determine course of action regarding the caves, including imposing a restriction on the number of people at a time who are allowed to visit the Glowworm Grotto.

*Visitors looking at what resembles a night sky, but is in reality the famous Waitomo glowworms*

## CAVE ADMINISTRATION

Two years after the Waitomo Caves were first explored, Maori Chief Tane Tinorou and his wife Huti realized the tourist potential of the site and opened the area up to visitors in 1889. Visitors were given guided tours of the caverns in exchange for a small fee. However, rampant vandalism followed, leading to the government taking over the administration of the caves in 1906. The land was returned to its original inhabitants much later, in 1989. Many of the people who administer the caves today are descendants of Chief Tane Tinorou.

The Waitomo Caves are divided into two levels which are 52ft (16m) apart. The dry upper level of the caves includes formations such as the Pipe Organ, the Banquet Chamber, and the Catacombs among others. The main entrance to the cave is also through the upper level. The most remarkable of the lower level formations is the Cathedral—a 59-ft (18-m) high rough-walled enclosed cavern that has astounding acoustics owing to its contours.

The Tomo, a vertical limestone shaft which separates the two levels of the caves, was carved out by an ancient waterfall. Today, the waterfall comes to life only when it rains heavily. The magnificent vertical drop of the shaft is illuminated to highlight the many layers of limestone and the finely scalloped walls. Believed to be the newest of the Waitomo formations, the shaft connects the upper level to the lower level caves and the Waitomo River.

The most stunning of the caves is, of course, the Glowworm Grotto. Like stars studding the night sky, the ceiling and walls of the cave are lit up by millions of glowworms that rest on them. This visual experience, many visitors say, is akin to a visit to outer space. Boats ferry travelers captivated by the luminescent sight through this grotto. This was the first of the caves to be discovered by Mace and Tane on their maiden journey in 1887. Today, a trip through the grotto serves as the conclusion for a visit to the Waitomo Caves.

# Index

# Acknowledgements

Front cover: Getty Images; back cover: Getty Images.

Abbreviations for terms appearing below: (bg) background; (tl) top left; (i) inset.

Automobile Associations Developments Limited wishes to thank the following libraries and associations for their assistance in the preparation of this book.

echinaromance 69i
Eisriesenwelt Caves 28, 29
Photolibrary 26, 27, 34tl, 34–35bg, 36, 37, 52i, 58, 59, 64, 65, 68tl, 68–69bg, 82tl, 82i, 83i, 90, 91, 106, 107, 164, 164–165bg, 180–181bg, 183i, 184i, 206i, 207i, 209i, 212, 213, 216, 217, 220tl, 220–221bg
Pictures Colour Library 182tl, 182–183bg
The Legendary Black Water Rafting Co, Ruakuri Tours 220i, 221i

All other pictures are sourced from Getty Images.